PERGAMON FRONTIERS OF ANTHROPOLOGY SERIES

EDITOR: Cyril S. Belshaw, *University of British Columbia, Canada*

Encountering Aborigines
A Case Study: Anthropology and the Australian Aboriginal

PFAS-1

Encountering Aborigines
A Case Study: Anthropology and the Australian Aboriginal

KENELM BURRIDGE

PERGAMON PRESS INC.

New York · Toronto · Oxford · Sydney · Braunschweig

PERGAMON PRESS INC.
Maxwell House, Fairview Park, Elmsford, N.Y. 10523

PERGAMON OF CANADA LTD.
207 Queen's Quay West, Toronto 117, Ontario

PERGAMON PRESS LTD.
Headington Hill Hall, Oxford

PERGAMON PRESS (AUST.) PTY. LTD.
Rushcutters Bay, Sydney, N.S.W.

VIEWEG & SOHN GmbH
Burgplatz 1, Braunschweig

Library of Congress Cataloging in Publication Data

Burridge, Kenelm.
Encountering Aborigines; a case study: anthropology and the Australian aboriginal.

(Pergamon frontiers of anthropology series, PFAS-1)
1. Australian aborigines. 2. Ethnology–Philosophy. I. Title.
GN666.B87   301.29'94   72-11991
ISBN 0-08-017071-4
ISBN 0-08-017646-1 (S)

Printed in the United States of America

For
J. L. B.
b. Canberra 25.8.51

Contents

Preface

Australia's Aboriginal peoples, so long cut off from the mainstreams of humanity's endeavors, are now beginning to tread the boards of the world's stage. Many scores of authors, anthropologists and others have introduced them to us, provided accounts of their problems, described their ways of life, analyzed their cultures, posed problems for future research. The Aborigines are strangers no longer. Hence this book. It extends a welcome to the Aborigines, attempts to bring researches on Aboriginal culture within a more general framework and perspective, and offers some suggestions as to why they have been written about so much.

My own personal and firsthand acquaintance with Aboriginal life has been short and entirely superficial. But this, I think, matters little in the context—and may even be an advantage. The book is about what others have thought is significant in Aboriginal life, and the kinds of problems which have seized the attention of anthropologists in particular. The reader who wants a more direct introduction to Aboriginal peoples themselves should consult, for example, the works of A. A. Abbie, A. Capell, R. M. and C. H. Berndt, A. P. Elkin, L. R. Hiatt, Ursula McConnell, M. J. Meggitt, D. J. Mulvaney, Marie Reay, W. E. H. Stanner, T. G. H. Strehlow, and W. L. Warner—a few names chosen from a host of professional anthropologists—and G. F. Angas, Daisy Bates, Mary Durack, Ion Idriess, Jack McLaren, Alan Marshall, and Bernard Smith—among the nonprofessionals—who will lead him into a delightful world of personal experience and impression. Again, anyone with half an eye who wants to know what the problems of Aboriginal research are, have been, or might be from the inside has only to sift through *The World of the First Australians* (Berndt and Berndt, 1964), *Australian Aboriginal Studies* (Shiels, 1963), *Aboriginal Man and Environment in Australia* (Mulvaney and Golson, 1971), and the works of C. D. Rowley. And there is little point in repeating, rehearsing and summarizing what has already been well done elsewhere. Nonetheless, the intellectual background and general assumptions guiding research have not always been clear, and as particular problems are tackled and fought over in professional circles the major questions from which they have been derived tend to drop from sight. So, what I have tried to do, in generally historical if idiosyncratic vein, is go over old problems and try to pose new ones by filling in some of the historical and intellectual background to Aboriginal studies. But the historical perspective should not be confused with history. It is simply a means of attempting to show where anthropology stands, and why anthropologists do what they do.

It would be impossible in a book of this kind to allude to all of the problems in Aboriginal studies, and, regrettably, many an important contribution has had to go unnoticed. Although the book is in no way a bibliographical essay, or a handbook for students looking for a thesis topic, most of the "starters" have been mentioned. Besides, for the specialist, John Greenway's bibliography (1963) is comprehensive up to 1959, and full references on any topic may be obtained as quick as thought from the Australian Institute of Aboriginal Studies in Canberra. On the whole, I have attempted to provoke thought by a technique of indirection rather than solve problems or tag them with markers.

There is one further point. As a subject or set of disciplines, Anthropology is wavering, beginning to atomize into numerous specialisms whose particular interests and problems could only be placed within the covers of a large symposium. Seen from these varying standpoints everything is bound to seem different, the skew wrong or mistaken. This one has to accept. But while I have kept my colleagues in mind, the book has a particular stance and is dedicated to my son, born in Canberra when that capital city was mostly grassland. He and others of his age have very positively occupied my thoughts. Young, vigorous and imaginative, the future belongs to them. They travel the world on a shoestring with an ease and nonchalance their fathers never possessed. They encounter all sorts, even communicate. If in a small way reading this book starts some into attempting to deepen the impact of casual acquaintance, or into trying to unravel the past, and presses others to reflect a little on peoples who, like the Aborigines, are so very differently situated, I shall be well satisfied.

KENELM BURRIDGE

Acknowledgments

Professor Cyril Belshaw, general editor of this series, suggested that I write this book. I thank him for the challenge and opportunity. Professor D. J. Mulvaney and Dr. Robert Tonkinson were kind enough to read a draft and have been most generous with their comments. I am most grateful for their help in making this a better book than it might have been. I thank, too, Professor R. M. and Dr. C. H. Berndt for their stimulus and encouragement to interest myself in Aboriginal studies; Miss Jennifer Gould for her valuable bibliographical assistance; The Australian Institute of Aboriginal Studies for financial assistance in making a short field trip in Western Australia; and the Canada Council for making it possible to visit Australian libraries. Finally, I thank the librarians of the Mitchell Library in Sydney, and the library of the University of Western Australia for all their help and advice whilst fossicking around the stacks.

Acknowledgments are made to the Oxford University Press, the Syndics of the Cambridge University Press, and Angus and Robertson for permission to quote from works under their imprint.

CHAPTER 1

Anthropological Man

1 INTRODUCTION

Since its inception in 1961 The Australian Institute of Aboriginal
Studies in Canberra has collected over 30,000 references to various
aspects of Aboriginal life. They range from the observations of Dutch
navigators in the first half of the seventeenth century to the present
time. For three hundred years varieties of individuals of European
cultural background have been describing the Aborigines and their ways
of life — Why? What questions have been explicit or implicit in their descriptions? This business of describing and asking questions of other cultures has become so pointed and specialized over the last century or so
that it has given rise to the various branches of professional anthropology —
Why have anthropologists, especially social and cultural anthropologists,
been interested in other cultures? Why have they been interested in
Australian Aborigines? What has been, and is, the significance of their
work? What are the unanswered questions that could form the basis of
future work, and what intellectual challenges lie in the material?

Attempting to answer these questions entails a movement of the mind
between the Aborigines themselves and their cultures, and the investigators and their cultures: a quadratic relationship whose intricacies the
mind has to hold and map. Aboriginal cultures are specimens of ways of
life, particular solutions to the problems of living in community. They
present scientific and intellectual problems that we recognize as such in
virtue of our own cultural heritage. On the other hand, the Aborigines

1

are people, not just problems. They are men and women, shaped in our image, part of ourselves. Their ways of life are strangely familiar, yet quite different and other. To understand this otherness we can go to live and work with them, or simply read about them. We can collect, measure, and document. Either way, perhaps, we may be allowed braver insights into the mystery of our being as man: reflections on what we once were, or a more accurate measure of what we think ourselves to be. If imagination founders, for what it is worth we may chalk up an addition to knowledge. At any rate, for those whose cast of mind has been shaped by European civilization, because the Aborigines are there—"out there"—some attempt, it seems, must be made to bring them within our comprehension as parts of ourselves.

Sir James Frazer, perhaps the most renowned of British anthropologists, never visited the peoples about whom he wrote so much. Reaching over time and space from his workroom, he asked himself a question: Why did he who would become Diana's priest at Nemi first have to pluck a branch from a tree in the sacred grove and then slay his predecessor? A straight answer eluded him—as indeed it must elude anyone who asks such a question. But, like his fellow classical scholars who regularly visited Italy and Greece, Frazer went to the lake of Nemi in the Alban hills, hoping perhaps to find some guidance in the atmosphere of the place. He was led into strange paths. His question, he found, was not simply an historical or antiquarian one. It embraced the evolutionary, psychological, and sociological implications of why this kind of thing should be done by any people anywhere. It drew him deeper and deeper into the complexities of being another kind of human being. Yet what started Frazer on his quest, why his question should have seemed to him so important, is difficult to answer. Why, once started, he should have continued is rather easier. It was the adventure itself that absorbed him, not its end. And though this is probably the truest and most general answer to any endeavor, like scholars and scientists in other disciplines, anthropologists and others who go to live among strange peoples have their own personal reasons or justifications for doing what they do. Thus, to take a more contemporary example, Richard Gould (1969, p.5) draws the contrast between ourselves, with a nuclear technology, and the traditional hunter-gathering way of life of the Australians. Observing then, that it is given to only a few anthropologists to see this kind of life at firsthand before it disappears for ever—to feel it and learn from it—he goes on to say: "This is the reason I came to the Gibson Desert . . . living and sharing experiences with these nomadic people is exhilarating but carries with it an inescapable feeling of loss . . . as if we were watching the last redwood or the last bison disappear."

The romantic impulse, the sense of physical and intellectual adventure, and the poetic juxtaposition of different kinds of human experience are clear. They serve the explicit and scholarly purpose of studying an unfamiliar way of life. But there is more in it than simply recording a way of life that seems destined soon to disappear — though this would be adequate reason enough. Because Gould asked himself how Australians lived, and set himself to study a way of life which, in a general way, was lived by our own remoter ancestors, there is the assumption that in learning what it feels like to be a hunter-gatherer we are rescuing a part of our own heritage as human beings. What of man the hunter-gatherer remains in, and is inextricably a part of, the men who stepped on the moon? Or, as Frazer might have put it, What part of me is in the King of the Wood at Nemi?

By contrast, Mervyn Meggitt (1962, pp. xvi–xvii) is much more specifically intellectual and scientific. His main object, he says, is to undertake a detailed analysis of Walbiri society in order to facilitate the placing of this central Australian people within an overall comparative framework. Within this broad approach, he goes on, he intends to deal with some specific problems: whether marriage is determined by reference to genealogical relations of kinship, or by reference to sections and subsections; the relative importance of locality, genealogy and subsection in relation to life crises such as birth, betrothal, initiation and death; the relation of kinship to totemic organization; the significance of unilineal descent groups; the changes that have occurred in response to contact with Europeans. To a layman unfamiliar with the technical terms of anthropology all this may seem rather baffling. Yet having braved the words — and they will have to be encountered again in later pages — a layman could surely discern that Meggitt's interest was directed to the details of a social organization that lie behind the convenient but more general expression "way of life." He is taking much the same direction as Gould, but he intends to go much further and he makes explicit just what detail he is going to cover. He is talking not so much to the public at large as to his colleagues. If here and there in his book something may be gleaned of his personal relations with, and interest in, the Walbiri people, he has ruthlessly subordinated them to the scientific and intellectual problems of a professional anthropologist.

Take another standpoint: an anthropologist as seen by the novelist, Xavier Herbert (1959). The anthropologist and his context are, of course, creatures of Herbert's imagination. Still, presumably they reflect in some part the novelist's experience of and with anthropologists. Set in the Australian outback, the tragicomic events of the plot, in which an anthropologist plays a major part, may be seen as a study of varying facets of fraud, chicanery and self-deception against the backdrop of what is thought of as a primitive and pristine honesty. "Perhaps he," writes Herbert (*ibid.*, p. 28) in introducing his anthropologist, "took up anthropology because he saw it as an easy means to easy living, a kind of racket, as indeed he made it seem with his blathering . . . and it is a fact that even scholarship, or rather the simulacrum of it, can be and very often is quite blatantly used as a racket . . . . Indeed there is nothing else in which handouts can be come by so easily, in the form of bursaries, scholarships, fellowships, foundations, grants – gravy, money for jam."

Neither trivial in itself nor about the trivial, Herbert's passage is satirical in the manner of Swift. He is concerned not only with delineating a character of his own invention, and stripping him of his professional pomp, but with ridiculing the revered institutions of a society which made him possible. Some anthropologists are, perhaps, simply careerists.* That is why they study Australian Aborigines – or anyone else that may seem opportune. But granted that our foundations, universities and other public bodies may make mistakes, that in real life they can be bamboozled by just the kind of charlatan which Herbert invented, we are left with the fact that in a society in which money is the basic measure of man, the people who run these bodies are still willing to disburse public or trust monies in support of the general endeavor of anthropology. Why?

The reasons why particular and individual anthropologists do what they do are legion. One is a romantic, perhaps, bent on escaping for a brief period the complexities and pollutions of life in an industrialized society. Another may be streaked with masochism. One or two may have failed to emerge from the chrysalis of boy scouting. Some feel that in probing the intricacies of another social order they may better humanity's lot. Others are captured by the intellectual, scientific, emotional and physical adventure of it all. Yet these and hosts of other personal and particular reasons for becoming an anthropologist should be subordinated to the sociological and significant. When the irreverencies, satire, charlatanry, romanticism, philanthropy, and academic cant are washed away, a nugget of truth remains. There is in European or Western culture, for whatever reasons contingently recruited, a firm commitment to the substance of

*See Berndt, C. H. 1964.

what is contained in the enterprise of anthropology in itself. If the present professionalization of the subject can be squarely placed in an increasingly complex division of labor related to a policy of universal education, there is also something more. Not something outside of ourselves, something artificial put on for the sake of appearances, something foreign, a burden shouldered for economic or other reasons, the spin-off from a transient imperialism, this commitment appears as an integral part of our European heritage. Anthropology — its substance and form — has a European signature. It is to what lies above and behind that signature we must turn if we are to understand why Gould — like many another — should be impelled to think he could perceive, grasp and then make articulate the importance of catching a final glimpse of the tradition al mode of life of hunter-gatherers such as Australian Aborigines; why Meggitt should have thought not only that he could analyze the social institutions of the Walbiri, but that it was right and appropriate that he should; why Herbert, appreciating in himself and his culture the nature of the impulse to anthropology, should attempt to bring it into a more general awareness through a story shot with wit and irony. No one could take it on himself to answer for the scores of individuals with their own particular motives and desires who have thought it worthwhile to study Australian Aborigines. Even if they were accessible and statisticized, that would be charlatanry indeed. But something can and must be said about the fact of anthropology, the phenomenon of anthropologists studying Aborigines — or anyone else.

Anthropologists do not go to the field with empty heads and without prejudice. They take with them what has been implanted in them; they go because of what has been implanted in them. If in some small measure an anthropologist may become a member of another culture and perceive the world anew, he can only do so through the lens of his native heritage, trying to answer questions posed in the home environment. Everest was climbed because it was there, and wherever there is a mountain people will climb it if they can. It is human to do so. But it is not enough to say that other cultures are studied because they are there. They have been there for others but yet not studied. Why should they be studied? Since this studying, anthropology, is intrinsic only to European culture and civilization, the answer must be found therein. Outside that context thought and imagination founder. No real answer is to be found in allowing events in time to "lead up to" a climax. And an appeal to particular political contingencies will not take us far. If there are features which distinguish the encounter with Australian Aborigines from those with

American Indians or Africans or Asians or the islanders of the Malaysian and Oceanic archipelagoes, each set of particularities seems to spring from a more general and deep-seated intellectual and moral address. It is possible to separate how Aborigines have been treated from why they have been studied. The register of contingent oppressions together with the more sustained record of service and self-sacrifice may be held as distinct from the continuing scholarly exploration and account attested in libraries. But in fact, as we shall presently see, the two aspects are intimately related. The one could not exist without the other. If there is an answer to our question that is not simply a "just so" story, it would seem to lie in the moral idealism which has linked and infused the correspondences of intellectual perception informing both the enterprise of anthropology and the European tradition on the one hand, and the contingencies of political action on the other.

2   THE REACH INTO OTHERNESS

The first thing that strikes the visitor to Australia who takes the trouble to go out of the cities into the countryside is the breathtaking beauty and variety of the natural environment. Roads, fenced paddocks, orchards and farmsteads make little impact on one's first impression: it is an open and rolling land whose woodlands, hidden clefts, and rising hills welcome the wanderer who knows how to use them. For scores of thousands of years the Aborigines have had this knowledge. They bent the land's resources to their purposes, acknowledged their fate when they knew there was nothing they could do. Stocked with insects, birds, reptiles, and marsupials — each with its analogue in the mammalian world overseas — the land was here desert, there marsh, or tropical jungle, or parkland, or snowy mountain, or sheltered cove. The Aborigine, his dog, a rat, and the flying fox were the only mammals. Few in numbers and moving from camp to camp, gathering with others in season for feasts, ceremonies and the settling of debts, the Aborigines lived through an eternity of time knowing only themselves, their land and its animals and plants. Then the white man came. No longer alone in their humanity, the Aborigines could find no way of refusing or entering a companionship that was alternately offered and withdrawn in contempt, could make little sense of the strange and unpredictable new environment of things, crops, people, and settlements. But they managed. They retreated to areas where the white man would or could not go, or, breasting the waves of the new culture, they were flung wounded and maimed into the flotsam.

For nearly two centuries the Aborigines have striven to retain the traditional ways which their forefathers bequeathed them; or they have tried to enter the white man's world on an equivalent footing. In the latter, they are beginning to succeed; in the former they have failed. Yet their cultures are not altogether dead. They have been preserved between the covers of books and journals. A few generations hence the descendants of today's Aborigines will discover that their traditional cultures were among the most voluminously if not most exhaustively studied in the world. Having by that time become more or less thoroughly Europeanized it is possible that they will take it for granted that their ancient ways of life should have been investigated. A considerable act of imagination will be required of them to perceive that if strangers other than Europeans had come to Australia the achievements of their forefathers would probably have gone unrecorded, lost in the mists of an unknown dreamtime. For if all cultures and civilizations have created and live in terms of fields of activity, knowledge and awareness which, though authentic unto themselves, can be described as though they fell very roughly into our own primary categories, only within European civilization and its derivatives overseas (Western civilization)* do we find that sustained and systematic concern for man and his creations—whatever his color and shape or whatever cultural or physical environment he might be inhabiting—which we have come to call anthropology.

All peoples are curious about strangers, investigate, explore, discuss, and lampoon them. Westerners are by no means alone in having traveled and told of their experiences in foreign lands among strange peoples. (See, for example: Abu Talib Ib Mohammed, Isfahani (1810); Hsuan-Tsang (1923); Ibn Batuta (1958); and Ibn Khaldun (1958).) But using these accounts to build up a taxonomy of social institutions and their inter-relations, and deliberately quitting the home environment specifically in order to do these things—these activities are exclusively a part of the European heritage. If today there are many anthropologists who are not European, it is because anthropology is but one of many European ways of doing things which their cultures have been adopting, or in which, as individuals, they have become so involved as to be, culturally, Europeans or as though Europeans. Though all cultures learn from their experiences of and with other cultures, and from time immemorial have been in-corporating those bits and pieces of other cultures which they find useful,

---

*Except where explicitly distinguished, or where the context makes clear that such a distinction is intended, "European," "European and its derivatives overseas," and "Western" are used synonymously.

and rejecting or attempting to reject those which they find repugnant, what is authentic to the European or "Western" tradition, and it alone, is a culturally determined appetite for learning about, and absorbing, other cultures and civilizations.

It can be and has been argued that this appetite and capacity is simply a by-product of European imperialism (see, for example, Gough (1968)). Yet history shows otherwise. For while there can be no doubt that the development of anthropology is intimately related to the European expansion overseas, this is but to restate one aspect of anthropology's European signature. Another and deeper perspective is gained when we remember two of the major uses to which Westerners have put their knowledge of other cultures: the construction of ideal or alternative forms of society, and the attempt to realize these different forms. Here the ancestry goes back at least as far as Plato's *Republic*. That same imaginative impulse which, leaping from the prison of its own social experience, attempted to describe another social order also searched for and found extant empirical examples on which it could build and embellish.

In a very real sense this impulse or inherent awareness of an alternative social order, imaginative or real, may be said to have "called anthropology into being." From the unself-conscious and haphazard to the self-conscious, explicit and systematic, anthropology has been realized as a distinct but integral part of this awareness. Implicitly or explicitly, satirically or otherwise, in a variety of literary genres, this awareness has tended to express itself as a critique of European society as it happened to be at a particular time and place. And the critique has always been intimately related to the ways in which the outward expressions of the sources and mainsprings of the European tradition have been changed, reformed or transformed. Which is to suggest that a significant part of the European tradition, its developmental experience, has resulted from continuing attempts to synthesize the traditional or interior cultural experience with that which is, or is considered to be, other than or outside of itself. Anthropology is part of this interplay, has been produced by it, has contributed to it. And anthropologists themselves are deeply marked by the larger processes in which they are, and have been, involved. When they investigate Aboriginal life, anthropologists enter their heritage, explore an alternative way of life.

Although it is conventional to place the beginnings of anthropology in the Enlightenment — that period when European expansion into new worlds had got well under way, and when Australian Aborigines began to become a part of ourselves — the attitudes and casts of thought that produced the present general subject and the disciplines within it have, as the passing reference to Plato has implied, a lineage that goes back to the ancient Greeks. Not simply to Herodotus, Thucydides, and Alexander the Great, whose activities in home and foreign lands involved investigating, recording, and learning from the ways and customs of both strange and more familiar peoples — though they are clearly and obviously significant enough — but to those philosophers whose struggles with the relations between the subject and object finally led them into the *logos*: that rational account of phenomena which separated subject and object in such a way that there could be thought to be an objective reality, and in terms of which all the data might be saved. Often contrasted with that participation in the oneness of things considered typical of Eastern forms of thought (see, for example, Young (1969)), this notion of saving the data through a rational and objective approach — where we ourselves are parts of objective reality — is commonly cited as the basis of what is distinctive in the European contribution, particularly in relation to its achievements in science and technology. Yet, without denying the point, it is possible to go a little further, to suggest that if this rationality is *distinctive* of European thought, the more common characteristic, from which perhaps the nobler contribution has arisen, is a dialectical engagement between "rational objectivity" on the one hand and the opposed notion of "participation in oneness" on the other.

If we consider for a moment the contrasts between, say, the cool rationality of a Plato or Socrates and the Dionysian rites and orgies; or the logical intricacies of Christian theology and its pietistic excesses; or the organized and rather worldly Church and the frequent millennarisms within it; or the sweet intellectualisms and science of the Age of Reason and its glossolalia and enthusiasms; or the scientifically industrialized society and the many movements back to nature and the land; the point is illustrated. Though in a particular period and situation one of the pair appears to predominate, and in different times and circumstances the other seems emphasized, the essential feature is that at all times and places within the European ambience, both at the level of the individual and at the level of the collective, each of the pair has been at work, generating a series of corresponding oppositions through their mutual engagement. Heart and mind alternately meet, synthesize, part company, and meet again. Embracing Aborigines and studying their cultures should be complementary but can be contradictory.

The intellectual achievement which created an opposition between rational objectivity and participation in oneness corresponds with that imaginative reach which can perceive and consider from a third point of view an opposition between things as they are and things as they are or might be in another realm of experience. When man first crossed the threshold and became aware of himself, he cut himself off from the natural world about him. Becoming morally responsible, obligated, man could no longer be like anything else in the world. But the impulse and desire to close the gap, to return to the paradisiacal world of no-obligation, to act in accordance only with the programmed instincts of nature, remains in all men. Partially bridged by expressing human relationships in terms of the identifications, similarities, and differences observable in nature, the breach between nature and culture, animal and man, and instinct and morality is further healed by a perception of the oneness of things. Participating in the One, all phenomena are refractions of the One. The natures of all beings and things and ideas are discoverable through a contemplative interplay, by analogy or opposition, between own being and otherness. Looking both inwards and outwards, while the components of own being can be projected onto the outer world the parts of the latter can be introjected into own being.

To this harmony of a diadic conversation the Greeks proposed an alternative: that purposeful movement toward the rationally objective which, implying a judgment on the diadic conversation from a third point, is opposed to the participatory life and has entailed a further severance from nature. This, times without number, individuals and groups within the European ambience have sought to redeem by giving free rein to the participatory impulses and emotions. Australian Aborigines, like so many others, have fallen victim to these opposed understandings. Monographs attest the warmth and sympathy as well as the system and specimen.

The early Christian Church, concerned as it was with organizing itself and translating a legacy of varieties of political, economic, and administrative powers into more specifically Christian moralities, could hardly do other than, generally, follow in the wake of its predecessors, the Romans, and their philosophical mentors, the Greeks. It gave, through its rituals, ceremonies, and local ordinances a certain scope within which the natural and emotional lives of its followers could be realized. But it was never content to leave it to saints or hermits and other religious to show by example and *ad hoc* teaching how a life that was both spiritual and moral could be contained within a synthesis of the opposition between the rationally objective and participation in oneness. Building on its Greek and Roman heritage as well as the gathered collective experience of its religious, it moved toward a distinctive theology built on a triad. Very briefly, and only so far as it is directly relevant here, God the Father and Creator, as concept, was rational and objective. He was the Reality in which all phenomena were comprehended, in whose being and awareness nothing was lost. Outside of ourselves and our social relations, He was "over there," comprehending all things which He himself had created and continues to create. Yet we puny humans were considered to be created in His image. We had the potential of participating in a small way in all the parts of His immensity. Still, He was outside us, apart from us, temporarily set aside by the Fall. Conceptually and emotionally, however, the apparently irremediable consequences of this were resolved in the Incarnation. God's immensity and "otherness" and "overthereness" became man and lived amongst us as man and Word. As Christ, as Jesus, the Son of God mediated between God and man, was in every man. Though Christ was the Second Person of an indissoluble Trinity which was still "out there," because Christ was in everyone, everyone was "out there" too. The Third Person of the Trinity reiterated this process of reconciliation. For while the Holy Spirit was "out there," an integral part of the Godhead, it operated not *on* but *in* man, only in man, and it did so creatively and imaginatively as well as, of course, spiritually and inspirationally.

Intellectually, the Trinity and the triadic conversation entailed in rational objectivity correspond with one another. Detached from the idea of rational objectivity, participation in oneness entails few conceptual difficulties. It comes as it were "naturally." Subject and the variety of objects it contemplates relate to one another in innumerable pairings. The mind perceives qualities of likeness or difference, analogizes, associates, refines, and generates a host of relations and distinctions. It is a subjective process, yielding varieties of albeit ordered impressions whose validity depends upon impact, usefulness and, finally, consensus. A critique is achieved by eroding the consensus, by demonstrating or by arguing according to specific rules that the data may yield other more profitable or aesthetically satisfying relations. Again, a decision one way or the other is ultimately reached by persuasion and consensus. All peoples think more or less in this way, and all peoples have their varying sets of rules by which, in different contexts or universes of discourse, the game may be played. But to reach out and say that "*This* is *a* or *the* Truth independent of a consensus" is an enormous claim. Yet this is precisely what rational objectivity means and entails. And within the European ambience this claim is made not once or twice in a generation but habitually. We make the claim when we appeal to logic, to mathematical truth, to revealed truth, to science. Though we might, we do not (as in other cultures in usual) necessarily make such a claim when we appeal to tradition, to the law, or to our own social experience.

The Greeks pinned their faith to logic and mathematics, the two faces of the key to the harmonies implicit in the universe, nature and culture. But so far as they relied directly on these alone they failed to carry the day against participation in oneness. To logic and mathematics, however, Christianity added the revealed truth. The Christian intellect, particularly as it adumbrated the materials of the New Testament relating to the Incarnation, succeeded in holding in both hands if it did not entirely reconcile the primary opposition between rational objectivity and participation in oneness. Indeed, Christian theology not only allowed, but taken in its fullness positively insisted that man step outside himself and view himself dispassionately (as God might) at the same time as it has decidedly affirmed the participatory life of interrelatedness in community. So that, for example, the practice of confession demanded not only an appraisal of one's acts in relation to others and a set of rules in which an approximation to godliness was thought to be manifest, but also in relation to the Godhead "out there." Nor may one miss the fact that this meshing of the rationally objective with participatory interrelatedness could, and can, also be expressed or achieved by entering another cultural ambience: seeing oneself and one's own from the standpoint of otherness. But to sustain the mind's movement out of its cultural nest to the point where it can regard its own native ambience with dispassion requires faith, faith in the validity and purpose of that movement.

Every field anthropologist knows the moment when, his own intellectual and cultural props slipping away, but not yet able to lean on the understandings of the other culture, he is utterly alone and wants to run home or "go bush" — become an Aboriginal and enter fully into the simplicities of nomad life. What supports his resolve are not only the discomforts and complexities of that life, but the residual and dogged conviction — born not of himself but of his culture — that he is doing something he ought to do. Without that culturally derived support, he would succumb. Faith and intellectual commitment are necessary. Without that the rationally objective cannot be maintained against the inertial human drift toward a viewpoint based wholly on participation and interrelatedness. Yet it is just that faith and intellectual commitment — expressed today in doubts about science and its attendant technology — which is beginning to falter. Without faith, the rationally objective becomes a chimera. Without the substantial if subjective values of the participatory life to bite on, the rationally objective becomes a mechanical idolatry. For while the rationally objective must necessarily grow out of the participatory values, and is grounded in faith, this faith in the ability of an intellectual construct to appreciate precisely the nature of things is forever exposed to the critique and stimulus of the heart: the intuitive and insistent perception of the reality inhering in the truth of things.

As a mode of appreciating the nature of things, science is a comparative newcomer. But it was built on Christian foundations which, continuing into the present, still play a crucial and essential part in the way anthropologists come into being and attempt to develop their subject. Consider for a moment St. Paul. He, his circumstances and what he did provide a convenient and archetypal anchorage. A Jew who was also a Roman citizen educated in Greek, Paul was an intercultural being, no other than truly Christ's man. His particular animadversions to the law, circumcision and the Messiah could, at best, be only dimly comprehended by gentiles. Yet they could not but arouse the hostility of Jewish communities whose distinctive cultural identity rested, in large part, in an opposite view of these features. For the exclusive community of Jews, determined to retain their identity in the Roman hegemony, Paul's further teaching—the Incarnation; the Resurrection; the new life in Christ and love; reliance not on the rigidities of the Mosaic law but on the Holy Spirit through Whom the law could be transformed, developed and transcended; the new man, product of the new law, extending his love and morality across cultural boundaries; the realization, through love and the Holy Spirit, of common humanity in Christ—was anathema. On the other hand, for the slaves and other displaced persons in the Roman world, for those who no longer possessed a distinctive identity to lose, and for those whose ancient traditions told of a dying and risen god, the message rang more sweetly.

Perhaps it was the Greek in Paul's intellect that led him to put his finger on those very features that could reconcile participatory relatedness in oneness with the intellectual perception of rational objectivity. If, as a Jew, Paul was a misfit or renegade, unacceptable to his native community, as a gentile, a peculiar mixture of othernesses—and prototypical of latter-day leaders of millenarian or adjustment movements— he worked in a world more or less ready to receive him. For this Roman world had already started, quite explicitly, to incorporate varieties of otherness into its ambience through the notion of natural law, the *ius gentium*, and the anecdotes, reports and books of its administrators and soldiers if not, more implicitly, through its triumphs, games, the importation of slaves and prisoners and the recruitment of mercenaries and auxiliaries to its armies. But Rome lost faith in its gods, its law, its purpose. As unable to meet its political, economic, and military difficulties as it was unable to provide that intellectual and religious framework which might contain and order the emotional and participatory needs of its varied communities, otherness overwhelmed it. From the disintegrating ruins those with faith, believers in the Incarnation, began to take over the reigns of power.

On one level it was only logical that, having accepted the Gospels and the Pauline legacy, the early Church should have incorporated certain books of the old Hebrew traditions into the sacred scriptures as the Old Testament. On another level, the incorporation of the books of the Old Testament into the sacred scriptures made it virtually obligatory that scholars and others with an intellectual bent of mind should come to terms with otherness. It is nothing less than astonishing that the Bible, the most influential book in European civilization, still a yearly best seller, should find such minor or no mention at all in histories of anthropology. For through the Bible and its interpreters all kinds of different European communities were brought onto common ground, came into contact with, and knew, the word of God as it was expressed in the myths, history, figures, and customs and activities of a strange non-European people. Not only was man considered to be made in the image of God, but it was through the variety of images of other kinds of man that European peoples were invited to seek the dimensions and mystery of God and of themselves. Not simply the symbol incorporating the totality of kinds of participatory awareness available in a particular culture, God was personal, universal, for all mankind, the incorporation at the level of the rationally objective of the participatory awarenesses of all kinds of cultures and moralities.

The mark of the educated European layman has always lain in his knowledge of the languages, histories, philosophies, and customs of the ancient Greeks and Romans. For the cleric a knowledge of Hebrew was an additional requirement. For all, a knowledge of the scriptures was essential. Today, developed and transformed in idiom, this same tradition of saving the data, of widening the intellectual and cultural horizon by incorporating varieties of otherness, is given expression in the study of Aboriginal cultures. Just as scholars once addressed themselves to the ways of life of the ancient Hebrews, Greeks, and Romans, and used the categories they derived from such studies to understand themselves as well as others and their interrelations, so now, albeit more systematically and perhaps mechanically, anthropologists seek to probe the mysteries of man's condition in particular places and cultural ambiences within a purportedly universalistic science of culture and society.

When, after the crumbling of the Empire, Europe was forced back on itself, on the defensive, virtually losing contact with the learning of the ancients, the books of the scriptures became the primary materials on which the intellect could express itself. The Bible was, perhaps, an appropriate vehicle for an ambience which had almost ceased to know the civilities and complexities of organized interurban life. "Almost," because Augustine's *City of God*, itself planted in revealed truth, the scriptures, Plato's *Republic*, and the urban ambience of the Romans, was also available. Moreover, scholars, poets, and chroniclers, who had come by their basic skills through biblical studies, the discipline of theology, and the learning of other languages such as Latin, Greek, and Hebrew, could not but be influenced by this education when they began to write (and translate into other European languages) of their own local traditions, epics, legends and experience in love, marriage, battle, business, and politics. If awareness of otherness, and a desire to incorporate that otherness into one's own being was not built into the nature of the European peoples, the Christian ambience certainly made it so. "There is much to be said," writes Anne Righter (1962, p. 23), "for the subtlety of a theatre in which Moses can enjoin obedience to the commandments of God upon an audience of Israelites who lived before the birth of Christ and, at the same time, with all the force and directness of the original incident, upon mediaeval people who, at the conclusion of a day of pageants and processions, will make their way home through the streets of an English town." Though in Spain and Italy this awareness and incorporation of otherness was reinforced by the presence of Muslim invaders, it was not until the Crusades (which, despite the material self-interest of its captains and leaders, would have been impossible to mount without a popular and grass roots sentiment about the Bible and its relevance to themselves) that Europeans as a whole realized a rather different dimension to those experiences of otherness with which they were already familiar. In going to the Holy Land they actually encountered peoples living very much the same kind of life as the ancient Hebrews had done. The Jew, familiar as townsman, merchant, and financier, an epitome of those whom Jesus had chased from the temple, could now be seen much as the Old Testament described him.

The European powers did not have either the physical and economic resources to sustain the initial motives of the Crusades, or the political unity that might have found those resources. But the political divisiveness of Europeans seems always to have been accompanied by that generalized impulse to appropriate otherness. The experience of the Crusades, political failures though they were, simply whetted the appetite for intellectual otherness. If Islam and the political order that went with it were rejected, the work of Muslim scholars and scientists was embraced. Though one result of the Crusades was the series of plagues known as the Black Death, they were followed by the Renaissance: a burgeoning efflorescence of the arts and sciences brought about by, among other purely indigenous factors, the rediscovery of the ancients and a peculiarly ethnocentric grasp of the relevances of the Islamic contribution to the European scene. More's *Utopia* and Bacon's unfinished *New Republic* were explicitly rooted in Plato's *Republic*. They were also descended from Ibn Khaldoun's *Muquaddimah*, Augustine's *City of God*, biblical and theological studies, and the works of medieval poets, chroniclers, and scholars. There was, in addition, a quite new element. For both More and Bacon seem to have owed much to the accounts of sailors, merchants, and missionaries who had started to make their ways to China and Japan.

Between them, More and Bacon mark the new beginning of what was to become a massive output of works devoted to the construction of alternative social orders. Some have been purely imaginative—reaching out from a limited self's experience to idealize, satirize, inform, or project a future. Most have drawn upon other contemporary cultures and ways of life. But, whatever their purpose, all are rooted in the European experience of otherness and in that culturally determined impulse to come to grips with yet further kinds of otherness. Every field monograph by a social or cultural anthropologist is an integral part of this long-standing European movement to bring new worlds into cognizance. There are the same imaginative stretch to incorporate otherness and make it intelligible; the same problem of translating a participatory experience into a statement that is rational and objective. Appreciating Aborigines as human beings has been accompanied by the attempt to communicate the culture in a rational and objective way. If an anthropologist was as observant as Herodotus or Marco Polo; as aware of the travels and travails of the human spirit as Dante; and as systematic as Aquinas or Bacon; his image of what he ought to be would be largely fulfilled.

More and Bacon took their cues from the creative ambience provided on the one hand by a formal, disciplined literary and philosophical education centered on the sacred scriptures, and on the other by the tales and stories of returned travelers. The latter provided the materials on which intellect and imagination could work, and, in turn intellect and imagination brought order to random tales and adventures. But lying behind this scholarly activity was a long wrought tradition of accounts of exploratory work. Christianity was always a missionary faith. With St. Paul as exemplar, Christian missionaries implanted the faith in Egypt and Syria, along the desert road to Samarkand and beyond, in Ethiopia and across the Indian Ocean to the Malabar coast. They were always busy in Europe itself, consolidating the faith. Though the Islamic expansion undid most of their early work outside Europe, the tradition remained strong. As soon as they could do so they were again making their ways to the ends of the earth. Continually infusing the European homeland with experiences of otherness, they wrote not as uneducated sailors might speak but as men trained in the mastery of foreign languages, disciplined in logic and theology, familiar with the Bible and the tales and legends of the ancients. As they had provided the soil from which the medieval morality plays had grown, so, after the Renaissance through to the present-day missionaries and clergy have prepared the mind for an appreciation of otherness. As teachers and educators they shaped the ambience in which Shakespeare's histories could become intellectually intelligible. As travelers who were bound to reflect on what they had seen and experienced, they provided the framework in which Othello, Caliban, and Prospero could be appreciated intellectually as well as morally. It has been the collective and accumulated experience of the missionary tradition, in short, which has prepared the European mind to accept rather than reject the strange or new experience, and then come to terms with it.

If there were in Shakespeare's times, as there certainly were through the centuries that followed, individuals who winced and tried to slip away when some ascetic missionary or poxy mariner grabbed their lapels and insisted on telling their tales of woe and wonder in other lands, the more pervasive and lasting reaction has lain in the attempt to order and so absorb the new experience into ever-expanding fields of awareness. Indeed, just this, attempting to transform a direct and raw experience into something of intellectual, scientific, and more general relevance is precisely what anthropologists set out to do. Moreover, those who set out to do this, whether or not they call themselves anthropologists, are anthropologists or have something of the anthropologist in them. The point is not simply that anthropology, until recently, and particularly in the nineteenth century, has relied on and used the materials provided by missionaries, traders, travelers, administrators, explorers and others, but that anthropologists, especially the field anthropologists of this century, like all others involved in the expansion of the European cultural heritage, have been and are imbued with missionary purpose. In part, this purpose consists and has consisted in a determination to bring to others, less fortunate, a better, wider, more civilized, more satisfying way of life: a deeper awareness of their own conditions of being as men and women.

How to realize this purpose is the rub. Still, however done, whatever the mode of giving may be, the offer becomes a resolve to find the means of incorporating another culture into one's own. Given some measure of success in this, the process of incorporation revivifies and transforms one's own culture into a more satisfactory and universalistic ambience. Active and purposeful participation in this cultural exchange and mutual incorporation rather than the activities of one dressed in clerical garb define the missionary endeavor. A positive interest in social reform and a better or more satisfying way of life, both in relation to his own and the other culture, have always been lively components of an anthropologist's equipment. When, in going to the field, he seeks to appropriate both for himself, his culture and posterity the whole of a strange social order, he tends to justify his intrusion into the affairs of others by referring either to what are in fact missionary ideals — albeit phrasing these ideals in a secular idiom — and/or to the impersonal appetite of science. On both hands he is being moved by the messianic theme. Anthropologists, indeed, represent a specialized differentiating out of some aspects of the missionary role.

To accomplish the missionary purpose, however, requires more than the impulse and determination to do so. Paul's experiences are, again, prototypical of what has happened times without number in the European experience. The peoples addressed object to the proposals being made. They do not seem to comprehend what is required of them. They may become excessively overenthusiastic. They misuse, twist or pervert what is given, told or taught them. It was not wholly Paul's fault that many of those to whom he preached sought to reenact the events of Pentecost, strayed into those very emotional, orgiastic, and morally rigorous activities which his own intellectual bent and charitable inclinations eschewed. Nevertheless, scores of missionaries, explorers, administrators, and anthropologists since Paul's day have been faced with attempting, both physically and intellectually, to deal with much the same kinds of activity. But where Paul was able to respond with letters, persuasive words and a charitable disposition, his successors have more often been forced to resort to force. Why, as Paul did, attempt to stifle or extirpate these repetitions or simulacra in one's own social ambience of that prime

Christian experience, the events of Pentecost? Why should these activities not signalize complete conversion or incorporation? If for Paul, who welcomed the gifts of the Spirit, it was a question of asserting order, decency, and charity against anarchy, excess, orgy, and uncharitable rigors, for his successors the same themes have been qualified by politico-economic motives and an overemphasis of the self-interested rationality that usually goes with them.

Summing up these varieties of "pentecostal" activity as overemphatic relapses into participation in oneness at the expense and defeat of rational objectivity does not, for the most part and strictly as summary, do injustice to the facts. Granting the crucial distinction between one who lacked political power and the means of physical coercion, and those who have it, what differentiates Paul from his successors, whether missionary or administrator, is that without the participatory values rational objectivity is worthless. What they have in common is the realization that without a grasp of the rationally objective an apparent incorporation would be merely illusory. For without that intellectual effort which, moving out of the constrictions of one's own time and cultural ambience can conceive of and appreciate the consequences of the unique historical event—through which all Christians become One in Christ—Christianity becomes a series of disjointed and unrelated if simple and happy get-togethers. Rational objectivity is a tough one. It puts the untutored mind to an almost unbearable strain. Particularly is this so when, as in the Christian tradition, this intellectual demand is accompanied by the equally firm injunction to love one another, help one another, and participate in the being of others. A crucial difference between European and other cultures is that whereas the authenticities of the latter are, for the most part, integral and almost organic developments of the communities concerned, in the former they are born out of otherness. The frequent recurrences of millenarian and similar kinds of activities within and on the peripheries of the European ambience, characteristic and integral to the European experience, bear witness to the difficulties involved.

For Paul, developing Greek ideas of history, history as distinct from myth, the Incarnation was an historical event, the culmination of a long wrought historical, not mythical, process. If the Resurrection was a mythical and not an historical event, all was vain. If Pentecost could really be repeated by almost any emotionally aroused group of people, then it was but the dramatic enactment of a myth, and the Holy Spirit a mere phantasm. For Paul, as for Christians down the centuries, it was, and is, absolutely essential that certain events actually occurred, historically, not only symbolically or mythically. Without the intellectual faith that could move out of its own ambience of time and place and affirm the historicity of these few events, and so the historicity of countless other events down the centuries, European culture might have collected together a host of myths, stories, legends, and accounts, but it is questionable whether it would have had history or a history in the sense that European culture has developed it. For if every nation or culture has a history, the business of history, properly understood, is discovering that history and making it explicit. What is distinctive in the European notion of history is the attempt, in spite of or with the aid of received traditions, to unravel a social matrix and series of events that existed and occurred within an ambience distinct from the present — and this by abiding by an implicit if not always explicit intellectual construct, methodology or set of rules concerning the value and relevance of the evidence adduced.

It matters little in the present context that we now know that much of the Old Testament is in fact myth — though it is the European notion of history, characteristically set against its own received traditions, which has made that knowledge possible. Nor is it of great moment that so much of so many reputed histories is myth: information at another level of awareness. What matters is that rational objectivity makes history possible. In spite of the intuitive perception that individuals' lives seem ultimately determined by chance or the random or arbitrary, a rational or logically interconnected account of man's affairs becomes conceivable. Further, through this rational objectivity what had been thought to be myth may be found to be not simply historically based, but in itself historical as well as mythical. If it is to the Greeks that we owe the notion of linear as distinct from cyclical or structural time, St. Paul's teaching put the seal on it. It was rational to deduce a relationship of cause and effect from intimately related successive events, and this especially when the events in question seemed to go together with a flux in social relations which could be recorded. The cultural tradition was provided not only with events and relations that, agglutinated in the mind, had or could have the qualities of myth, but with events and relations that could be fixed in time, separated, and shown to be or not be directly related to one another. Although it was, and remains, inevitable that another social ambience, or developmental process, past, present, or future, cannot but be seen through — and so colored by — an author's own social ambience, the idea that this other social ambience might be appreciated apart from, as well as in terms of, one's own social ambience, that the means existed to reach toward God or the divine and perceive oneself, one's past, or another as

God might have done, has from the beginning been firmly rooted in the European intellectual heritage. Only this makes it possible for us to think that we can unravel something of the Aborigine's past.

Bearing in mind that expressions of rational objectivity have always been accompanied by the opposed notion of participation in oneness, the encounter with other cultures raised problems that remain with us to this day. The early missionaries asked themselves three main sets of questions: Were these strange peoples, so similar yet so different, representatives of man, one with themselves, or were they something other? If they were indeed men and women, how had they come to be where they were as they were? How should they be treated and what should be done with them? Like all peoples whom we know something about, Christian missionaries had, first, an ethnocentric, social or cultural definition of man. It was a variant of that definition, common to all cultures, which can be subsumed in the phrase, "The potential of entering by due process into the full range of awareness of the rights and obligations offered by the culture." In general, the longer the line of ancestors or ancestresses associated with the ingroup or native culture, the greater was the potential of a particular person becoming, or being thought, fully man. The stranger the individual, the more remote the possibilities of his entering by due process into the rights and obligations of the culture, the less the potential of being considered fully man. In addition to this universal and moral if ethnocentric definition of man, however, Christians lived and acted within terms of the great chain of being, a legacy of the Greeks. Within this framework, which held that every type of thing or existent, animate or inanimate, had one or more properties in common with another type of thing or existent, it was entirely possible that a creature very like a human being could exist without, in fact, being man. However, complying with the demands both of rational objectivity and religion, the Christian definition of man, going directly to descent from Adam and Eve, and then, later and qualifiedly admitting the possibility of polygenesis, was grounded in a knowledge or awareness of God or the divine. This awareness could be deduced from the evidence of articulate language, religious activities and, more particularly, moral sense: the articulate discrimination between right and wrong action.

In the first question "Are they human?" together with its ancillaries, "As human as we, In what ways different?" we can see the beginnings of an enormous literature concerned with the religions, customs, rights, obligations, moralities, and languages of other cultures. These same topics, much elaborated and differentiated into a variety of specializations though they have become, lie at the core of anthropology today. If there are some anthropologists whose engagement with their fellow human beings is liminal, all join in paying at least lip service to a deep respect and love for others. This they do because it is in this respect and love that the subject is grounded.

The second question has probably led to more contention and bitter feelings between concerned scholars than the first. For while the answer to "Are they human?" might be directly intuited and later rationalized or referred to an intellectual construct or set of rules, the question how and why a people had come to be where they were as they were had to be answered rationally, historically or quasi-historically: before being referred to an intellectual construct or methodology, evidence had to be retrieved from the past. In the case of a literate culture with the evidence of documents, monuments, and remains, the historically minded could and did set to work with a will. In the case of a nonliterate culture, however, the problem was how to make the past reveal itself as history in the European sense.

It seems to be a universal in human affairs that when asked to account for, or explain or explicate an event or relationship, there will be a resort to some kind of historical or quasi-historical mode. Within the European ambience, both in a general as well as in the more especial sense, an historical or diachronic mode remains the crowning explicans of human experience. It presupposes some appreciation — reached through a synchronic mode — of how things are. Yet though the problems deriving from the definition of man might include, they do not necessarily require, a notion of how things came to be as they are. We can say something pertinent about the thought and activities of a strange people in a synchronic mode without having to account for how things came to be as they are. Still, the job seems somehow unfinished. In the absence of written records however (and we may note that there are many more nonliterate than literate cultures) the synchronic account coupled to imagination had to suffice. A means of making history (in the European sense) reveal itself, some way of entering a disciplined and rational diachronic discourse, was required. But these means, though present in embryo in the Graeco-Roman period and through the Middle Ages into the Renaissance as generalizations on the apparent patterns of historical events, did not come into their own until after the Enlightenment.

Two relevant features of the Enlightenment may be mentioned here. The problems deriving from the questions asked by missionaries, as well as the more general problems about the nature and origin of society being investigated by scholars in their studies, though they fed into each other, began to be differentiated into separate disciplines and subjects, each with its own set of methods and rules of evidence, each becoming more and more systematic in its methods and purposes. Hitherto central to all study and educated discourse, the study of man, though framed within the stabilities and harmonies of the great chain of being and seen in relation to God, the angels, spirits, intelligences, living things, nonliving things, existents and matter, became differentiated from the study of nonhuman phenomena, and itself began to differentiate into a variety of specialist fields. The study of man in his social ambience was detached from theology and the term "sociology" – the systematic study of the forms of society, literate or nonliterate – was invented. At this point, for many, social and cultural anthropology began. Second, the sustained critique of Christian teaching – and it was traditional Christian theology alone which held rational objectivity and participation in oneness in a crucial synthetic balance – placed rational objectivity and participation in oneness in a taut and unsynthesized opposition. Whilst some addressed themselves to the worship of reason, rationality, sober judgment, and the development of what was to become science and scientific method, others engaged in orgies of participatory sexual promiscuity, murder, mayhem, and religious enthusiasm. Many alternated these opposed and contrary kinds of activities in their own individual lives without in any way allowing the one to bear on or influence the other.

The events of the French revolution illustrate not only the separation of these primary themes in the European heritage, but also, eventually, their uneasy accommodation and juxtaposition rather than synthesis. Continuing into the present, this juxtaposition means that an individual may choose or be impelled to one rather than the other. Held apart in this way, a synthesis is rarely achieved. It has always been relatively simple – though fast becoming less so as the consequences become more evident – for the scientist engaged in the study of nonhuman phenomena to separate his investigations from his personal and social relations, to live two lives, to be wholly rational and objective in the one whilst in the other he remained subject to whimsy, chance, and the pressures of accepted usage. But to live like this has always required faith, complete confidence that the results of rational investigation would inevitable benefit the quality of the sum total of social and personal relations. We are now at the point – as in the Enlightenment in relation to Christian teaching – when the evidence seems to show this faith to be not as firmly grounded as had been supposed. And again, as in the Enlightenment, battle has been joined. While the protagonists of science plead the virtues of rational objectivity in human as well as in nonhuman matters, antagonists found movements and create new communities based almost wholly upon the participatory values. Nor is this present lack of a culturally enjoined or determined synthesis a dilemma from which anthropologists and other social scientists have been able to escape. It affects both their own lives and the studies they make of others. And because, unlike the investigation of nonhuman phenomena, the study of human affairs necessarily involves a moral relationship between investigator and investigated, entails an answering back, the dilemma has usually been contingently and implicitly resolved at the level of a naive or uncertain political stance generally favoring the *status quo*.

From the outset, though sociology was conceived as the rationally objective, scientific study of the forms of society, the participatory values deriving from the moral relationship found expression. At one level the purposes of study were rationally objective: to find out. At another level the purpose of finding out was to change, to build a more perfect, a more rational form of society in which each individual could wholly fulfill himself. Inevitably, sociologists brought to their investigations and constructions varieties of moral stance and political idealism. Inevitably, too, the kinds of moral stance and political idealism could hardly do otherwise than take departure from what was already familiar. Even though the increasing numbers of utopias and works on political economy relied heavily on published descriptions of other cultures, the themes that bound them together and gave them coherence were taken directly from Christian teaching and systematics as well as the contemporary political scene. Social science has always rested on ideological assumptions.

It was the same with that branch of sociology and anthropology known as social anthropology. With the more systematic expansion overseas of European peoples, missionaries, administrative officers, antislavery groups and aborigines protection societies, alarmed at what was happening to many subject peoples, addressed themselves to the twin tasks of recording as systematically as possible the customs, social institutions, and languages of these peoples, and attempting to ameliorate the conditions under which they were living. On the one hand, by investigating, describing, and analyzing strange cultures and languages, and so "saving the data," they gave expression to rational objectivity. On the other hand, by siding with these peoples against the inroads of settlers, merchants, and land expropriators they allowed the participatory values to take shape in moral and political terms. Nevertheless, separating *people*, with whom one necessarily comes into a political and moral relationship, from their *culture*, which on the face of it seems readily accessible to rationally objective study, has never been easy. Inevitably, what is said of the one reflects on the other. A political bias becomes implicit if not explicit.

As the intense and exciting intellectual and emotional activity that was the Enlightenment gave way to a rather calmer period during which the new knowledge could be put to use through the opportunities offered by the industrial revolution, a means by which history might be made to reveal itself in rough or approximate fashion without recourse to documents, came to hand. Until about 1860 those Europeans whose work brought them into contact with primitive peoples asked the same sets of questions as had been asked down the centuries. Where there was European settlement the question of what to do with the natives, and how to treat them, was usually of most pressing concern. The answers supplied were, on the whole, generalized, deriving directly from their own cultural ambience rather than from some explicit systematic designed for the purpose. Like the scientists who investigated nonhuman phenomena, those whose work took them to faraway places attempted to describe, identify, and name the activities they saw taking place around them. Some tried to adduce the interrelations of the activities they described. Many made wild guesses as to how things had come to be as they were. Mostly, however, because they could do no more with the evidence available, they made synchronic studies. For that crowning diachronic explicans they were forced either to infer or invent a plausible quasi-history, or use models derived from the transformational processes observable in plants, animals, and individual human beings. But the publication in 1859 of Darwin's *Origin of Species* marked a change for which neither Darwin nor his book were wholly responsible. Long gestating, appearing several times since the days of Heraclitus and Aristotle but never accepted, so often the stillborn child of the great chain of being but now to take life and find a welcome, the idea of an *evolutionary* pattern in affairs was seen as the key to the secret of how things came to be as they were. At last something significant could be done with the accumulating data.

More useful in the hands of natural scientists than for students of culture, evolutionary theory nonetheless gave specific direction to both kinds of study. Close inspection of the differences between otherwise similar classes of plants and animals led into the idea—based upon the model of similarities and differences in human families, where the qualities and characteristics of a particular individual were attributed to this or that ascendant relative, or compared with other relatives in the same or descendant generation—that at some time in the past these similar classes had a common ancestor or origin, and that variations had come about through a process that combined ontogenetical development, natural selection, and differing environmental pressures. Vague and imprecise as these terms were, the enhancement into principle of the general lines of participatory family gossip, and their application in a quite different context, was generative and stimulating. With this illumination it became possible to place different types, species or subspecies on a "family tree." By plotting the variants of a general typology on a time scale, by correlating categories of simplicity, complexity and differentiation with categories of time—earlier, later, before, after—it seemed possible to track back through time to a plausible origin. It was also possible to come forward and so trace a possible developmental or evolutionary process. Either exercise could feed into and qualify the other so as to achieve a fit. Given acceptance of the general principle of evolution, internal criticism and dispute turned on the nature of the "fit," on relative position on a descent, evolutionary, or developmental line, or on relative placement as a "collateral."

If to some the logic of evolutionism, Darwinian or Spencerian, was spurious and based on false premises, to most it was neat and decisive. Few of the conceptual tools used by anthropologists today do not derive from the painstaking work of scholars nearly all of whom worked within an evolutionary framework. Yet despite many refinements over the years, evolutionary theory has never been wholly acceptable. For although, as a heuristic device, it could yield very persuasive hypotheses as to the way in which institutional forms *might* have developed, and provided investigators with a wealth of insights and guides as to what to look for, it could not be said that this or that was the way it *had* actually happened. In a sense, evolutionary theory bore the same relation to history as myth. Indeed, it could be argued that the soundest basis for accepting the validity of evolutionary theory is that it was grounded in the kinds of transformational truth that are in fact revealed by myths; that because, like myth, it was generated at the level of collective participation, then made rational and objective, it was the better suited to revealing social as distinct from scientific truths. Yet, because of the way adherents were expected to operate, evolutionary theory belongs—though many a historian might deny it—to the rationally objective. Ideally, it entailed a separation of subject and object, and a movement of the mind outward to the point where the separate ambiences of subject and object could be appreciated and interrelated in terms of an impersonal theory or intellectual construct — whether God or Nature lay behind it.

Nevertheless, whether as myth or pseudomyth, as a set of propositions about the transformations of social institutions — where real myth dealt with the transformations in human experience within a particular cultural context — evolutionary theory seemed to many to be a bad or false myth. The historians were joined by those whose attitudes of thought were rooted in participation in oneness. Expressed at first in religious terms, and later in more specifically moral and political terms, hostility was centered in what seemed to be the necessary — and if not logically necessary then the likely or directly experienced — consequences of evolutionary theory in the context of the interrelations of political and social groups. It is one thing to assert that cultural or social forms, and people, are conceptually separable, quite another thing to keep them separate and pretend that what is said about the culture does not necessarily reflect on the people, the individuals involved. So, for many scholars and laymen evolutionary theory seemed to carry with it an ineluctable hierarchy of higher and lower forms. Which implied separate origins, separate lines of descent, inherent and unalterable relative differences in capacities of comprehension and competence. In relation particularly to north European cultures, other peoples could be and were thought of as inferior types of man. Further, though these inferior peoples might advance in the evolutionary scale, since the superior would also advance the differences between them would probably remain much the same or become even more exaggerated. Peculiarly appropriate to a society in which the rich got richer and the poor poorer, and to a business ethic which held survival, fitness and success to be dependent upon superior moral capacities for hard work, foresight, risk-taking and initiative, evolutionism, given the imprimatur of science, was as convenient to the tasks of imperial expansion as it was supportive of those maintaining or gaining rank or status at home. Sociologically, the adoption of cultural evolutionism marks the shift of power from eighteenth-century aristocracy to the nineteenth-century business tycoon, from a stable elitism to a competitive elitism.

Because Anglo-American expressions of evolutionism were so much creatures of circumstance, opposition to it was muddled. Some fundamentalist Christian sects, for example, opposed evolutionary theory because it seemed to contradict the Bible. On the other hand, wholly committed as they were to carving out a place and identity for themselves, founding new communities in recently discovered lands, they adopted much the same attitudes toward primitive or nonliterate peoples as many evolutionists. Grounding their faiths in the Old Testament rather than the New, they took departure from Hebrew exclusivism and the story of Noah and Ham. They were the elect. Nonliterate peoples were and always would be hewers of wood and drawers of water. For more traditionally oriented Christians, however, mankind was descended from Adam, was one, had language, moral sense and so an idea of godhead, was shaped in the image of the creator, was as-god, had the opportunity of redemption, could be taught how to enter into and exercise the full range of rights and duties available to a Christian. And it was this stream of Christian thought and attitude which, combining with its otherwise estranged offspring, liberalism, set its face against varieties of racism. An uneasy alliance carried on currents of economic expansion and political ambition, the combination found expression in antislavery movements, aborigines protection societies, and the determination not only to build a better kind of society but to teach, train, and bring all within the fold of many kinds of abundance.

This matrix of mixed premises and aspirations, which derived from the demands of science and rational objectivity on the one hand, and the participatory values on the other, is still embedded in anthropology as a subject. It is intrinsic to asking what is the purpose—and so what are the premises and methods—of studying ethnographic materials. During the first half of the nineteenth century scholars and laymen began to meet to discuss, in intellectual vein, problems and questions that we now regard as falling within the scope of general anthropology. Later, these discussion groups of friends and acquaintances were to merge and form the national institutes and associations through which the variety of interests within the subject could be organized and developed. At first these societies were largely historical and antiquarian. But those who met and read papers to each other—historians, classicists, lawyers, churchmen, missionaries, civil servants, colonial administrators, army and naval officers—were virtually a new class of educated professionals who were beginning to take their place in a liberal and bourgeois world. They set the pace in founding the various societies through which, in addition to their memoirs and travel books, a knowledge of other cultures had begun to be disseminated to a widening literate audience. They brought to the discussion of ethnographic materials their own several and developing professional canons of method and purpose. If the lawyers were interested in abstracting from a cultural matrix the sets of rights and obligations which governed the maintenance of a social order, and others were interested in language, or whether there was a belief in a supreme being, or the social organization, or whatever it might be, all were concerned with how things had been in the past, and how they had come to be as they were. They were by no means cosy groups. Criticism was fierce and pointed, particularly when discussion centered on the topics on which they were bound to be divided and in which they were most keenly interested: scope, purpose, and methodology.

Which aspect of Aboriginal life should be professionally studied for what reasons by what methods were not issues wholly related to status and careerism. Rational objectivity and the participatory values were not in a synthetic balance and, moreover, scientific technique and technology had begun to drive a wedge between "scientific problem" and "intellectual problem." For medical men, trained in biology, wedded to evolutionary theory and accustomed to regarding man as one of many zoological species, there could be little compromise. The developing subject had to be based in biology and biological techniques. If the truths revealed were uncomfortable, so be it. Truth was paramount. But for others the consistency of biological "truths" lay more in the arrogance of those who asserted them than in the "truths" themselves. Besides, there were many kinds of truth, and only a few of them were necessarily biological. In England in particular these issues gave rise to quarrels, resignations and expulsions from learned societies, and the formation of secessionist groups (see Stocking, 1971).

In the upshot the biologists and evolutionists carried the day. Although many historians and antiquarians seceded, finding a more amiable intellectual environment in folklore societies, some remained associated. Together with the lawyers, missionaries, and colonial administrators they formed an influential but disunited opposition to the establishment of biologists. Some of them went along with evolution either as a heuristic device capable of posing problems for investigation, or as a type of explicans to be adapted to social or cultural facts, or both. But there were many who objected to biology as the explicans of culture. In the first place it meant that no one who was not trained in human biology could be considered a competent anthropologist. This, considering the naiveté of many biologists regarding culture, seemed outrageous. More important, if human biology could explain by reference to the upright posture, brain case, speech organs, opposable thumb and other features of the biological organism what it was that made culture possible, it was not a sufficient explicans of the enormous variety of cultures and social processes that were rapidly filling the horizons of knowledge. Similarities could be taken for granted, it was variety and difference that needed explanation or, at the least, systemic description.

With the advantage of hindsight we can appreciate that, within an intellectual ambience characterized by successive separations of varieties of discourse and literary genres, what was going on in these early discussion groups and societies was a competition for the adoption of a particular style and method of dealing with the data and making it relevant. Jurists, historians, philosophers, political-economists, literary critics, linguists and others in humane studies as well as physical and natural scientists had found their niches. The accounts and speculations of travelers, merchants, explorers, administrators, missionaries, and military gentlemen were well-established genres. If establishing the study of man required, first, abstracting and differentiating from these varied enterprises those features which would provide a coherent and scientific field of discourse, it also needed an orthodoxy of method, scope, and general purpose. Each group of contestants brought to the arena a specific expertise which had been developed for a purpose other than the investigation of culture or the forms of society. Each had adherents and followers. None was able to gain the day for more than a short while. The contest continues, albeit in a more indulgent atmosphere. There are now too many varying and competing approaches, methodologies and purposes for any one particular school to be the specific target of another. Rather has the intellectual argument shifted into more explicitly political alignments.

Never in complete eclipse, the biological explicans has, over the years, alternately diminished in influence only to return with renewed vigor and persuasiveness. For man is indeed an animal, and, because it seems to evade the moral issues of will and purpose articulately expressed, the biological approach might also avoid the pitfall of political bias. On the other hand, it was and is precisely that part of man which distinguishes him from other animals that is and was of interest to those interested in culture. They were concerned with the varied expressions of man's symboling and imaginative faculties, in his articulate moral sense and purpose. These features, it was and still is held, are not susceptible to biological explanation or "reductionism." Yet if the separation of biology and culture as distinct universes of discourse is convenient, the challenge of science resides in asking whether that convenience is appropriate.

The core topics of anthropology were, and remain: man's origins and present status; kinship; social organization; religion (which includes myth, ritual, and modes of thought). Given that over the years different methodologies and viewpoints for dealing with these topics have been developed, the first could be said to lie within the competence of the general field of biology. Even though it could be held that the discovery of a pile of bones without clear evidence of culture was the discovery of something other than man, what was sought were the evolutionary links between man and animal, and particularly that threshold where a manlike creature actually became man. But the studies of man, people or population groups do not necessarily coincide with each other or with the investigation of culture or society. As an artifact is distinct from its maker, and can be analyzed in relation to other artifacts, so other aspects of culture may be studied, diachronically or synchronically, without reference to the biological makeup or origins of their creators and users. The second topic, kinship, could also be said to lie within the biological competence because, actually or putatively, it seemed to be grounded in a biologically explicable courting and mating system. Within the restricted vision of the middle and professional classes, marriage, subject to explicit rules and therefore open to systematic investigation, seemed synonymous with mating which, if not wholly random, was and remains resistant to reliable and systematic investigation. Except in the case of primitive peoples, who were thought to be for the most part prisoners of their environment and natural endowments, social organization could be conceded to historians and others who believed that man's fate and progress lay at least as much in his own hands as in the stars or Nature.

There was a further point which biological evidence could make. The obfuscating curtains of organized religion had to be torn aside. While they remained man's spirit and creativity were hopelessly entrapped. All Christian religious emphasized the close connection between kinship, the family and religious values; and studies of other cultures were beginning to show that the relationship was even more intimate than had been supposed. Particularly was this so in the case of the Australian Aborigines. Kinship, marriage, being born, growing up, and dying were inextricably buried in a matrix of religious or protoreligious values. If it could be shown that mating, marriage, and kinship varied with biological makeup and environmental conditions, or that religion belonged with a primitive state that could be biologically determined, then it might be possible to show revealed religion as the sham it was supposed to be. Ever since the dawn of the Enlightenment organized religion had been under heavy fire, and, with the acceptance of evolution, it seemed that the battle was almost won. But again, protagonist and antagonist tended to talk past one another. Each wanted the whole, neither was content with the part. Too many Christians held blindly to history, to the dogma that the Old Testament account was made up of literal and historic truths. They had forgotten, too, much of the import of the New Testament: that man realized himself in surrendering to divine law—which must include the implications of man as animal. Indeed, no organized religion could hope to survive for long if it denied the animal man. On the contrary, it is precisely the antitheses between animal man and the requirements of living in community in a cultural ambience that all religions seek or should seek to resolve.

Much time, energy, and opportunities for the posing of more fruitful problems were lost in these disagreements and in the attacks on established religious orthodoxy. Still, this is and was consistent with the traditional role of the substance of anthropology: the positing of alternatives through otherness. If anthropologists along with most of the natural and physical scientists of the time were guilty of intellectual vandalism in relation to their heritage, they yet managed to collect an enormous amount of data on different cultures. With this data they developed the concepts which burden the anthropologist today. Withal, though most of them paid lip service to science, they wrote not to an audience of natural or physical scientists or technologists but to those who, like themselves, were interested in the human experience as it was to be gleaned from literature, classical and biblical studies. They had to adapt their style of discourse and vocabulary accordingly. If there were some natural scientists who knew, or who had heard of, men such as Sir Edward Tylor or Sir James Frazer, or Morgan, Andrew Lang, Bachofen or Westermarck, it may fairly be doubted whether there were many who were familiar with the content of their works. On the other hand, the literary, historical, religious, and philosophical worlds knew their work well. Even allowing for the growth in professional parochialism, much the same is true today. Those trained in the natural and physical sciences only rarely take up social or cultural anthropology, though of course a few turn to human biology and prehistory. Nevertheless, recruitment is mainly from the humanities, from those disciplines which have always dealt with man's articulate awarenesses and purposes. Indeed, where the evidence depends at all on the spoken word these competences are crucial whatever other kinds of skills an investigator may possess.

Evolution had its impact on anthropology because of the way it brought order to biological facts, because those trained in biology took up anthropology, and because, going to the animal in man, it seemed to have the potential of dealing positively with what seemed prior, most basic or elementary in man's condition. From the Greeks and through European history, culminating in the Enlightenment through men such as Lamarck, Buffon, and St. Hilaire, ideas like evolution had constantly been appearing as a framework for the understanding of social or cultural phenomena. It was as constantly rejected because, like a myth, it had to be taken on faith and was opposed to history. Until applied to biological facts it did not have the appearance of a rationally objective framework. Even then it was not suited to historians dealing with time scales and ranges of data too narrow for evolution to apply effectively. It was, and remains, too glib and simplistic for philosophers attempting to elucidate the principles by which the historical process could be understood. If some were tempted to an explicans based on racial superiority, on the whole they were not interested in cranial measurements, monogeny or polygeny, races as species, man's relation to apes and monkeys, and other topics that seemed to be becoming anthropologically relevant. They were interested in what man had done, proposed to do, failed to do, and had had to do in particular circumstances; what he had thought about, how he had expressed himself, what he sought, how he had managed. To be sure, Marx and Engels used the data that evolutionary theory turned up. But their idiom was Hegelian. Whatever the driving force, spirit or physical resources, if man was animal rather than word positive and ordered explanation was vain. Chance or God ruled.

By about 1890 evolutionism began to wane so far as the accounting for culture was concerned. There were too many flaws, too many well-established historical facts which simply would not fit the developmental framework. Still, in little more than a couple of generations a basic taxonomy of social institutions had been established: a culture or social order could be described in terms that were thought to be specific. And the diffusionists who now came to the fore had no choice but to use this taxonomy. Advocated by the historically orientated whose interests centered on the ways in which peoples had migrated, and how ideas, customs and techniques had spread, diffusionism was nevertheless bereft of any coherent framework of ideas that could order the data to hand, or pose fresh problems. But for the diffusionists themselves this was virtue rather than vice. Hooked by the supposedly scientific nature of what was called "inductive method," they set out to find the facts. Theorizing could follow. If this was all well and good for literate peoples, or where there was documentary evidence – Alas! Nonliterate peoples had no history that the number of researchers and current techniques could reveal. Consequently, within anthropology the question, "Where did they come from, and how did they come to be as they are?" came to be answered by recourse to numbers of varied and *ad hoc* hypotheses which grew more and more exaggerated as time passed. As a set of interrelated and organized disciplines, anthropology lost direction and became the plaything of the interested amateur, an easy prey to assertion and opinion.

Not until toward the end of the first quarter of this century did the study of culture again cohere into a more or less specific universe of discourse. This is not to say that between 1890 and 1925 no good work was done. Far from it. Frazer was industriously immortalizing himself. Rivers and Boas, giants both, were at work. Malinowski and Radcliffe-Brown had already started to formulate the ideas whose development was to have such an impact later on. As then, so at present. Those who thought of themselves as anthropologists were looking for bases of cooperation or definitive grounds on which they could part company.

In some ways this period of halting uncertainty is difficult to understand. For those interested in culture Marx, and through him Engels, had provided very reasonable formats within which anthropological data could be made intelligible and relevant, within which problems could be developed and investigated. Specific criteria by which a developmental process could be measured were offered. The events of history were given a pattern in terms of social relations. Through marxist thought the data of anthropology, made strange and esoteric by the evolutionary taxonomy, could be incorporated into the general terms of European philosophical discourse whether the conversation turned to history, technological innovations, bride-price, or the relevances of patriliny versus matriliny. It was not to be. Marxist thought was political theory, and anthropology was science, a mode of operation in which political biases supposedly had no place. Clinging to the taxonomy of evolutionism was but a symptom of the commitment to science and, implicitly, revealed anthropologists as determined to take their cues from developments in biology.

Then, too, there was the political climate in Britain and America and, to a rather lesser extent, in Europe as well. Arising from this, the negative feature, that Marx preached a revolutionary doctrine that could only be rejected by firmly established and conservative bourgeois scholars, seems not as important as the more positive feature: that in a world of imperial and economic expansion primitive or nonliterate peoples were definitely not of oneself but quite other, not to be discussed in the same breath as civilized and literate peoples. Meshing in with the political and racist implications of evolutionary theory, with the esoteric taxonomy that confirmed and preserved that otherness, with what was implied in the white man's burden, with the commitment to science, with the contingent needs of manipulating and dealing with subject peoples, with the practical difficulties of collecting data, the subject itself seemed to demand a radical distinction between We, scientists in a cool upper world of rationality, and They, prey to superstition, political bias, self-interest, economic exigencies. Science, supposedly, was above all this. In fact, of course, science served political ends, and scientists, unwittingly for the most part, cooperated toward those ends. A prosperity based upon technological expertise and competence shielded them from politics and convinced them of their apolitical nature and dedication to truth and science. It was left to particular individuals, mainly Christian missionaries to give expression to the political implications of the moral relationship inherent in being there and asking questions. Not until the late twenties and early thirties, when anthropologists started going to the field as a matter of professional routine, did anthropologists begin to realize the full extent of their responsibility. The moral, social, and political implications of Aboriginal conditions of life in relation to the larger community became quite explicitly a part of anthropology.

Shortly after the First World War, and mainly under the influence of Malinowski and Radcliffe-Brown, social and cultural anthropology found new direction. Whether under the label "functionalism," or "structuralism," or "structure-function," or "culture pattern," the overriding assumption was that parts of a social order or culture were integrated, interconnected and interdependent. Operationally the main problem was how this interconnectedness could or should be demonstrated. Given that social relationships were in, or tended to seek, an equilibrium, three main analogies were used to characterize the equilibrium and the ways in which social relationships cohered: the organismic, the architectural, and the mechanistic. But if social relationships could be analyzed or intellectualized as though they were interrelated organismically, or as in a building, or as in a machine, how far the analysis was an artifact of the analogy, and how far it corresponded with the empirical reality were always topics of criticism and reassessment. There were, moreover, differences of opinion as to the bases of culture or society, and whether or not such assumptions were even necessary. Malinowski's view that culture was based on certain biological needs—food, regulated sexual access, shelter, security, relaxation, mobility, growth—found little support in others. For the culture-patternists, culture was the artifact of man, and its sources and patterning were to be found in the interplay between history and the psychological effects of the modes of courtship, sexual access, conception, birth, and early child nurture. On the other hand, there were those who held that since, existentially, man was the child of culture and society, the participant in a number of interrelated collective representations which were there before he was born and which survived his death, it was necessary only to analyze the interrelations of these collective representations. The origins and bases could wait.

Though integrationist and functionalist theories continue to be influential, their heyday was in the period between the twenties and fifties. Marxist thought, based upon opposite assumptions, upon necessary conflict, alienation, and competition for resources, was little heeded. Evolutionary theory, though always appearing in geneticist and extensionist forms, was generally relegated to the background. It was, indeed, a necessary doctrinal introduction to the subject, a link with the more firmly based science of biology. Otherwise, it was held in temporary abeyance. There were more urgent tasks to face. If the simpler peoples of the world were not studied now, civilization would overtake them and their cultures would be lost forever.

Integrationist theories had, and still have, many flaws. But there is no doubt that in all their varied expressions they were preeminently suited to, and resulted from, intensive fieldwork — the *sine qua non* of professional anthropology over the last half-century. Necessarily synchronic in general mode because it was, in the main, the directly experienced field data that had to be rationalized, integrationist theory bypassed the conceptual difficulties involved in reconciling the diachrony and synchrony. The American culture-patternists, it is true, specifically included history in their conceptions. Being psychologically based, the diachrony was given further expression in geneticist and extensionist constructions. But the interpretations of history and the developmental process produced by the culture-patternists cannot be said to have been wholly persuasive, and the confusion between history and evolution was further compounded. For the British functionalists and structure-functionalists, on the other hand, evolution became a nonproblem, and history was formally set aside. In part this last was a reaction from the exaggerations of the preceding generation of diffusionists. It was also because, unlike the peoples which American culture-patternists were studying, well-documented histories of the peoples the British were studying did not seem to be available. Most important, however, was the overriding practical need for reliable and intensive fieldwork studies. Still, geneticist and extensionist notions kept finding their way into analyses; many monographs and essays had to resort to straight history as a background to their synchronic analyses; and "social change," a supposedly scientific substitute for the supposedly unscientific study of history, became fashionable. But except as a mode of recording changes that had occurred, social change, like diffusionism, has never been able to cohere into a set of interconsistent ideas capable of eliciting principles of change or the historical process.

Generally, despite the examples set by Hegel, Marx, and Weber, anthropologists have never found it easy to reconcile the diachrony with the synchrony otherwise than through varieties of adaptations of evolutionary theory, or the resort to straight history. The events of history, if not wholly random, are at least particular and not susceptible to generalization except on the basis of a specific doctrine about the nature of history. But since the adoption of such a doctrine would have entailed a defined political stance at the expense of a supposed detached and scientific viewpoint, anthropologists generally felt themselves debarred. Moreover, the urgent need for fieldwork seemed to make the choice exiguous. History dealt in flux, with changes in social relations and the social order, with the logic lying behind those changes, with processes of disintegration-reintegration. It seemed much more important to demonstrate interdependencies and integration—all those features that made for stability, permanence, and the *status quo*. On the other hand, despite the very real conceptual difficulties involved in integrationist theories, they and the fieldwork experiences that went with them can be seen as a part of that process of absorbing other cultures that we have suggested is authentic to European civilization. The fieldwork experience could not but narrow the gap between "We" and "They." Even though the supposed "objectivity" of science—understood by all too many anthropologists as entailing merely a rather special kind of diadic relationship between subject and object—still implied a separation between "We" and "They," the experience of living with and befriending the people studied, of collecting, analyzing and publishing data under the moral constraints of friendship and mutual confidence, has made most if not all anthropologists very much aware of the political implications of the moral stance they adopt in their work. Those people over there, near-naked Aborigines seated by the camp fire, were becoming, or have become more explicitly a part of "Us."

At the present time integrationist theories would seem to have more or less exhausted themselves, and anthropology itself is beginning to disintegrate into a variety of specialisms. Just as, in the nineteenth century, evolutionism seemed to provide the most comprehensive and general framework capable of including varieties of specialisms, so now, ever tempting an intellect itself bemused with shifts of power and status, evolutionism is coming into its own again. It demands a faith which may be lightly given, pleasures the mind with easily placeable data. Still, the moral, political, and conceptual dilemmas involved in separating people from culture, and in linking the cultural to biological and psychological or ethnological and ecological levels, have not been resolved. The way fieldwork data is gathered — by asking questions, obtaining answers, and direct observation of activities — necessarily entails analyses on two levels: what is said, and what is done. Inevitably one is led into discussing the relations between modes of thought and understanding on the one hand, the forms of society on the other. The distinction between evolution and history remains confused: the different kinds of supposal involved intersect and overlap in irregular patterns. The purportedly scientific account of man and society is still riddled with conveniently ascribed overt or covert purposes, functions, and causes — which must lead into questions of origin and history. Finally, at the core of the subject and implied in the reach for otherness, lies the choice of alternative basic assumptions about man and the nature of society.

What is man? Whence his coming, becoming, and going? Breaking these questions into their components, and then trying to find answers by searching the features of Aboriginal life, is why anthropologists study Australian Aborigines. The answers may be elusive. But without that reach into otherness the questions could not have been asked.

3   A EUROPEAN SIGNATURE

To understand why anthropologists have studied Australian Aborigines it has been necessary to make a summary excursion into the nature of anthropology's European signature. Had Europeans had another kind of history or intellectual heritage, or had they been cut off from that heritage in such a way that the past might never have existed, then Europeans might have embraced the Aborigines, destroyed them without compunction, left them to fend for themselves, or entered almost any kind of relationship with them that was consistent with overwhelming power on one side. But it would be going against the grain of all that we know of other contact situations in history to say that the Aborigines would have been studied. Their cultures would have been lost for ever, the drama of Aboriginal life would have been played to an empty house. The very fact that we take this kind of study for granted shows that it is integral to the way we are. Without that European signature the substance of anthropology is impossible to imagine. The enterprise derives from the Graeco-Christian synthesis. It was contained in that reach for otherness implied in the opposition between rational objectivity and participation in oneness, in the juxtaposition of Plato's *Republic* and the Bible, in a theology born of comparing the messages of the Old and New Testaments in the light of Roman law and Greek philosophy, in the theological synthesis of the *Republic* and scriptures in Augustine's *City of God*. The heirs of Herodotus, traveler and recorder, and of St. Paul, prototypical Christian missionary, have provided the materials for growth. The problems of the relations between the "here now" and "that other," the present and the past, the synchrony and diachrony, would seem to have grown out of the attempt to combine the great chain of being, Greek, with the Christian notion of history. If, inevitably, it seems that myth was the mediating element, assumptions with the qualities of myth still mediate between history and evolutionism.

Nurtured in an ambience of otherness, European civilization seems to have found, and still finds, authenticity in successive reaches into otherness. On the one hand, this has meant interacting with and learning about other cultures — absorbing them, feeding on them, synthesizing and reaching out again — within the terms of a generally diadic relationship governing word and deed. On the other hand, it has meant evaluating the resultant of the diadic encounter against an intellectual construct of more universal relevance. The problems which Europeans have sought to resolve in studying Australian Aborigines and, indeed, other peoples have been problems that are, on the whole, intrinsic to the European intellectual heritage. Problems deriving from the data itself have at once qualified the European viewpoint and been absorbed and transformed into European problems. Emphasizing rational objectivity, philosophers, theologians, scientists and historians have adumbrated the questions posed in generally abstract, intellectual terms. The same questions have been explored in mythological vein by dramatists, travelers, novelists, satirists, and utopians. The monographs of social and cultural anthropologists straddle or participate in all of these genres in varying degrees. They attempt to contain the participatory values within a rationally objective framework; mythological assumptions are the mediating elements. If the peculiarities of the demographic features in relation to the topography of the peninsular European mainland may have had something to do with this distinctive European address, it is much more certainly rooted in the intellectual effort which, conceived by the Greeks and ordered in Latin, flowered in the Christian environment. Exhorted to preach to all nations and bring them the good news, Christians were also in possession of Plato's notion of the ideal or alternative social order. They were expected to engage the participatory values, see Christ in all kinds of men and women, and see themselves not simply as others might see them but as they were, as God might see them. This last required what the Greeks had bequeathed: the intellectual perception whereby it became possible to save the data and take a rational and objective view of oneself, others, and the world.

The synthesis that brought rational objectivity into the secure and fruitful embrace of universalistic participatory values belongs specifically to traditional Christianity and its theology. Lacking that theology, or a substitute equally capable of containing given grounds of being and knowledge as well as their most pertinent critique, the synthesis is not easy to maintain. Unless it is firmly seized by the participatory values, rational objectivity must, in time, either wither away or, if grasped but not synthesized, create those tensions to which we now are heirs. Although there can be few fields of European endeavor which do not bear the impress of these tensions, because anthropology in each of its divisions is a subject invented only by Europeans, and practiced only by those participating in European cultural values, it may be supposed that it contains these tensions more pertinently. What has happened since the Enlightenment has been a proliferation and differentiation of problems deriving from the main tensions. The participatory values are expressed in the implicit or more explicit comparison with ourselves, in the moral relationships we are bound to enter when engaging with other human beings, in the political attitudes derived from the nature of the moral engagement. Rational objectivity is achieved through intellectual constructs which cannot but take departure from political and moral biases. Evidence is weighed and evaluated in the light of these constructs.

The technological skills which have made possible the kinds of investigation associated with the natural and physical sciences, and which these sciences have, in turn, developed almost beyond measure, still play only a minor part in social or cultural anthropological investigations. It is possible to make in a few days a journey that would, in the past, have taken many months. There are mechanical aids such as tape recorders, cameras, typewriters. Doing the job has become much faster and less painful. But not necessarily more thorough. Especially for the human biologists and prehistorians, scientific technology has vastly extended the range and accessibility of empirical data. Yet up until the present, social or cultural anthropology—our main concern—has remained on the whole a literary genre. The data is empirical, its collection, relevance and interpretation systematic: models of interrelatedness are borrowed from the natural and physical sciences and fruitfully used. Still, as a collectivity anthropologists have not brought to their investigations that sustained attention to smaller problems which is characteristic of the natural and physical sciences. Partly this is because those who study culture are what they are: political creatures who seize upon what takes their imagination. It is also because, while the natural and physical sciences are fed with billions of dollars, anthropology, expensive as it is, does not provide a living for many. The truth is that, compared to the natural and physical sciences, the financial investment in anthropological research hardly brings a sensible return. What is learned is mainly hidden in libraries, disseminates slowly, and is not methodically pursued and followed up.

An age of specialization has not left anthropology unaffected. Scholars find their niches by concentrating on particular topics, places, and peoples. At the same time, because in the words of Clausewitz, who was conscious of the extension of the political process, "it is particularly necessary that in the consideration of any of the parts their relation to the whole should be kept constantly in view" (Rapaport, 1968, p. 101), there is a continuous search for an overall and coherent framework of ideas which might, for example, as well contain and deal with economic affairs as it might describe and analyze kinship systems, religion or social organization. In a sense it is a search for the coherence of medieval thought or, indeed, for the kind of coherence to be found in the cultures of the small or nonliterate communities which anthropologists generally study. European civilization has always been composed of scores of subcultures, each engaging with others within the terms of a dialectic framed by rational objectivity on the one hand and the participatory values on the other. But the unity of European civilization is by no means a uniformity. The dialectic continues therein as it does in anthropology itself. Whether they set their sights on some small mountain-girt European community, a coral atoll, or Australian Aborigines, those who study other cultures make the process explicit. But again, the intellectual absorption of strange cultures does not necessarily make for a uniformity.

The process of investigation, of attempting to translate the terms of one culture into those of another, of implicit if not explicit comparison, constitutes an engagement whereby both parties undergo change. The interplay between the two cultures — "We" and "They" — continues until a third set of terms comes into being: another culture. Hence the requirement not simply of *any* intellectual framework expressing the dialectic between rational objectivity and the participatory values, but of one that envisages the ultimate synthesis or third set of terms, that can accommodate expanding awarenesses on both hands. The framework that cannot accommodate expanding awarenesses is stillborn. On the other hand, the moment an anthropologist disengages the dialectic, abandons the participatory values and starts simply to collect data which he hopefully feels to be free of moral relevance, he starts on a road that at best leads nowhere and at worst goes somewhere like Dachau in the forties. Whether study is directed to their animal nature, the symboling of communicative faculties, social relationships, or the links between these fields, people are moral creatures who beget moral problems. Seeking the truth about them and the environments they spin around themselves carries the burden of unleashing new evils and new moralities. How to keep the techniques of discovery subject to an address which acknowledges just this is a continuing if often covert imperative.

CHAPTER 2

Australian Man

1 ABORIGINAL STUDIES: PERSPECTIVE

Australian Aborigines were brought into the European ambience later than most other peoples.* From early in the seventeenth century until the first settlement in Australia in 1788, European knowledge of the land and its peoples was confined to the observations of sea captains who were, for the most part, engaged on other business—usually extricating themselves from the consequences of a storm or faulty navigation whilst investigating the commercial possibilities. Luis Vaez de Torres, the Spaniard, observed some Aborigines as he came through the straits that now bear his name; and Willem Jansz, Jan Carstenz, Abel Janszoon Tasman, J. E. Gonzal, and Martin van Delft are some of the earlier Dutchmen who recorded their impressions. For Torres, charitable and eager to justify his hard-won expedition, the Aborigines—or at least the islanders of the Torres Straits—were "clean, cheerful and grateful." But the Dutchmen were none of them enthusiastic. It was left to the English buccaneer, William Dampier, to make them known. In Mulvaney's words (1958, p. 135): "It was not the Dutch explorations but the poaching of William Dampier in [Dutch East India] Company waters which made Australia and its natives generally known; his *New Voyage Round the World* was a best-seller of 1697." With Dampier's *tour de force*, the Australian case rested for seventy years. Intellectual curiosity—aroused

*For accounts of first contacts and the main outlines of anthropological research in Australia, see in particular: Abbie, 1969, pp. 17–27; Elkin, 1935, 1939, 1958, 1959, 1963, 1970; Moorehead, 1966; and Mulvaney, 1958, 1971a.

43

perhaps by John Locke's *Two Treatises on Government*, and *Human Understanding*, published in 1690 — was temporarily assuaged. Further snippets of information did not significantly qualify Dampier's ample observations. The Australian coast is notoriously inhospitable to shipping and, at least until the nineteenth century, was always most hazardous to approach in the clumsy ocean-going vessels of the period. Political and commercial appetites, hardly whetted by the reports received, remained dormant. Still, those seventy years were years of intense intellectual effort and productivity in Scotland, England, France, and The Netherlands. They constituted the very heart of the Enlightenment, and Captain Cook's first voyage (1768–1771) was one of its major climaxes. Conceived primarily as a scientific expedition, to observe the transit of Venus from Tahiti, further purposes were added. Captain Cook was instructed also to look for the reported southern continent, annex it if he found it, report on its products and inhabitants, and establish good relations with the latter.

In due time Cook found the southern continent. He went ashore, explored. "We are to consider," he wrote in his journal (Cook, 1955, p. 397), "that we see this country in the pure state of Nature; the Industry of Man has had nothing to do with any part of it, and yet we find all such things as nature hath bestowed upon it in a flourishing state. In this Extensive Country it can never be doubted but what sorts of Grain, Fruits, Roots, &c., of every kind would flourish here were they once brought hither, planted and cultivated by the hand of Industry; and here are provender for more cattle at all seasons of the year that ever can be brought into this Country." He went on to describe the Aborigines and their way of life, as we shall see, in glowing terms.

Nevertheless, what Captain Cook, and indeed Sir Joseph Banks also, had to say about the Aborigines was completely overshadowed by the botanical, geographical, navigational, and political implications of the voyages. Besides, that interest in other peoples and strange cultures which had been restimulated by Rousseau's *Social Contract* (1762) was wholly taken up with the very epitome of the noble savage, the wonderful Polynesians. Polynesian visitors to London and Paris were lionized. Accounts of them and their ways of life, and the treatment accorded them, had all the brittle glamor of Hollywood in the nineteen-thirties. Nor did European settlement on the Australian mainland even the balance. Not an initially attractive people, the Aborigines struck few romantic chords in the minds of convicts, soldiers, and administrators. Successive governors, to be sure, were acutely aware that the Aborigines were, or soon would be, a "problem." Developing a penal colony in an environment of bona fide settlers, fortune hunters, scallywags, and a demand for cheap but well-muscled labor in a strange and unknown country brought its own more pressing conflicts. Besides, the land was not an immediate Lady Bountiful. It had first to be known, then coaxed, and later carefully husbanded.

The Aborigines, faced with ever growing numbers of settlers encroaching on their lands, soon lost their first wondering innocence and began to show the human face of corruption. Gin, rum, prostitution, idling, and filching furthered the process of disintegration. To the settlers the Aborigines were a nuisance, by turns exasperating, comic, or dangerous. They killed valuable stock, could or would not do the kind of work required of them, got blind drunk, had nothing to trade or proffer, could contribute nothing to the enterprise of developing a colony. Quite soon, too, it seemed to become clear to many settlers that the Aborigines were a dying race, scheduled for extinction in Evolution's onward progress. For some, hastening the process could be rationalized as obeying the dictates of Evolution or History. Even some of the missionaries who sought to stem the tide a little by setting up schools and what we would now call "relief centers" were enmeshed in the idolatry. Indeed, it was not until the fifties of this century that the dismal auguries of Evolution and History were discovered to have reversed themselves. The Aboriginal population is increasing rapidly. Yet in spite of or because of the Aborigines' expected early demise, administrative officials, travelers and sojourners, settlers, missionaries, explorers and others reported briefly on physical characteristics, general ways of life, modes of government and social organization, property, marriage, language, relative intelligence, whether or not Aborigines believed in a supreme being, and the possibilities of civilizing the Aborigine—the same general topics as had concerned travelers down the ages, including William Dampier and Captain Cook. So that although the period between 1770 and 1870—years which Elkin (1963) has called a phase of "incidental anthropology"—was by no means barren, there was no positive and coherent direction in the questions that were asked, and no positive system in the answers that were given.

In Europe and America, however, all sorts of things were happening. The years between 1858 and 1871 saw not only the establishment there of many anthropological societies and journals dedicated to the systematic study of other peoples, but the publication of numerous seminal works which, like Darwin's *Origin of Species* (1859), brought order to an immense, confused and confusing mass of material. In 1861 there appeared Bachofen's *The Matriarchate* and Maine's *Ancient Law*. T. H. Huxley published *Man's Place in Nature* in 1863, and M'Lennan's *Primitive Marriage* and Fustel de Coulanges' *The Ancient City* were published in 1864. The following year Tylor published his *Researches into the Early History of Mankind*. Lubbock's *Origin of Civilization* came in 1870, and in 1871 Darwin's *The Descent of Man*, Tylor's *Primitive Culture* and Henry Morgan's *Systems of Consanguinity* were published. Yet these are only a few representative samples, particularly relevant to anthropology, of an enormous output of literary works, learned and otherwise, in the half-century between 1843, when Herbert Spencer published his *Proper Sphere of Government*, and 1893, when Spencer completed his *Principles of Ethics*. The learned middle classes had arrived, printers and publishers thrived, writing a book gave status.

The period was one of growth and intellectual energy. Genres such as literary history, the novel, social commentary, criticism, essays, satire, early science fiction and utopian tracts differentiated and developed their particular styles and idioms. Anthropology, which in its substance was older than, and had participated in all these genres, also began to be differentiated as a distinct discourse. What had been a generalized and loosely ordered intellectual activity combining a variety of styles and interests had, by 1870, become a distinct area of study and investigation with clearly formulated problems. Publishing in Adelaide in 1879, Taplin, a clergyman, gave a rationale for what was already an established awareness among educated Australians. "It is of great importance (he wrote) that we should gain a knowledge of the customs and folklore of the Aborigines. Not only is it useful as the subject of scientific inquiry, but as a means of benefitting the natives themselves. We shall deal with them much more easily if we know their ideas and superstitions and customs" (Taplin, 1879, Preface). Thus briefly could Taplin draw attention to the scientific, political, and welfare or participatory aspects of anthropology.

In fact, evolutionary theory had for some years been giving direction to scientific inquiries in the field as well as in the study. About 1870, A. W. Howitt, who had had a quite considerable if casual acquaintance with Aboriginal ways of life, but who became conversant with some of the literature mentioned above, started a correspondence with Henry Morgan. He joined forces with L. Fison, a missionary who was also in touch with Morgan, and, fired with enthusiasm, addressed himself to problems of kinship and social organization. *Kamilaroi and Kurnai* (by Howitt and Fison) appeared in 1880, and Howitt's more mature *The Native Tribes of South-east Australia* came in 1904. But the period between was one of continuous work in which Howitt, whose correspondence with Morgan led to the designing of more and more fulsome and complicated questionnaires together with hints and instructions on how to gain the desired information, was but one of many who now had a clearer idea of what might be done and how it should be done. Method was becoming important. Close analyses of data took the place of more or less random impressions, anecdote, and speculation. Between 1870 and 1910 R. H. Mathews published some two hundred papers, most of them dealing with kinship, marriage classes, and social organization. Other authors were E. M. Curr (1886); R. Brough Smith (1878); George Taplin (1879); William Ridley (1866 and 1875); John Fraser (1892); T. Worsnop (1897a and b); W. E. Roth (1897); and John Mathew (1899 and 1910). Perhaps the most important and influential works of the period were those by the Professor of Biology at the University of Melbourne, W. B. Spencer, who regularly corresponded with Tylor, Marett and others at his home university in Oxford, and F. J. Gillen, the Postmaster at Alice Springs, who knew the Aranda people well. Working together the professor and the postmaster published *The Native Tribes of Central Australia* in 1899 and *The Northern Tribes of Central Australia* in 1904.

Elkin (1963, pp. 6–10) divides the fifty years from 1870 to 1920 into two phases: a "compiling and collecting" phase (1870–1900) and a phase of "fortuitous, individual field projects" (1900–1920). Intellectually, however, it seems clear that the first and more active phase took its impetus from the evolutionary theories of scholars in Europe and America, and that as evolutionism fell into disfavor and diffusionism took its place Australian studies hesitated and began to fall off. Thought to exemplify the earliest and most primitive condition of mankind, Aborigines and their cultures lent themselves to evolutionary studies. On the other hand, academically respectable though they had become, the diffusionists could do little with Aboriginal cultures apart from providing a series of competing hypotheses as to possible migration routes from the Asian mainland.

The wheel has turned. Now that we know more about the ways in which Aborigines communicate with each other, adopt each other's customs and forms of social organization, and travel from one region to another to buy and sell artifacts, myths and songs and rituals, the problems which the diffusionists posed, but had neither the evidence nor techniques to tackle adequately, have come into their own again. Today the prehistorian, with something approaching adequate funding and logistic support, finds that digging deep for a piece of bone or charcoal, or a shaped flint or some surviving pollen, can be as rewarding as unearthing the treasures of long forgotten riverine kings. A recent report on the discovery in Australia of some human remains reveals that between 25,000 and 32,000 years ago an individual was cremated—though not completely so. The bones of the neck and back were little more than singed, and the condition and distribution of the recovered fragments indicated that the burnt skeleton was thoroughly smashed after the pyre had been allowed to cool. In some cases the direction of the blows could be deduced. It was further discovered that the terrestrial and lacustrine fauna were the same then as now: a continuity of some 25,000 years! (Bowler *et al.*, 1970). Dr. Watson might huff incredulously, but what more might a venturesome Holmesian mind require than such a combination of scientific technique and informed imagination?

As useful for evolutionist theses as it is for diffusionist studies, the kind of work described above is becoming more and more popular and widespread. It combines doing and thinking. Given that the search is systematic, discoveries have system or pattern written into them. But is what is discovered necessarily part of a system or pattern? Evolution, by attempting to combine criteria of more/less with criteria of yes/no, is precisely a mode of deriving pattern or system from such otherwise random data. And pattern itself depends upon purpose which, in turn, is derived from the more ancient notions of divine and historical purpose. On the other hand, diffusion appears on the surface as contingent and arbitrary; and the problem of deriving *principles* of cultural transmission or of peoples' movements and migrations from the empirical facts of diffusion—as distinct from simply generalizing on the facts—remains evasive. Where evolution evokes pattern, diffusionism evokes the random and demands both the worst and the best of imagination. Consequently, the logic or systematics of cultural transmission and population movement, to which town planners, urban sociologists, market researchers and others have been turning their attentions, have not since W. H. R. Rivers' *History of Melanesian Society* (1914) much occupied social or cultural anthropologists. Still wary of moving into fields where their predecessors overreached themselves, they have tried to map out recent cultural movements, but have, on the whole, confined themselves to the implications or consequences of diffusion. As yet infirmly grasped, as empirical instances multiply the new dimensions of this old field of study must soon become a specialized concern.

Despite that uncertain pause in Australia itself around the turn of the century, the fruits of fieldwork amongst Aborigines reached their widest continuing audience since Dampier with the publication in France in 1912 of *Les formes élémentaires de la vie religieuse* by Emile Durkheim. Although we now know that much of the material used by Durkheim was (unknown to him) worse than flimsy, so that the image he projected of Aboriginal life seemed distorted, the conceptual framework that produced the image has been grasped as relevant and significant. It said something about culture or society in general even if what it said about people, the Aborigines, was not wholly convincing. If Aborigines appeared wooden, like puppets, further development of the framework might enliven them, bring them closer to the lived experience. And this might need the magic of a fairy tale. For fleshing the people is, for anthropologists, subordinate to the intellectualization of the meaning and relevance of culture or society. Given a knowledge of the nature and mesh of particular social relationships, not one culture but many might be the better understood. There can be few anthropological studies today which do not in some way stand upon the theoretical insights of Durkheim. He transformed the distinctive character of Aboriginal life into general categories.

Hard on Durkheim's heels, in 1913, Bronislaw Malinowski who, unlike Durkheim, was actually to see some Aborigines, staked his first claim to fame with *The Family Among the Australian Aborigines*. One wonders how much attention this work would have attracted had the war not swallowed it up. Looking back, Malinowski was fortunate. The war took him to the Trobriands, and there he found the material that was grist to his intellect. Ill-suited to kinship analyses, logical exercises into which Australian studies inevitably lead, and which he frankly disliked, Malinowski might not have shone so brightly against, for example, Howitt and Mathews. He excelled in the anecdote, his intellectual perceptions rested closely on the people he knew. And just this concern for people, for the textures of sensible life rather than the abstract relations which might be derived from them, was to characterize Australian studies in the years that followed. Inescapably, the Aborigines and the logic of their social relations became more distinctive and "other."

With the end of the war and in its immediate aftermath, Australian studies reached a low ebb. That vital link between fieldwork and reflection in the study—exampled in the partnerships of Howitt and Morgan, and Spencer and Marett, and which Malinowski synthesized into the single field-scholar—was broken. Then, in 1925, as the result of a resolution of the Pan-Pacific Science Congress held in 1923 in Sydney and Melbourne, the Department of Anthropology at the University of Sydney was founded. Australian studies took new life. The first professor at the new department was A. R. Radcliffe-Brown, Cambridge scientist, a pupil of W. H. R. Rivers, fieldworker in the Andaman islands in 1906–1908, follower (later) of Comte and Durkheim, and the most zealous of anthropological missionaries. Harking back to the eighteenth century in his conviction that proper method would yield a sociological science whose discovered laws would enable governments to control the processes of social change, (Radcliffe-Brown, 1931), Radcliffe-Brown preached his good news in five continents, leaving his converts to carry on the good work. In current jargon Radcliffe-Brown was a "structure-functionalist." His message was, in effect, a means whereby the field data could be collected systematically and made to assume a coherent and consistent pattern. Although, explicitly, he urged the adoption of the methods of natural science, he was louder in the word than brave in the deed. Both in his monograph on his first fieldwork venture — he published *The Andaman Islanders* in 1922, having already published a variety of essays on Aboriginal life — and in his other work he followed the logic of the word and the idea rather than the implications of the empirical behavior he might have observed. This choice, rather than the perception that until we know how things are we cannot begin to ask how they came to be as they are, would have forced him to turn his back on history had he not already been inclined that way. On the other hand, the commitment to science, particularly biology, required that he not lose sight of evolutionary theory. This paradox he was never able to resolve.

Looking back, with all the advantages of hindsight, it is easy to point to inconsistencies of method and errors of ethnography in much of Radcliffe-Brown's work. In particular, but like many another, he failed to appreciate that while harmony, consistency and wholeness may inform an intellectual or analytical framework, they are not necessarily properties of the empirical reality. If much of his method was cribbed from the work of Howitt, Mathew, and Mathews, what cannot be gainsaid is the positive drive and impetus he gave to the subject over a period of some thirty years. A great showman, he and not Mathew, Howitt, and Mathews inspired pupils, laid a permanent mark on Sydney, Capetown, Chicago, and Oxford. Regarded as a great teacher, he provided relevance when it was most needed, a framework of ideas within which fieldworkers as well as theorists in their studies could approach a bewildering mass of ethnographic material and weld it into meaningful shape. While Malinowski revealed with dramatic force the participatory understandings to be gained from the serious study of a "simple" people, Radcliffe-Brown offered a rationally objective framework within which the participatory understandings could be fixed and interrelated. It was due largely to Radcliffe-Brown's stimulus and challenge that, in Australia, Aboriginal studies picked up and became more and more the systematic concern of learned institutes and less and less dependent on the enthusiastic amateur. Before taking up his post in Sydney, Radcliffe-Brown had written three papers on Australian social organization (1913, 1918, 1923). In 1931 he published his now classic *The Social Organization of Australian Tribes*. And from Radcliffe-Brown's day to the present, using much the same approach, fieldwork studies among Australian Aborigines have been pursued unremittingly by increasing numbers of Australian and other scholars.

In spite of all the hard work, however, the steady garnering of more and more detailed ethnographic material, apart from the work of Radcliffe-Brown himself the intellectual profile of Aboriginal studies has not been such as to leave an impress either on other disciplines or on anthropologists working in other fields. Indeed, within anthropology itself the greater names have been made by scholars working in fields remote from Australia. Whether this was due to the Aborigines, those who beheld them, or to quite extraneous factors is matter for argument. In fact, in Australia, accepting the stimulus of others, research on Aboriginal life went ahead. Documenting in relation to the Australian material the ideas, mainly, of Malinowski and Radcliffe-Brown, work went on within what is cheerfully called the British empirical or pragmatic tradition. The distinctive American approach, "culture-pattern" studies, was never really put to the test in the Australian environment. Between the wars M. F. Ashley-Montague took up a long-standing problem brought to a head by Malinowski (1913) and in 1937 published *Coming Into Being Among the Australian Aborigines* (1937), a work devoted to the problem of paternity among certain Aboriginal groups. Also in 1937, W. L. Warner wrote *A Black Civilization* (1958), a book rich in data on ceremonial life, and whose contents in other respects were to provide the basis for the celebrated "Murngin controversy" (pp. 236–244). A. P. Elkin published in 1938 what was to become the standard work on Aborigines, *The Australian Aborigines* (1938); and in 1939 Phyllis Kaberry published *Aboriginal Woman, Sacred and Profane* (1939). In 1925 G. Roheim, recruiting to the scene the stimulus of Freud and his associates, published *Australian Totemism, A Psycho-Analytic Study in Anthropology* (1925); and H. Basedow, who had been working and publishing since shortly after the turn of the century, published *The Australian Aboriginal* (1925), The Journal *Oceania*, sponsored by the Australian National

Research Council, and founded in 1930, became the repository of detailed fieldwork analyses.

It is worth pausing at this point to consider briefly the kind of effort put into anthropology and Aboriginal studies in Australia. Although, as the name *Oceania* suggests, Aboriginal studies competed with general essays and material from Melanesia, Micronesia, and Polynesia, the proportion of Aboriginal to other studies in the journal over a sample thirty year period is 28%. A little low, perhaps, but there were of course other journals hospitable to Aboriginal material: *Mankind*, the journal of the Anthropological Society of New South Wales, founded in 1931; *Walkabout*, the journal of the Australian Geographical Society, founded in 1934; *The Australian Museum Magazine*, founded in 1921; *Anthropological Forum*, founded in 1963 at the University of Western Australia; and *The Australian Medical Journal* were, and remain the most important. If for thirty years the Department of Anthropology in the University of Sydney held the field alone, Aboriginal studies have never been the exclusive concern of professional social or cultural anthropologists organized into a department. Museums in the capital cities, pitifully underfinanced, were centers of amateur interest. It is due to the devoted work of a handful of professional curators that scholars today have been provided with the necessary basis for work in prehistory and material culture. The work of F. D. McCarthy, of Sydney, has been particularly notable. From the twenties until the present time the South Australian Board for Anthropological Research has financed a number of expeditions — including the J. B. Birdsell–N. B. Tindale expedition of 1938 — which in their totality have had a scope wider and more diverse than that normally associated with a university department. Although it did not have a department of anthropology, the University of Adelaide encouraged Aboriginal studies through a variety of other departments. T. G. H. Strehlow, C. P. Mountford, and N. B. Tindale are great names in the field. Elsewhere, however, despite the work of Howitt, Spencer, Wood Jones, and Thomson, all of whom worked from Melbourne, of Roth, who worked from Brisbane, and of Daisy Bates who, working from Perth, advised Radcliffe-Brown (see Salter, 1971, pp. 156, 176), the more general and amateur interest in Aboriginal studies was not such as to focus funds into particular and sustained professional departments. Perhaps it was thought there was little point in spending money when, as it seemed, all that needed to be done in relation to a dying people was already being done.

It could be, and often has been urged by interested professionals that this apparent lack of interest in founding university departments reveals a basic lack of imagination and thrust. Yet, on a per capita basis, Australia was certainly no better or worse supplied than were Britain or the United States between the wars. In Australia, particularly, the economic conditions of the thirties made it extremely difficult, in view of other more urgent claims on the public purse, to justify the permanent earmarking of funds for anthropological research. There is little doubt that if the department at Sydney had not been founded in the twenties, in the euphoria of postwar boom, it would have had to wait for another twenty years or more. It is important, too, to appreciate the lay and general rather than professional interest. The former is intrinsic to the European heritage and may find expression in a variety of genres and activities whether or not they happen to be focused in particular kinds of professionalism. The second is a self-conscious awareness and channeling of some parts of that general interest into particular professional molds. The amateur interest is a continuing one which sustains and is – or ideally should be – sustained by the narrower professional concerns. But to maintain a cadre of professionals, public monies, competing against other priorities, are needed. What is impressive in an era of economic recession, soup kitchens, and unemployment is that they were found at all. It was not until after the Second World War, again in conditions of economic boom and growth, that a near sufficiency became available. The founding of The Australian National University (1947–1950), in which was included a Research School of Pacific Studies, saw the arrival in Australia of a noted theoretician as professor of anthropology: S. F. Nadel. Tragically, he died before he could make any lasting impact. And although he turned his department's attention toward the islands, particularly New Guinea, Aboriginal studies also found a new home and center. Rather later, departments of anthropology were founded in Perth and Brisbane, and one is presently being started in Adelaide.

On the whole, therefore, and again on a per capita basis related to gross national product and other priorities, the Australian funding of Aboriginal studies has been and is as, if not more, generous than wealthier and more heavily populated countries have managed. Still, a few is not many even if that few is relatively large and its members hardworking. At the political as distinct from the intellectual level, however, things were allowed to drift.

After the war, led by the indefatigable Elkin, whose *The Australian Aborigines* had gone into a second edition in 1943 and was to be followed by a third and fourth in 1954 and 1964, much more began to be published. In 1945 Roheim came again with *The Eternal Ones of the Dream* (1945).

T. G. H. Strehlow's *Aranda Traditions* appeared in 1947; D. F. Thomson's *Economic Structure and the Ceremonial Exchange System in Arnhem Land* came in 1949; Leonard Adam's *Primitive Art* appeared in 1940–54; and Ursula McConnell published *Myths of the Mungkan* in 1957. C. P. Mountford, W. E. H. Stanner, A. Capell, N. B. Tindale, H. Petri, E. A. Worms and others published copiously in *Oceania* and other journals. R. M. Berndt, who had started publishing in 1940, came into flower, soon to be followed and joined by C. H. Berndt. Their output over more than twenty years can scarcely be matched.

Nevertheless, from the thirties into the sixties Aboriginal studies suffered from a dearth of new ideas, new ways of looking at the material in hand. There were, perhaps, just too few professionals to generate that interchange of ideas which might give birth to a new synthesis. Besides, for many young professionals – who had cut their teeth on Aboriginal studies – the greater academic prizes seemed to lie elsewhere. With the exception of three studies (Worsley, 1955, 1961; Rose, 1960), marxist thought had but little impact. Structure-function, integration, interconnectedness, social change, and the political leanings to the *status quo* which went with them held the field. Not a few anthropologists felt that, intellectually, the target had been reached. All that remained to be done was to adumbrate the theoretical framework and stud it with more and more detailed ethnographic material. What to do about the Aborigines as people was vigorously debated. But the issue engendered more passion than coherence; the participatory values were not reflected in intellectual concision and persuasiveness.

Then, in the early sixties, another Frenchman who had not been to Australia, Claude Lévi-Strauss, found in Aboriginal studies a means of demonstrating intellectual advance and excitement. With *Le totemisme aujourd'hui* (Lévi-Strauss, 1962; translated, 1963) Aborigines and their cultures became of more immediate intellectual rather than social concern. Now Lévi-Strauss had not stumbled on new ethnographic material which had lain hidden over the years, nor had he intuited from the Australian data an idea which had been denied to others. What he did was to review the evidence in the light of a notion of structure which, based upon definitional logical categories of inclusion and exclusion, and inviting the investigator to discover the principles of mediation between opposed pairs, projected a fresh image of the ways in which Aborigines thought and acted, organized themselves and viewed the world about them. But this notion of structure did not burst full-grown from the mind. The lineage was Hegelian, collateral to Marx, born of an endogamous marriage with work being done in linguistics. In short, it derived from the main streams of European thought, reached out in its synthesis to the peculiar Aboriginal otherness — strange and "out there" — and sought to incorporate it in terms that were valid for both Europeans and Aborigines. By means of this intellectual construct Aborigines became more like Europeans, and Europeans became more like Aborigines than they had, perhaps, thought they were.

How true is the image? For Dampier and many another sea captain preoccupied with the hazards of bringing a ship close inshore in order to find fresh water and victuals, the Aborigines were miserable, rude and uncouth. To Cook, on the other hand, who happened to strike land in the vicinity of the most beautiful harbor in the world, the Aborigines of his journal were just those noble savages in a state of nature which current ideas had led him to expect. Each was projecting from his own social ambience without the aid of a well-defined intellectual construct which would yield a measure of rational objectivity. Durkheim, however, had such a construct. Through his work we are invited to see in Aboriginal culture the social processes that, in evolutionary time supposedly did, and in the present supposedly still do, produce what we call religion. Radcliffe-Brown, working within a generally Durkheimian framework, had his Aborigines neatly organized for marriage, breakfast, and dinner. Herein, according to him, lay the roots of religion: environmentally derived, an arrangement for sharing resources and ordering reproduction. For Lévi-Strauss, on the other hand, Aborigines might seem to be college professors absorbed in the logical niceties of homologous differences.

Each of these images of the Aborigine or human is distorted. Truth is a large word. On the other hand, how useful or valid is the intellectual construct of the culture — from which these images are derived? Despite the herculean efforts of field ethnographers who, knowing the Aborigines at first hand, have appreciated the skew and sought to find the evidence to put the record straight, what has caught the imagination of the scholarly world and public at large are the force and persuasion of the intellectual construct rather than the lineaments of the people themselves. What Aborigines actually do and think and feel is in a sense as irrelevant and trivial as anything anyone does or thinks or feels in the course of his daily round — until, that is, all the doing and thinking and feeling reverberate with intellectual excitement. Life among nonliterate peoples often tends to be dull and dulling. Just as washing the dishes, ironing shirts, or a roadside conversation with a tramp can be quite forgettable experiences without the aid of a gifted dramatist or novelist to make them memorable, so it is with the simpler peoples and their anthropologists.

An examination of the several papers presented at the 1961 Research

Conference of the Australian Institute of Aboriginal Studies in Canberra reveals that the main topics engaging scholars in the Australian field are: the antiquity and prehistory of man in Australia; the physical characteristics of Aborigines; genetic and biometric studies; languages; ecology, equipment, economy and trade; social organization; religious and artistic life; population trends; relations with Europeans; and (of course) the social position of women. All of it is nutty, sober stuff: a summary of what is known, could be known and ought to be known about Aboriginal life. With each paper presented by an expert in his field it is taken for granted — as what professional would not so do — that the work involved is self-justifying. As indeed it is. But when Meggitt writes (Shiels, 1963, p. 216), "I can only assert that *none* [*sic*] of Australian fieldwork ... has produced data upon which can be based what I take to be a valid structural-organizational analysis of Australian society" he underlines the fact that what had been missing from Australian fieldwork studies was just that intellectual grasp which would enable a fieldworker to find the kinds of data which would yield the kind of analysis he advocated. Like beauty, data lies in the mind which contemplates it.

Using some randomly selected bibliographies, the most popular or most frequently (22%) cited authorities are contained in general works which discuss or allude to most of the topics below. Art, drama, and dance take second place at 19%, followed by social organization (15%), and religion, totemism, and myth (14%). Physical anthropology, assimilation and culture contact, and ecology and economics vary between 5% and 6%. Language and linguistics, sexology, dreaming and intelligence, and sundry other matters come to about 3% each. So that while the spectrum is broad, there is a concentration on social organization, religion, myth, and totemism: traditional key topics each of which is directed toward the sort of question an informed and educated mind might ask. A rather different picture emerges from an examination of *Oceania* over a thirty year period between 1935 and 1971. The greatest coverage is given to myth, ritual, religion, and totemism (20%), followed by kinship and social organization (18%). Prehistory and physical anthropology come in at 16%, culture contact at 15%, art and drama at 13%, linguistics 9%, economics and technology 4%, ethnographic reports 3%, and law and other matters 2%. The same key topics are well in the lead, but language and culture contact — professional topics — have a far greater share of the space.

John Greenway's *Bibliography of the Australian Aborigines* (1963) lists 10,283 books and articles in periodicals, 763 journals or periodicals, and 554 tribes. Of these listings roughly 17% are concerned with physical anthropology and related topics; 14% with religion, totemism, and magic; 12% with material culture; 11% with kinship and social organization, and mission activities; 6% with mistreatment of Aborigines, and with popular travelers' accounts; 5% with myths and legends; 4% with psychology and mental capacities, and medicine and disease; 3% with music, song, and dance; and 6% with sundry other matters. Abstracting culture contact from mistreatment of Aborigines, travelers' accounts and mission activities give a rough figure of 23% — the largest single category. Linguistics, abstracted from "myths and legends" and included in "sundry other matters," are a relatively small proportion of the whole. Nevertheless, in a few years A. E. Capell succeeded in surveying the whole field of Australian languages and laid the basis for future, more detailed work. Prehistory, which can be abstracted from "physical anthropology" and "material culture" — and which did not find organized expression within a university department until the late fifties — would appear to have a fair share. Glancing at the studies funded by the Australian Institute of Aboriginal Studies over its first ten year period, linguistics and prehistory come into their own. There were eighty-six projects in linguistics, fifty-six in social or cultural anthropology, fifty-one in prehistory, and twenty-six in human biology. The remaining forty projects were divided between ethnomusicology, material culture, archival work, research assistance, academic positions, radiocarbon dating, music discs, cinema films, and dance notation (see Australian Institute of Aboriginal Studies, Annual Report, 1 July 1969–30 June 1970, and Australian Institute of Aboriginal Studies, Newsletter, Vol. 3, No. 2, April 1971).

Greenway's bibliography is in itself impressive evidence not only of Australians' interest in the indigenous peoples, but of an interest shared by European intellectual circles as a whole. The sustained importance of human biology or physical anthropology and the growing significance of linguistics and prehistory in the affairs of the Institute are not simply a reflection of the fact that these kinds of studies are relatively easy to cost and account. They flow into each other in obtaining the record of prehistory. On the other hand, the projects funded under the rubrics of social and cultural anthropology are not only difficult to cost but have been by far the most expensive. They entail maintaining an anthropologist in the field and in the study for periods of months, even years. Then there are publishing costs to be borne.

Why this wide range of interest, this expenditure of Australian public monies? In a strictly economic sense the return of the investment made is negligible. The value in national prestige is small. Outside pressures to ameliorate the sparse living conditions of Aboriginal peoples find their response in separately budgeted funds. The conclusion must be, either that Australians and others are silly or irrational, or that the study of Aboriginal life, particularly its values and qualities, carries the mark of a peculiar compulsion and integrity. What has been lacking have been the political will and energy to engage the participatory values more effectively.

The publishing policy of the Institute follows the line taken by the editor of the Viking Fund Publications in Anthropology in the 1969 Annual Report of the Wenner–Gren Foundation for Anthropological Research: to "provide the academic world with data that would otherwise remain concealed, and that our criteria should be not so much academic or theoretical brilliance as scholarly ability and integrity, and the potential value inherent in the data, rather than in the manner of presentation." (Australian Institute of Aboriginal Studies, *Newsletter*, Vol. 3, No. 2, April 1971, p. 23.) Though the presumption must be that work of "academic or theoretical brilliance" will find no difficulty in finding a publisher, the passage cited poses an important problem. What sort of place is there in anthropological research for the simple and apparently unadorned collection of data?

A partial response is given in a volume published to mark the tenth anniversary of the inception of the Australian Institute of Aboriginal Studies (R. M. Berndt, 1970). In this book, specifically not representative of *all* that is being done in the Australian field, more than half the space is devoted to myth, religion, and totemism — modes of thought — and a significant section to what may be done with old data. The rest is concerned with demography, kinship, history, and social change. So that the questions thought to have the greater importance are, very roughly: What are the categories and consequences of Aboriginal modes of thought? Is a particular piece of evidence dead when the thought that gave it relevance has passed away? Lévi-Strauss was by no means the first to apply himself to the categories and consequences of modes of thought, nor will he be the last. But the answers he has given are of such a kind that it will be some years before the full implications can be worked out. In answer to the second question, there are many who would assert that data collected under one set of conditions of problem and intellectual viewpoint are quite useless or positively misleading to those with different intellectual viewpoints working under quite other conditions. Because data has relevance only within a particular context, they would say, a change of context alters its relevance and makes it so flexible as to be meaningless.

Except for the simpler kinds of data, such as those of identification, one might easily go along with this. On the other hand, it was precisely this process of applying new thought to old data that enabled both Durkheim and Lévi-Strauss to make the intellectual advances they made. Despite the distortion in relation to the supposed empirical reality in the initial stages, it was not long before the empirical reality began to fill with new relevances.

Within this brief survey of work in the Aboriginal field, it is impossible to ignore the fact that the most spectacular intellectual advances in Australian anthropology have been stimulated by syntheses in the European homeland. Evolutionism, the eighteenth-century inheritance, the Durkheimian synthesis, the influences of Radcliffe-Brown and Malinowski, the psychologies of Freud and Jung, and the structuralism of Lévi-Strauss have been the dominating spurs to activity. Each sought to bring purely European or Western concerns — the critique of organized religion, the relative priorities of social and psychological determinants, supposed differences in modes of intellection — to the test in the Aboriginal environment. The contributions of Howitt, Mathew, and Mathews, anticipating so much of the methodology that was to come, went unsung in Australia, and are only now being celebrated elsewhere. The labors of Elkin, Stanner, R. M. and C. H. Berndt, McConnell, and Warner in general ethnography, religion, totemism, and myth, of Capell and Strehlow in linguistics, song, and myth, of Rose and Worsley in social organization, of Mountford, McCarthy, and Tindale in material culture, ethnology, and prehistory — to mention but a few — have fleshed out, developed and qualified intellectual syntheses derived from abroad. Among the younger faces Meggitt and Hiatt have carried on the good work, bringing to the scene a more critical approach than their elders. Aborigines and their cultures are too universal an anthropological interest to expect that intellectual advances should necessarily come from those most familiar with the people themselves. Yet the material is there, waiting for the hands that can mold it. If we glance briefly outside the confines of social and cultural anthropology, however, we can see in all that prehistory is beginning to entail the development of a cooperative endeavor — bringing together scholars from a variety of diverse disciplines — which may well lead into great things (see, for example, Mulvaney and Golson, 1971).

One would not normally make a point of assessing the contribution of conationals in the study of indigenous peoples, but the particularities of the Australian case seem to demand it. Not only have Australians done most of the work but the relationship between the first and later

Australians has been such as to merit this kind of treatment. The deeper one goes into the trees the less one is aware of the shape of the wood. Close familiarity with the ethnographic detail breeds caution, inhibits the taking of an intellectual risk. Between the intellectual synthesis — which cannot but overlook the existence of certain particulars, and which attempts to reveal the logical principles evoked by what appear to be the more significant particulars — and the grittily tenacious mind which holds fast to all the particulars, there is a gulf which no persuasion or rhetoric can bridge. Still, both are necessary to the process of scientific investigation. If the former presents a large truth whose flaws are known, but which is capable of revealing further truths, the latter fastens on a collection of small truths believed to be flawless, and which may, in the end, topple the synthesis. Yet until all or most of the small truths are patterned or synthesized they cannot of themselves challenge the synthesis which has ignored them.

Evolutionary theory was known to have flaws. But it brought order, revealed much that had not been known, and posed further problems. It was defeated not by the amount it ignored but by the significance of what was ignored. The same may be said for the syntheses of Durkheim and Radcliffe-Brown, and perhaps will be said with more conviction than at present of the Lévi-Straussian synthesis. Yet it would be misleading to suppose that these writers had produced syntheses of most that was thought to be known about Aboriginal life. Rather have they judiciously selected, discarded, and integrated what they deemed pertinent. And it is scarcely an accident that the criteria of significance reach out to show how, on the one hand, Aborigines and their cultures can reveal to ourselves what it is to be ourselves, and on the other hand invite us to participate in an otherness that is strangely yet distinctively human. Without such syntheses, which make the stranger intellectually and morally relevant, intelligible and accessible to those who have not interacted with him, anthropology would be a haphazard and entirely ethnocentric collection of curiosa: at best trivial, at worst an unpardonable trespass on the integrity and patience of those being studied.

2   THE SKEINS OF LIFE

Long ago, when this oak was young, Hornblower sailed, and Washington was a man, the emu honked, the wombat burrowed and the kookaburra laughed in a timeless land where the car park stands, the buildings tower and sheep and cattle graze. Then time came. The land was divided, trees were cut, grains plated, animals husbanded. But the wheel of the dreaming went on turning, gathering the enormous bowl of heavens compassing the divers shapes and colors of a seemingly endless sweep of land into the focus of one perceiving dot. From the sunbaked center to the coasts where the seas move in from infinity to a creaming line of breakers, gum trees march across the land as far as the eye can see, ever whispering to those who care to listen. As each seawave is never twice repeated, so these trees stand, straight or bent, gnarled or twisted, white bark, grey bark, red bark, peeling bark, grey-green glossy leaves: like the sea, monotonous to many, of compulsive fascination to others. But whether one speaks of the forests of the south and north, or of ochreous deserts cupped in barren red or blue or purple mountain tops, or scrubby plains, or sunbaked grasslands, or jagged jumbled rocks, or quiet pools and lakes, flooding rivers, almost stagnant streams—the lofting dome of the sky embraces, relaxes, smiles, thunders, flashes, growls and broods over what seems an utterly lifeless land. But look again. The glistening particles in rock and desert sand and gravel flash and change their colors as the light changes, as the walker moves. Billions and billions of little ants, big ants, red ants, black ants, giant ants—busy, busy, busy. No plant or shrub or tree that does not speak. When at nightfall the stars reach down from their blue-black bed to prick the eyes, the hollow emptiness fills with rustles which the dullest ear can catch. A land to be passed over in patience by train or plane, a land of storm and drought, a land of uncertain temper, peeling bones and moon's detritus. A land unpromising if too eagerly embraced, yet also a land responsive to the understanding touch.

This touch the first Australians had. They gave themselves over to the land, and the land gave to them what sun and drought and rain allowed. They knew the land, they knew each shrub and plant and tree and rock upon it. They knew the seasons, knew the streams, knew where water seeped under the drought-hard earth. They knew when and where to find ripening bush fruits, wild tubers, corms and grass seeds. They knew where to fish, how to find the stingray, how to make the turtle give himself up, how to keep a shark from troubling them. They knew where wallabies played, where kangaroos fed, how lizards ran into spinifex and earth, where a bandicoot dug and hid. Purposefully, they walked over the land, making camp where they knew food ought to be waiting, moving on when they had had their fill. The ancestral beings who had made the land and its animals and plants, who were in the stars, quickened the foetus, made it human and brought a babe into a world hedged with morality. These beings guided them in their moving, showed them where to go, demanded in return that they be men with the wit to know where not to go. They brought rain when properly asked with due formality and ritual. Then overnight, or with the lapse of hours the hard and naked sundried earth glowed with blooms. Fish swam, frogs croaked in pools that had just now been bare declevities in pink and purple desert. Sprung with life renewed from the dreamtime ancestors' hands and sweat and spit and frothing sperm, the land was theirs, their own, for them to know and nurture. So they knew the land and everything on it. As they belonged to the land and to everything on it, so the land and everything on it was for them — if they did right, were wise, followed the law, nourished and enriched and enlivened the land and its animals. Sometimes the land withheld its favors, for no reason God wot, like a woman perhaps. So to die was but death and a new life to come. Meanwhile, their duty was to survive, to live on lest they betray their trust and the land die. Douse the fire, strike camp, move on, find the last lizard, that cluster of grubs under rotting bark or in roots underground, the last withered berry . . . And because they survived, the land lived on. Yet they and their dogs, the rat and the flying fox were all of their kind. If they failed the ancestors, none would survive. They alone were responsible.

At one with the land and all that lived or moved over it, still they were different, wholly alien in their own home. They knew they could think, could speak, knew right from wrong. They knew themselves men and women in a land of marsupials, reptiles, insects, fish, birds, and plants. Yet this was their home, their heritage. To approach, embrace, and become part of their land and its animals and plants they had but their wits, their imagination, their will to be masters under the ancestors who had left it all for them. They learned the land, its plants and its animals. They used the stone and served it with embellishment and paint. They dressed the stone with their being, their past and their future. Through dance and ceremony, rituals, mutilations, masks, decorations, and the secrets handed down from their ancestors, they could enter for a while into the very being of kangaroo, wallaby, emu, turtle, eagle, crow . . . and in so doing kangaroo, wallaby, emu, turtle, eagle and crow came into and participated in them. As they moved into the thunder, the lightning, the rain, clouds, so these, inevitably, moved into them. No frenzy this, no childish absorption of the world into self. The articulate thought which perceived itself only in virtue of its alienation sped to the object whose contemplation made the thought known to thought, returned to the self and so back again to the object, weaving the threads binding subject to object. So the alienation brought by awareness was made whole by thought.

They moved and camped in families, coming together from time to time into companies managed and organized by the elderly and capable, regulated and ordered according to the Law. Each child came to know something of the patterns his parents had woven, each man as he grew older came to know more and yet more. Such wisdom they treasured and revered. As the years rolled by some of the threads were lost or abandoned. So new wisdoms grew out of and replaced the old, new threads were woven between themselves, the land and its life. Suiting the word to the thought, and the deed to the word, they and the world they perceived became as though one, a home in which they belonged, which belonged to them and their forebears — who had made it when only dreams existed, who had made them and who even now were remaking them, the land, its animals and plants from the stuff of dreams they shared with their descendants.

When Captain Cook, a practical and commonsensical seaman who seems to have relied upon Banks for intellectual injections, wrote of Australia and its inhabitants as being in "the pure state of Nature" he shared in an intellectual romanticization characteristic of some anthropologists. The romantic transforms the real into dream, imprisons the real like a fly caught in dark amber. To follow out the implications of the dream only severs the Aborigines from ourselves. Thought of as in "the pure state of Nature" the Aborigines could be in a paradisaical state, as with Adam and Eve before the Fall. Or, if human, they could be thought of as primitive in a sense that debarred any meaningful communication between ourselves and they. They might, indeed, be thought of as so much nearer the animal than ourselves as to be considered more animal than human. Still, when Cook's commonsense and true nature assert themselves the Aborigines become human. "From what I have said of the Natives of New Holland," he wrote (Cook, 1955, p. 399), "they may appear to some to be the most wretched people upon Earth, but in reality they are far more happier than we Europeans; being wholly unacquainted not only with the superfluous but the necessary Conveniences so much sought after in Europe, they are happy in not knowing the use of them. They live in a Tranquility which is not disturb'd by the Inequality of Condition: The Earth and sea of their own accord furnishes them with all things necessary for life, they covet not Magnificent Houses, Household stuff &c, they live in a warm and fine Climate and enjoy a very wholesome air, so that they have very little need of clothing and this they seem to be fully sensible of, for many to whom we gave Cloth &c to, left it carelessly upon the sea beach and in the woods as a thing they had no manner of use for. In short, they seem'd to set no Value upon any thing we gave them, nor would they part with any thing of their own for any one article we could offer them; this in my opinion argues that they think themselves provided with all the necessarys of Life and that they have no superfluities."

In Cook's day there were, it is conjectured, some 300,000 Aborigines. They were nomadic wildbooters, scattered in small groups over the subcontinent, gaining a living from hunting, foraging for wild-stuffs and fishing in environments that could be tropical or temperate, lush downlands, desert, parkland, thick forest, estuarine, mountainous, broken, or beach. They engaged in trade and barter transactions between themselves; trade routes and ceremonial exchange cycles interlaced the countryside; and in the north there were fairly regular contacts with Indonesian traders who came to Australian shores to fish for trepang. Where the Aborigines came from is not known for certain. A consensus is forming that they came into Australia from the Asian mainland via the Indonesian islands, dispersing through the subcontinent from points between the Kimberlys and Arnhem land. Precisely when they, or their forebears, came to Australia is another matter. Archaeological evidence points to the existence of man of some kind in Australia for something like thirty thousand years. Whether these early inhabitants of the country were the ancestors of the present population, or quite distinct from them, is not known for sure — though it is probable that they were their ancestors (see Mulvaney, 1969; Mulvaney and Golson, 1971, Chapters 21–33).

Despite their relative isolation from the mainstream of man's development on the Eurasian land mass, in a biological or zoological sense the Aborigines are today generally agreed to be representatives of modern man. They are not, as was once thought, more nearly Neanderthalers. Differentiated among themselves as to genetic and blood grouping endowment, and, to a layman's eye, clearly differentiated as to physical aspect, in relation to their neighbors outside Australia the Aborigines as a whole may nevertheless be considered as roughly of the same major racial stock. Again, although within Australia it is possible to distinguish over two hundred languages and several varieties of culture, in the wider context it is the homogeneity of language and culture that becomes significant. Prone to European diseases and ordinary human temptations, deprived of their lands and food resources by European settlement, hunted and imprisoned or killed for interfering with the Europeans' sheep or crops, their social orders shattered, selling their women and taking to the rum bottle, in the course of rather more than a century the total Aboriginal population had dropped to a tenth of what it had been supposed to be in Captain Cook's day. Now, having perforce virtually given up the traditional nomadic life, gathered into government and mission stations and settled on reservations, having mated and intermarried with Europeans and with Japanese, Chinese, Filipino and Malay fishermen and pearl divers in the north, the population, both full blood and miscegenated, is increasing rapidly.

It should be emphasized that physically and/or culturally it is a different kind of population that is increasing. Aborigines are becoming other than they were. Quite soon, anthropologists will have to speak of the "Aborigines" and their cultures in a strictly historical sense. In the meantime, because so much of a traditional way of life survives in the new, general surveys have to make use of a double fiction: that there was a general and regarded as classical traditional way of life; and that this is or was a stable standard by which to measure the present. Yet neither fiction is in any way convincing. If in the past, to Europeans, there seemed little sign of the Aboriginal communities *developing* in the European sense, they certainly interacted with each other and *changed* in a variety of particulars. It is doubtful whether, for any one group, a generation's cultural experience was a replica of the one preceding: the potential of changing experiences, of an internal dynamic toward change, was implicit in the general situation of rather different cultural groups in contact with each other. On the other hand, it may be taken that such changes in the cycles of cultural experience occurred within fairly narrow limits.

One of the inherent sources of confusion in anthropological literature is that once a people has been identified, even wrongly identified, and written about, they become fixed in the printed word, pinned to the book like a butterfly in a drawer. Yet human beings are forever curious, experimenting with new ways, adopting the customs of others, misremembering the past. Why else grasp the rum bottle? Because men and women are so susceptible to the bright and new, and do experiment in spite of the urgings of more conservative elders, cultures are never wholly stable. They are in constant flux. But against this empirical reality, which ethnographers in the field have constantly emphasized, intellectual appreciation requires that we halt things in mid-stride as it were and say "Look — there it is, *that* is what it is like." We know it will change, we know it will be different when we look again. The glimpse has to suffice. Because no one can ever know all the empirical reality that is available in any one slice of time, let alone collect and identify each changing piece, that glimpse has to carry its burden of general and lasting — that is, intellectual — relevance.

If then we know wrongly or incorrectly, at least we have something which the future may straighten. So, accepting the caution, we may turn to describing the Aborigines and their ways of life in general terms, attempting to bring them within the range of ordinary comprehension.

The Aborigines were, it seems, always organized on a small scale, the largest tribes or subtribes consisting of no more than a hundred to fifteen hundred souls, and averaging some five hundred persons. All over the subcontinent, whether in the tropical forests of north Queensland or the Northern Territory, the deserts of central Australia, or in the temperate downs and woodlands of South and Western Australia, Victoria and New South Wales, the regular organized group rarely seems to have comprised more than about thirty or forty persons. Such groups, often described in the literature as "hordes," were composed of families related to each other by virtue of a well-known system of descent, patrilineal for the most part. A tribe or subtribe was composed of several of these "hordes." Apart from the dingo, a species of wild dog which seems to have come into the Australian mainland about eight or nine thousand years ago, the Aborigines kept no domesticated animals. The dingo itself was only partly domesticated. For though it bred in and around the environs of a camp, it also bred in the wild, whence the pups were captured and brought into the camp to be domesticated.

The Aborigines worked in stone, utilized wood, fibers, animal fur, skins, and bones. Though the list of the material furnishing of their cultures is relatively slight (as might be expected of a nomadic people without flocks or transport) artifacts were proficiently executed and served their various purposes. Wherever they lived the rhythm of life, whether at the level of the family, the horde, or the tribe, was characterized by a continuous process of concentration and dispersal. Families broke up to go hunting, fishing, or foraging, gathered together at dusk, broke up again after a few days, rejoined each other for minor domestic purposes, dispersed again, and reconcentrated at longer intervals for ceremonials and rituals popularly known as corroborees. These might involve not only the horde, but other hordes and subtribes as well. Moving thus from camp to camp, the bulk of their food was gathered by the women: hunted foods formed a relatively small part of the diet. In the far northern and southern extremities of the subcontinent, where the rains can be heavy, Aborigines built fairly substantial huts of saplings covered with bark, turf, skins, or leaves. But for the most part they built no permanent dwellings: only temporary shelters and windbreaks which they might occupy for periods of a day or so to a few weeks.

Nomadic habits and the freedoms of the great outdoors die hard. Although it could be said that in the past the nature of the country and the distribution of the food supply enforced a nomadic way of life, the evidence for "enforced" is little more than an inference from the assumption that because things were so, therefore there was every reason for their being so. Today, gathered together as they are in the permanent dwellings of mission and government stations, Aborigines still prefer to sit outside their houses in the shade of gum trees, in the lee of windbreaks, around a smouldering camp fire. They still maintain a rhythm of movement. They visit kinsfolk, friends, or cult-members in other government or mission stations, spending days or weeks with them. They go into the nearest township to drink, or get themselves imprisoned so that they can visit friends and relatives already in prison, and feed at government expense. Corroborees, festivals and rituals can only be arranged and organized through a constant interchange of visits and information. If indeed at some unimaginable time in the past the nature of the country "enforced" a nomadic way of life, it is unlikely that the first Australians were other than hunter-gatherers when they came into Australia from an environment that must have been very different. And today it is the quality of the social relations born out of that way of life that seems determinitive. Unwilling to engage in continuous interactions with particular neighbors and kinsfolk, individuals and families make a break, move off, engage a fresh set of interactions, move on, embrace another social environment, and eventually return home again. The values of the traditional social or cultural environment, the engagement of successive and different interactional contexts defined by variable spaces, are persisting in spite of quite different physical circumstances. It is to this, the continuing engagement of the participatory values in different contexts, one feels, that Europeans respond when they express affection for Aborigines.

The paucity of the number and varieties of artifacts in Aboriginal cultures, combined with what appeared to be certain rigidities of ritual, belief and general outlook, has led some to suppose that Aborigines were virtually incapable of any further development (for examples, see Strehlow, 1947, pp. xvi–xvii, 6; Birket-Smith, 1957/60, p. 51; Lommel, 1970, p. 233). Yet such evidence as has been brought in support of the contention has been overgeneralized and extended both in space and time. Today, young Aborigines are quick in learning new techniques. In the past, electrical insulators from the transcontinental telegraph, or beer bottles thrown from a train or left at a campsite by a jackaroo, lent themselves to traditional skills and were so utilized. In the north, it is thought by some,

Malay trepang fishermen taught Australians how to make clay pots. But, because clay pots were fragile and unsuited to a life of movement, Australians themselves had no use for the pots. If we ask what features of Australian life brought prestige and influence in the community, what earned admiration and respect for a man or a woman, the possession of material artifacts is low on the list. Nor did those technological skills in which Europeans take such delight and pride earn more than the finished product was worth.

It is this meager technological achievement, perhaps, which has led Europeans to rate Australians as low—or even lowest—in the evolutionary hierarchy. Yet, as Cook pointed out, they had "very little need of it." We do find, however, that prestige and influence depend, and depended, on skills of intellect and imagination. Technical, hunting, geographical, and navigational skills certainly did, and today still do, play an important part in a man's total makeup. But the emphasis has always been on an accurate knowledge of the law, of myths, rituals, and ceremonial procedures, the framework of an articulate awareness of man's experience. If we distinguish the literate from the nonliterate awareness, on this sort of criterion the Aborigines are the equal of any. Further, accepting that this valued experience derived from the quality of relationships in a nomadic way of life, we can perhaps appreciate that innovations which went contrary to the experience, or whose realization entailed the adoption of different kinds or qualities of social relationships, would tend to be rejected.

Though trade rings or ceremonial exchange cycles are known to exist in the northern parts of Australia (see Thomson, 1949; Falkenberg, 1962, pp. 143–198), and probably existed in the southern and other areas before the traditional ways of life were so quickly broken up, it has not been shown that participants do, did, or could derive any direct and concrete economic benefit from them—unless, of course, one takes a holistic view of the meaning of "economic." On the other hand, those who participated in these exchanges do, and did, derive prestige from the rate of turnover of valuables which, not convertible into other forms of wealth, were exchanged and passed on to others in the ring. This rate of turnover was itself dependent on a knowledge and awareness of social situations and relationships, on cunning, foresight, and the ability to seize advantage from a fruitful experience of particular individuals living in certain ways, subject to sets of rules, and exploiting the resources of the environment. No dullard could hope to maintain a reasonable rate of turnover. Only the quick and acute could do so. Again, although it has been held that some

Aborigines in northern Australia used women as a form of wealth (see Hart and Pilling, 1960, pp. 51–77) and as a means to extending their influence, it is clear from the internal evidence that if he is to put himself into a position to exert any influence over and through women, a man should first conform to what his elders required of him: the demonstration of intellectual and imaginative skills exercised according to the rules or customs. Yet the very fact that women should be coveted and used for political ends should give us pause. Aboriginal women are as strong, hardy and active as their brothers. But the latter created and maintained the political environment and its relevance. If the use of women by men seems to have been a universal in human affairs, might Aboriginal life indicate why this should be so? It is clear that for the Aborigines it was more important to exercise power through and over people rather than things. People are and were more important than things. But if we are to answer the question why, in the Aboriginal case, it was men rather than women who created and controlled the regularities of the social environment in which the people could survive as humans rather than animals, we need to look further than babies.

Most Australian communities were, and remain, small but generally informal gerontocracies which left little scope for the senile but, in varied situations, gave seniority of experience its due. They were managed by those capable and older middle-aged men who had grown shrewd and knowledgeable, who held the secrets of rituals and ceremonies, who had earned their prestige and influence in the community by demonstrating their awareness and knowledge of their own community's assumptions about the nature of man. They were men who, relating received assumptions — essentially that body of belief and experience coupled to purpose which we call "religion" — to their own personal and pragmatic experience of life, were able to turn them to account. In doing so they not only fulfilled themselves but, to greater or lesser extent, mirrored in the flesh the community's image of what a whole man should be. Yet if intellectual skills were, and are, largely exercised in religious fields, in myths, rituals and ceremonies, in probing and hypothesizing about the meaning of things, in attempting to plumb the depths of human experience in order to find or confirm the purposes of life, this did not mean that the religious specialist *per se* necessarily had the most prestige and renown. He might not be able to put his knowledge to use, his wisdoms might be too narrow, dogmatic, and specialized. Besides, thought to have a greater knowledge of, and closer contact with, just those powers or beings which men know least about, the specialist could be, and often was, subject to possession or trance. In such a case the ordinary rules of society were, so to speak, held in suspension. A man in trance, or possessed, was not held responsible for his actions. Conversely, he who was a master of the prescribed imaginative and intellectual skills, but who spurned the community rules, asserting his skills against them and those who abided by them, was both feared and shunned. He became, and in many situations today still becomes, a sorcerer or criminal, an evildoer who holds in scorn what members of the community hold to be good and true. If ordinary men steered between the poles of being subject to trance or possession, and knowingly and purposefully doing evil things, the men who managed affairs were generally those with well-rounded characters, shrewd men whose intellectual and imaginative capacities were balanced by political acumen, economic and domestic skills.

All Australian Aborigines observe an incest taboo, and the rules for regulating marriages are generally exceedingly complex. Here their import may be stated quite briefly. They delimited the area of choice of spouses, divided the community into groups and categories of persons between whom there were prescribed potential ritual, economic or sexual relations, and allocated responsibilities for the nurture and training of the succeeding generation. Albeit somewhat qualified, the same sorts of rules and conventions persist in today's settled communities. These rules are, and were, integral to the ways in which Aborigines represented to themselves the nature of their being, and they were closely related to views on the conception and birth of children. Some Aborigines were thought to be ignorant of the part played by the male in conception. And although there are grounds for supposing that this alleged ignorance is a facet of that tradition which has generally sought to find in Australian life anything which might seem strange or peculiar to a European, it is certainly the case that at least some Aboriginal peoples overtly denied the significance in conception of male sperm. Was this ignorance or something else? Close observation of the breeding habits of the kangaroo, where postpartum conception is frequent, and where, in the wild, it was not always possible to observe the initial mating and thereafter keep track of the female, could easily have led into the idea that in nature, at least, some kinds of birth without the aid of a male were possible. Again, experience of impotent males and barren women, or incompatible couples, would hardly lead them or anyone else to conclude that there was a direct causal link between sexual intercourse, fertilization, and the birth of a child. Thus, rather than resort to an idea of chance or statistical probability (which we tend to do), Australians affirmed that if, in most cases, a man had to "open the way" into a woman, conception itself was due to a third factor, a creative power whose identity was determined by the relation between morning sickness or the first kicks of the babe in the womb and a dreaming, a vivid thought, or an environmental feature such as a rock, plant, animal, or meteorological phenomenon. And this creative or causative power was associated with, or identified as one of, the ancestral beings or divine powers of the creative dreamtime—who created and create all things. On the other hand, social fatherhood, the responsibility for nurturing, sheltering, feeding, and teaching the child was assigned to the husband of the mother.

The lands of a tribe or subtribe were divided into a number of inter-digitated sites or localities each of which was associated with one or more named creative or destructive divine powers whose relevances and interrelations were, and are, expressed in myths and the rituals and ceremonial which enact the myths. Membership of a patriline, or the place of birth, or the place where a father or grandfather was buried, generally determined which particular divine powers, cycles of myths, ceremonies, and rituals should be an individual's particular concern. Those who had such a set of concerns in common were joined together into a ritual or religious society or cult. They "owned" the sacred sites and were responsible for maintaining and passing on to the succeeding generation, as a sacred trust, the body of knowledge they had developed. These sacred sites or localities might be included in, or overlap with, the lands associated with a horde. But all over Australia the exploitative association of lands in relation to the horde, and the ritual or religious associations of specific localities in relation to a patriline or cult group were kept distinct.

While tribe and subtribe are simply European categories indicating varying numbers of hordes within a linguistic group, horde, cult group, and/or patriline indicate indigenous groups or categories which, being generally exogamous, necessitated marriage into other hordes, cult groups, or patrilines. In addition, among many Aboriginal peoples there was a further division of society known as the section or subsection. The section or subsection system might comprise several neighboring tribes or subtribes, and each horde within the total body would contain members of the different sections or subsections. Each of these groupings and categories played a part in the regulation of marriage. If we add to these the categories of kin relationship, we are given a fifth variable in the regulation of the all-important institution of marriage. The relative significance of these five variables is, and has been, as our quotation from

Meggitt (*above* p. 3) has indicated, one of the chief problems of anthropological concern. For while "tribe" and "subtribe" are simply anthropological conveniences, the horde, cult group, section and subsection, patriline and kinship are translations of substantive Aboriginal organizational categories. Each of them divided or grouped people by reference to different criteria. Though sets of kin, not necessarily based on consanguineal relations, could change with adoptive practice, and though the horde was an existential and unnamed group of cooperators whose composition could change over relative short periods of time as members split off, joined other hordes, and then, perhaps, returned to their former horde, patriline, cult, section and subsection memberships seem to have been relatively stable. As a whole, however, the complex derived coherence from, and was underpinned by, sets of religious attitudes or assumptions which are not easily separable from economic, political, kin, cult, section and subsection activities.

Earlier writers tended to describe the total social order as "totemistic" or representative of "totemism" because, in naming so many of their groups and categories, as well as their culture heroes, divine powers and ancestral beings with reference to natural species, meteorological phenomena, or topographical features, these things seemed to be involved in the very being of the people themselves. That is, Australians seemed to be an example of the way man had lived when in a relatively undifferentiated state. Closely related to ideas about the "state of nature" and the "primitive," and deriving directly from evolutionary theory which held "differentiation" to be the criterion of stages of development, just what was involved in this apparent assimilation of humans with their environment has posed a host of problems of interpretation and analysis.

Growing boys and girls learned from practical experience and demonstration how to hunt, forage and gather wild-stuffs, dig for tubers, spin thread, carve, work stone and make a variety of artifacts. They learned and internalized the categories of relationship. They soon became aware of cult and section groupings and, since particular kinds of behavior were attached to particular kinship categories, they were soon made aware of the range of kinship categories and the patterns of behavior associated with them. As they became familiar with the features of their physical environment, so they got to know about the divine powers, ancestral beings or heroes associated with particular localities. Relatively undifferentiated in babyhood, boys and girls realized early that certain tasks were for males, others for females; that cult activities were mainly for initiated men to the exclusion of women and children; that there were particular occasions when women and children not only could, but had to join in; that if women did most of the hard, backbreaking tasks — such as digging for corms or tubers — associated with community life, men did most of the exciting things and were, above all, responsible for managing community affairs. As children matured, so their growing powers, their effectiveness and usefulness in community, were signaled by a series of initiatory ceremonies. These, involving mutilation of the skin and sexual organs, circumcision and subincision, tooth evulsion, branding, cicatrization, trials and ordeals as well as more formal instruction as to the meanings contained in myths, conferred upon the growing child wider sets of rights and obligations. Arranging and carrying out the initiations were the responsibility of the elders of the relevant religious society or cult of which the child was a member in virtue of his first stirrings in the womb. For boys and for men these initiations were of the greatest importance. They enabled them to "become men," to play their parts in the management of community affairs. Educative processes sealed in ritual forms, initiations provided the opportunity to gain in knowledge and awareness, to come to know something of man's place in the cosmos.

Aboriginal women do not appear to have led a rich ritual life — but perhaps they had a much richer life than a male orientated anthropology could perceive. If their main role seems to have been to do well what the men expected of them, they were by no means minor characters in life's play. They fed the community, had little need of illusion. Their needs and desires were the fixed points from which the management of affairs took departure. Their whimsies and fancies were the shifting shoals which men had to accommodate or accept if they were to direct the ship of community with any usefulness or efficiency.

From their religious elders young people learned of the "dreamtime" before men were, how the incorporeal beings or divine powers of the present once had sensible form, laid out the contours of the land, created the flora and fauna, provided the techniques whereby nature's bounty might be available, and then, at last, made men out of themselves and what they had created as their own beings merged into the mists of time. Nonetheless, these beings or powers are always present, sensibly manifesting themselves from time to time much in the way they did when they were engaged in creating the world. As was evident to the Aborigine, creation is both a continuing fact as well as a unique historical or as though historical event. Created once and for all time, the world and everything in it dies and yet renews itself or is recreated. The parched desert, baked and cracked after years of drought, bereft even of ants, comes to life after rain with lush grasses and a myriad blooms. Animals foregather, feed, mate and die as the land reverts into desert again. Dearth succeeds plenty as night follows day, as the sun rises and sets. With each death the human community died for a while, and with each birth the promise of life was realized. Throughout the year, as births, deaths, marriages, and initiations were celebrated, the human community together with its wealth, rules, and assumptions about the nature of things, died and was recreated. Holding together our own "big bang" and "steady state" theories about the origins of the universe, for the Aborigines the world was created, and *that* creation steadily continues: created and creating were one.

Just as the kicking embryo proceeded from the divine creative powers associated with a locality, so, sometimes, these same powers were taken to derive from, or were explained in terms of, a still greater power which, located in the sky, and generally associated with thunder, lightning, rain, flood, and the rainbow—themselves very closely associated with the serpent, phallus, stream, and semen—was thought of as the very life-source of all things. But if this "life-source," howsoever conceived, tended on specific occasions to be concentrated in a particular thing or phenomenon, more usually the multiplicity of creator powers remained a multiplicity, each with its own sphere and proper ambience of being. The idea of Oneness, of a unity, was contained not in an idea or manifestation abstracted from or subsuming the millions of particulars observable and experienced, but rather in the multiplicity itself. All taken together made an integrated and organic whole. As the fact of birth was a corporeal proceeding and separation from the incorporeal divine powers of the dreamtime—which though it existed *then*, still exists today—so the life cycle was a series of ritualized exits and entries from one field of moral being to more extensive fields of moral being and responsibility. Death signaled the passage from moral being into a reaggregation with the powers of the dreamtime. Between birth and death the period of sensible and corporeal moral being was, for each individual, a transient and distorted reflection of that mode of being from which man had come and to which he must ultimately return. It was a man's duty to attempt to minimize the distortion, to so manage his moral life and that of the community that the spheres of the divine, the natural world, and the moral world corresponded with one another, bore witness to the harmonious integration of the multiplicities which made up the whole.

For the Aborigines sickness might be, but was more often not regarded as simply physical illness. Sickness evoked death, and, like ourselves in relation to what we define as a mental or psychological illness, since man was defined as moral rather than animal, sickness tended to be regarded as a lapse from appropriate moral being rather than a distemper of animal condition. Australians had a *medica materia*. For particular kinds of sickness there were prescribed medicines and techniques. Bleeding, binding, salves, packs, minor surgery, and amputation were among them. But if it is an overstatement to say that behind every technique of allevia- tion or cure there was the feeling that it was the sick person's moral lapse that had to be cured rather than the physical symptoms, moral condition was generally regarded as more important than physical condition. The consequences of mere physical hurt or illness were rela- tively minor. But since moral lesion cannot exist in isolation, but must relate to others, the consequences reverberated to include all those who had had contact with the sick person. It was essential to try to find out all that had happened, and then try to put the sick person's mind at rest.

After death, especially if moral obligations remained outstanding, that incorporeal or immortal part or quotient of man which was destined to join the powers of the dreamtime might stay close at hand and manifest itself to kinsmen and others as a ghost or similar kind of being until, appeased through rituals, feasts and offerings, it was able to continue its journey into the dreamtime. The death of a man with malice or vindic- tiveness in his heart, with some score yet to pay, was matter for great concern. His ghost would remain close to the living for some while, would annoy, hurt and injure the living until laid or set at rest. If we now need our playwrights to remind us that ghosts are not necessarily figures dressed in white sheets, but have much to do with memory and con- science, the Aborigines recognized that while the good may take care of itself the evil that men do lives after them. This evil they attempted to define and contain in specific ritual activities. At the same time, death and its attendant rites provided an opportunity for renewing and revivifying the moral order—not simply by way of restatement but in the form of taking political initiatives.

The Aborigines were faced on the one hand with numbers of free- moving and self-willed powers, creative as well as destructive, of whom the beings of the dreamtime were prototypical, and on the other with the world of nature, a profusion of animals, plants, topographical features, and meteorological phenomena, each with its ordered modes. Enjoying some of the powers of the divine world, and some of the powers of the natural world, man had moral being, was subject to obligation: the conduct of affairs in full awareness of a basic reciprocity in social interaction. Man, moreover, was quite alone in knowing how space and time limited him, in his awareness of death and obligation, in his self-conscious expectations of reciprocal conduct from his fellows. If the activities of wallaby and wombat and the occurrences of lightning and rain had been ordered and set by the dreamtime creators, each in its nature, it was in man's nature to regulate his own affairs, his being, in an awareness of his articulate moral rules. Man had to find out, then cherish and maintain his knowledge of the variety of modes of being in the world, so that he could know how his own moral mode of being could be affected by those other modes of being in which he participated. This knowledge was revealed to man partly through dreams — often vehicles of political ploy, statement and decision — but mainly through his myths.

If we cannot say that every single facet of Aboriginal life was faithfully set down in the corpus of myths belonging to a particular community, we can be certain that little of importance was omitted. "All ... technical skills," writes Ursula McConnell, "the arts of hunting and cooking, all nature's gifts, and observances of ritual and ceremonial, are made explicit, and kept intact in the social mind by the recital and dramatic portrayal of the creative and inventive activities of the *pulwaiya* [the dreamtime beings, the characters of myth] by whose sanction they continue to exist and function" (McConnell, 1957, pp. 17–18). Essentially oracular and informative, but not necessarily didactic, myths revealed to the Aborigines how they might realize their moral being. For though a myth might set out in fine detail the varieties of foodstuffs and resources to be found in particular localities, and might narrate the consequences of disposing of them, it was discreetly ambiguous as to how a particular man should dispose of them. For however like men the characters in a myth might appear to be, they were not men, not subject to moral obligation. Listening to a myth was one thing, understanding it was quite another. Australian myths provided word maps of localities, told of the powers associated with the localities, encapsulated in words committed to memory most if not all of the data available to Aboriginal culture. But making sense of this data, understanding it, was just what the elders of a ritual society specialized in. On listening to a myth and so becoming aware of an objective world of entities outside himself, but rather like himself, so that he might identify with them, a man was forced to decide in the light of his own pragmatic experience, and his knowledge of others and the rules of his community, how he himself should act. The religious elders set themselves the interpretative task. From them — and no doubt from time to time in the past there were competing schools of interpretation —

the initiate learned not only the content of a myth but how to interpret it and so make it work for him. Further, in acting out the myth in a ritual situation, during corroborees or in initiation ceremonies for example, a man became himself a part of the myth, not only representative of a dreamtime being, but, for the duration of the enactments, that dreamtime being itself. As the anthropological committal to the fieldwork method itself implies, there is no better way of understanding something than to be it.

More than any other feature of Australian life, it is these ritual enactments of myth which have led those who have lived with Aborigines to stress the essential unity of their life-style. Nor can there be much doubt that being at one with nature, the divine beings of the dreamtime, and with one's fellows was the main theme of Aboriginal life. The activities entailed in attempting to achieve this unity plot the life cycle. But of course, because Aborigines are human, the path is neither smooth nor absolutely bounded. As in all communities, there are wrongdoers, those who cheat, those who are determined to take more from life than the rules of their culture properly allow them. Despite a relatively free and easy attitude toward material things, particular things did and do belong to particular people. At the point at which a casual borrowing became a theft the reaction was as sharp as it would be among ourselves. But in traditional life there were no policemen, no formally constituted courts, magistrates and the rest. The matter had to be resolved by direct action, by quarreling it through with the aid of kinsfolk, by involving all in the community with the responsibility of settling the affair. Homicide, and some kinds of adultery in some circumstances, were regarded as serious crimes. Again, fixing the blame and taking appropriate action, initiated in the first instance by the injured party taking direct action, almost invariably became a community matter. The standard punishment for an adultery was a spear driven into the thigh. Homicide invited a revenge killing on the part of the kinsmen of the murdered person, compensation, or the resort to sorcery — by means of which the suspected murderer could be made seriously ill, or killed, by the use of a variety of mystical techniques.

The efficacy of these mystical techniques rested on a complex series of factors. Everyone participated in the assumption that they were, or would be, effective. The murderer, himself participating in the assumption, would know that the techniques were being employed. This was the basis on which, through a gradual erosion of his self-confidence, or a continued pricking of conscience, a guilty man might be persuaded to cooperate in his own destruction. Thus, made wary by the knowledge that measures were surely being taken against him, the guilty person might begin to see physical signs of these measures. The sorcerer would no doubt help him to perceive that things were not as they usually were. Little accidents might balloon in importance, a slight headache—bound to occur in the nature of things—might be given an otherwise unwarranted importance. Gradually or more quickly, as the guilty person became more and more suspicious of every little thing, he would isolate himself from his fellows, isolate himself from the life-giving oneness of things. Outbursts of temper against those who only meant well, roughness of manner in his social relationships—all would add up to growing difficulties in finding food, friends, sympathy, and human companionship. This in the end killed him or made him sick until, with due action and thought, he could work his way clear of what we might call a severe paranoid condition. Yet if we are not clear in our own minds precisely what we mean by a paranoid condition, we might perhaps miss the essential point of what seems to have taken place in Aboriginal life. By withholding its consent the community deprived a wrongdoer of his manhood, deprived him of his capacity to participate in the moral order. This reaction the wrongdoer had already invoked when, in acting as he had done, he cut himself off from his fellows.

The picture of Aboriginal life that is sometimes given—by Cook among others—of a simple and natural engagement with arcadian bliss should be treated with caution. It is as silly and patronizing to speak of the Aborigines as superhuman or blessed or vested with a pristine innocence as it is to regard them as subhuman, in league with the devil, or having inferior intelligences. They were and are as corruptible as anyone. Some Aborigines are, and were in the eyes of other members of community, what we would call criminals. Envy neither was, nor is, absent in Aboriginal life. Cheating and lying are as common there as anywhere. Political ambition might lead to excesses. If the desire for power was controlled, as it is in any community, there were, and are, always those who seek to outflank the controls in order to get what they want. Young men still tend to be aggressive, compete with one another, and have to be brought to order by their elders, who have to recruit the cooperation of the community as a whole. Recognizing by reference to the traditional rules that random acts of self-willedness cannot be in harmony with the rules and conventions, Australians have always taken pragmatic and forceful action appropriate to the circumstances.

The relatively narrow cultural horizons of Aboriginal life certainly limited the range of both opportunities for, and varieties of, corruption. But once these horizons are widened Australians have not been any slower than others to explore the new opportunities. Though today the elders must at times refer to the local policeman and the apparatus of courts, prisons, and magistrates which lie behind him, in their own lives the rules which govern their social relationships and interactions are legitimized by the assumptions buried in myth—the "old Law," as the Aborigines say, distinguishing the traditional social order from the new one in which they are becoming more and more involved. But as horizons widen and it becomes less and less possible to restrict the ranges of experience, so the "old Law" must gradually yield place to the complexities and opportunities offered by the new.

When an Australian visited a shrine—it might be a hillock or outcrop of rocks—to look at, or even venerate, sacred objects of stone or carved wood known in the literature as *churinga*, he was doing hardly more or less than a serious minded European who visits St. Peter's, Nôtre Dame, or Westminster Abbey. For just as visits to these Christian shrines bring Europeans into close, intimate and self-conscious contact with their traditions, both religious and national, whether or not they consider themselves Christians, so the *churinga*, suitably incised and inscribed, reminded an Aborigine of his origins, traditions and conditions of being, and, be it only for a few moments, made him an integral part of the stream of his tradition. Like the Christian confirmation, the series of initiations which an Aboriginal youth or maiden underwent were, for them, religious and sacramental acts which signaled and legitimized growing powers and responsibilities. To meet these last they had to grow in awareness. The moan of bull-roarers at night during a ritual ceremony may be described by Europeans as signaling the presence or immanence of a particular dreamtime being. In this form, distanced as the reader usually is from the situational qualities, one is inclined to dismiss it as just another native superstition. No less, however, does the music of the Mass signal the special immanence or presence of God, did the beating of timbrels evoke an awareness of the meaning of Jehovah. Among Australian Aborigines the dance is still sacred: the ordinary rules of community life are laid aside, dormant, and new rules, rules more consistent with the divine nature of the activity, are brought into play. For in the situation of the ritual dance men are no longer just men. They represent, act out, and in a sense become that which is thought to be eternal: the truth of things.

Though all Australian art is essentially religious, particular drawings, paintings, incisions, carvings, and pieces of sculpture are not necessarily sacred or set apart from other dimensions of life. "Religion" is a category far wider than "sacred." To rank as true art, the creative work must surely show forth the religious impulse, the purposeful probe into the truth of things, the transcending of both appearance and the technological competence. Questions of aesthetic appeal aside—and here we ought to remember that aesthetic appeal itself depends on appreciating a thrust into the truth of things, so that a differently perceived truth goes with a differently appreciated aesthetic—when we contemplate Australian Aboriginal art we at once become aware of its diagrammatic force. Whether communicated by rhythm of line or pattern or color or all together, Australian art tells a story, seems more concerned with describing and transmitting adequate representations of the principles which govern the Australian condition of being than with representations of what the eyes may see and apprehend directly. Austere, portraying a thing or animal or event or story, but also making plain the underlying structures of these subjects, Aboriginal art gathers the emotions and transforms them into an intellectual response to what is, in addition, an intellectual statement. Juxtapositions of colors and forms first seize the emotions. But because to an Australian the composition is meaningless outside a context of myth, the dreamtime, ancestral beings and the ordinary experiences of daily social life, the representation enforces reflection as a preliminary to the aesthetic judgment which considers the harmonies of mind and emotions. At this point, perhaps, awareness of being what one is comes closer to positive knowledge.

The Aborigines did not take their powers of intellect, mind, and will for granted. Claiming what we would call telepathic capacities by means of which they could communicate with each other, or kill or injure one another, they are and seem always to have been much concerned with the proper exercise of intellect or mind or will informed by moral awareness: in sum, the implementation of the Law. This it was that distinguished the Aborigine as human, and marked him out from the dreamtime powers on the one hand, and the natural world on the other. A life's objective was the union of these parts in accordance with the Law. Qualities of intellect and mind and will, properly and fruitfully exercised in moral awareness, bestowed prestige and commanded respect. Where the circumstances of European penetration made a traditional tribal life impossible, the breakdown of cultural ties and the means of transmitting the cultural heritage have resulted in a wretched and meager life lived on the peripheries of the European environment—shanty or slum life. On the other hand, in circumstances where it has been possible to carry on a traditional life, no people have in the past so set their faces against changes in their social systems as have the Aborigines. New techniques have been acceptable, so also a variety of artifacts. But to take to cultivation, or to sheep or cattle herding, as a community, would have entailed such an elaboration of property rights, rights of inheritance and succession, and political institutions as would have entirely nullified the significant and important concerns of traditional community life.

That today and over recent years Aboriginal peoples have in fact taken more and more to sheep and cattle herding on European owned stations, and now live in more or less settled communities, is due to the impossibility of continuing to lead a tribal life. With their hunting grounds under cultivation, or enclosed, with the depletion, too, of animal life, the survivors of once distinct groups have been forced to reaggregate in particular centers, and there attempt to create a new way of life. Because it is all they know, elders strive to maintain syncretic versions of the old Law. But to the youths and maidens of today this old Law is becoming less and less convincing. Quite as eager as young people elsewhere to grasp the opportunities offered by a technological civilization, young Aborigines are now in the process of attempting to think out the alternatives before them.

As one might expect of a people whose traditional mode of livelihood went with organization into small groups, political and economic institutions were overtly simple and, indeed, barely recognizable. But this did not mean that political and economic life was simple. On the contrary, on both hands it was most complex, hidden and embedded in what would seem to an outside observer to be purely ritual or religious activities. Birth, death, initiation, funerary and mortuary ceremonies were not only occasions for joy, celebration, or grief, but for the settlement of old debts, the engagement of new debts, and the explicit statement or promise of allegiance, loyalty, service, rivalry, support and obligation. Dreams were not necessarily private experiences. They received public expression in song lines with political overtones; dreams were sources of political activity. Myths could broaden out and change to include new experiences. Although very little has as yet been done on the relation of myths and dreams to Aboriginal political life, the internal evidence points to a rich vein. Again, although the values and rules relating to the local group or horde, kinship, section, and subsection seem hard and fast, the incidence of "wrong marriages" as well as expectable economic exigencies would lead us to suppose that they provided the framework for political activity. Indeed, just these political implications seem to lie behind Meggitt's statement concerning why he went to study the Walbiri. Nevertheless, it is to the close "fit," the formal integration of the rules relating to different spheres of life that fieldworkers have drawn the reader's attention.

Aboriginal life was and is intensely personal. The traditional Law was strict, life's course was precisely plotted. This same Law, adapted as it was to face-to-face relations in circumstances of shifting but limited numbers of interpersonal interactions, revealed to an Aborigine how he might be precisely himself: an Aborigine. Working together, the Law and personal interactions have inhibited the Aborigines' entry, either as individuals or as communities, into the loosely structured and characteristically impersonal ambience of the greater society.

A European or, indeed, any member of a civilized ambience or open society, becomes habituated to being something other than he is. It prevents us from appreciating the enormous leap that is entailed in moving from a closely ordered familial and personal life into a complex of loosely arranged and depersonalized roles. We become used to wearing different masks, different hats, as varieties of situations succeed each other. We have our ways of creating opportunities when, for a few hours perhaps, we can be ourselves. But not many of us know our way around all our available spaces, and, until recently, outside his own Law an Aborigine could only be a stray in these spaces. There were no landmarks, no coordinates for thought, controlled emotional response or prediction. If the open society provides a greater range of opportunities for self-realization than the closed, it also provides as great a range of temptation to deny one's potential. The prescriptions and restrictions of the Law combined with the exigencies of a nomadic life and small population units made the Aborigine what he was.

To an Aborigine myths were, and to some extent remain, as revelation. They revealed to man the nature of man and the world in which he lived. They provided the terms within which an Aborigine might understand himself and his condition. Human activities and the features of the physical environment not only explained themselves as existential facts, but, so far as they occurred in myths they were also vehicles through which, in the light of his own pragmatic knowledge and experience, a man might explain to himself the interrelations of the divine, physical, and moral worlds. In their own ways expert psychologists all, Aboriginal assumptions and practices regarding the birth and nurture of children, the strains of puberty, and the problems of mutual adjustment—keyed as they were to elaborate systems for the regulation of marriage and the marital relationship—might be the envy of many a European practitioner. Immured in their self-justifying and therefore self-maintaining systems of interpersonal relations, as though aware that there was no profit in gaining the world at the cost of losing their own souls, Aborigines have tried to cling to their traditional ways so far as circumstances have allowed.

If older generations have often been as rigid in their adherence to the forms of traditional Law as many a Christian to the shibboleths of a particular sectarianism, the young want a new law. They do not seek an identity that will mark them off as Aborigines locked to an anthropologically romanticized dreamtime. They want to take their places in the world as Australians, as capable of dealing with small town or city life as their ancestors dealt with forest, desert, or beach. Life on a cattle, sheep, or mission station can be cozy and comfortable. It can also be exploitative and demeaning. Rounding up sheep, or herding cattle, or mending a windmill have their own satisfactions. Being a stockbroker, or priest, or fortune teller, or tennis player could be as fulfilling. The young, that is, want to do and be what they feel is in them to do and be, and they are learning the means of realizing their desires (see, for example, Wilson, 1964, 1970).

3   "WE" AND "THEY"

Stripped to the bare skin and deprived of centuries of cumulated culture, we and the Australian Aborigines might differ from each other in certain minor biological aspects. As plain men and women, morally aware and capable of rationalization and intellection, we and they would be much the same—if mutually opposed. Of different tribes and with different normative moralities and cultural backgrounds, we and they would be mutually hostile and suspicious. Further, the nature of our cultural heritage in relation to theirs accentuates the difference between "We" and "They," makes us acutely aware of the disparity in conditions of being. We have infinitely more social and cultural spaces to experience. Our ancestors gave us the means to preserve and develop the experience of past generations, created systems of retrieval in libraries, gave us a cultural memory independent of oral traditions. The notion that we could, by means of an intellectual construct, save all the data and preserve it has widened the gulf between ourselves and nature, and "We" and "They." Yet that very notion has made us take the first step toward knowing them. The greater step, that of understanding and embracing them, has been taken not in virtue of our bare human skin but because of the Christian moral imperative to love one another.

Lacking that moral imperative, which comes not from the animal but from the self-conscious and articulate perception that the animal should grow into and develop the moral idea, strangers are wary, recoil in suspicion. The sameness that is clothed in an otherness is everywhere instinctively rejected. Obedience to the Christian imperative has never been easy. It goes against the grain of the animal. A continuing moral and intellectual challenge to overcome the instinctual rejection of otherness has been the burden of our heritage; and through two millennia the imperative has been going through the process of becoming more and more generally realized. The process is slow, but the greater wonder lies in the fact that it is taking place.

To reach out into otherness and know, to reach out into otherness and embrace — these are the mainsprings of anthropology. Some of the authors mentioned in the preceding pages have emphasized the knowing — how to know more of the otherness more acutely, more accurately, more economically and elegantly. Others have emphasized the embracing. Few have not combined both aspects in varying proportions. Taken together and in all we can perceive a dialectic which, inherent and integral to European civilization, has been extended outward into varieties of realms of otherness. As we, individuals all who seek our sovereignty in interactions with others, play out the terms of our own dialectic, another dialectic — between ourselves and those others out there, who may neither perceive nor realize individuality as we ourselves do — gradually and subtly alters the positions and terms in which the former dialectic was engaged. Having given otherness initial placement, both dialectics are engaged. But sooner or later relative placements shift, and both dialectics have to be engaged anew. This is the process of absorption. This is how we and they broaden in outlook, perceive each other differently, come in time to share a common heritage.

CHAPTER 3

Transitional Man

1 PLACING ABORIGINES

Australian Aborigines have been frequently described as "one of the most primitive of peoples," meaning that in most respects they and their cultures represent an earlier, more ancient, simpler or less well developed or differentiated form or type. The usage is still common, though many anthropologists now tend to avoid the word "primitive" and substitute for it "simple" or "nonliterate" or even "preliterate." Mainly, this is because pejorative connotations such as "rude" or "coarse" or "vulgar" that, in context, have become attached to "primitive," do not appear to do justice to the facts, tend to set Aborigines apart as a distinct species, and so positively obstruct policies of integration or assimilation. However, since no such pejorative connotations attach to "primitive" when it qualifies, say, Italian art; and since there are always some who will attach pejorative connotations to the substitutes for "primitive" in relation to other cultures, avoiding the word "primitive" does not resolve the problem. This is, briefly: What kinds of relationships do Aborigines and their cultures bear to other kinds of people and their cultures, and how may we express them?

So far as it is held that Aborigines and their cultures are particular representations of the spirit of man they are, like ourselves, but men and women, and their cultures, like our own, are attempts to realize particular insights of that spirit within the constraints of community life under given conditions. But the fact that, on the face of it, Aborigines and their cultures are different from ourselves and our culture, and differ from

85

others and their cultures, raises the questions of how to define the differences and the relevance of these differences in relation to the many similarities. On one level – the normal practice of all expanding cultures known to history – the reaction to difference has been to permute combinations of disgust, admiration, enslavement, destruction, trade, or exploitation. In addition, but on quite other levels, there is the reaction that attempts to give the strange people and culture some placement in relation to other peoples and cultures. This last, a habitual and sustained systematic accounting unique to European or Western civilization, is rooted in European man's attempt to make the world he lives in appear to his intellect a rational and ordered one governed by moral law. This alone makes possible the narrower and more parochial statement that if anthropology is, as it claims to be, a study of man, his cultures and forms of society, then, unless the subject is to degenerate into a number of particularist and unrelated studies, Aborigines and their cultures must be placed in relation to other peoples and cultures.

Even if we neglect the moral implications, making such a placement has never been a simple matter. Peoples and their capacities for change and development are difficult to separate from cultures which, when they change, become almost impossible to distinguish as developing cultures on the one hand, or quite different cultures on the other. Further, while there exist categories and criteria by which cultures can be distinguished from one another typologically rather than geographically – for example, by reference to technology, or politico-economic organization, or kinship structure to mention a few – consensus on the usefulness and moral implications of particular criteria has rarely been general. But, accepting that there are difficulties, they arise not so much from the nature of the material as from the natures of anthropologists and their subject which, in turn, are rooted in the European intellectual and moral heritage. It is possible – just possible – to imagine, as one is frequently invited to do in science fiction, a situation in which every culture or community could, on scientific criteria, be designated a type in relation to other types. But as soon as we withdraw from the imaginative objectivity of the novelist's world the image begins to crumble. Other kinds of reality take over. We realize that science fiction and much of social or cultural anthropology are kin. People change, and so do their cultures. Characteristics of biological descent begin to interfere with and qualify purely cultural features. Typologies built upon varied criteria are offered, temporarily adopted by some, criticized and rejected by others. Political and moral attitudes toward fellow human beings affect and influence particular kinds of placement — can there, indeed, be any more decisive criteria of exclusion and inclusion in relation to human groups than the political and moral?

Then, too, whether conscious or unconscious of it, the past holds us prisoner. We remain gripped by the received traditions of the scriptures, particularly the New Testament. We are heirs to that great imaginative construct, metaphor or supposal which, rooted in Homer, Plato, Aristotle, and the Neo-Platonists, flowered in the Middle Ages, was part of the very fabric of Renaissance life, and persisted through into the Enlightenment: the Great Chain of Being.

Very briefly, as reminder and to pursue a thought from the first chapter, the great chain of being visualized the cosmos, the fantastic plentitude of God's creation, as composed of a multitude of existents each of which shared one or more attributes or properties with another. With the Godhead at the apex, every created thing was related to other created things according to the Divine purpose, and could be arranged in a hierarchy of classes or orders. Within this framework all creation, from angels and heavenly bodies to the smallest particle of dust, was ordered, each created thing had its proper place. Between one type or class of thing and another, however, there were bound to be transitional or intermediate types or classes. There was no gap, no vacuum. The heavenly bodies showed forth a constancy and harmony and order in which the mathematical medieval mind rejoiced. On earth, however, this same harmony was expressed more generally in flux or change — the changing seasons, processes of growth, the changing fortunes of men and communities. While the moon was thought to describe the boundary between the generalities of constancy and the generalities of flux, the further the distance from earth the more was flux qualified by constancy.

The orders of angels, defined as intelligences — though opinion as to their corporeal or incorporeal nature was hotly contested and veered from one side to the other — stood between man and God, and inhabited areas of space at varying distances from earth. Those furthest away, the highest ranking, only rarely made themselves visible to men. The lower ranks, nearer to earth, made themselves visible more often. Indeed, lest it be thought that angels, spirits with intelligence, whether corporeal or not, were or are *a priori* figments not requiring accounting for, it should be remembered that the appearance in the sky of angels, or beings like angels, seems to have been common certainly into the sixteenth century. (Lewis, 1961, p. 111.) Between man, defined as corporeal with intelligence and rational and moral understanding, and the plants, which had existence and life, were the animals, defined as having existence, life, and corporeality but not intelligence in the sense of rational, articulate moral understanding.

It should be emphasized that the great chain of being seems never to have been a static construct, but was continually being developed, qualified, and criticized. Whether as metaphor, supposal, or general assumption about the way things were, it was a fact of life, a tool of understanding all the way through the Middle Ages to the closing years of the eighteenth century. Nevertheless, there were always fecund intellectual and metaphysical difficulties. Since God was Perfect Being, and omnipotent, in what sense, if at all, could he create an imperfect thing? Given that moral and spiritual imperfections in man derived from the Fall, and that there was no gap, no missing link in the great chain of being—Was Caliban an animal, man, or some intermediate species? Was he, on the other hand, in some sense like the inhabitants of Bedlam, a lunatic, a man whose apparent derangement might be cured? Were some types or races of man perfect *of their kind* but lower on the scale in relation to other types or races of man, albeit they had corresponding human imperfections? Did the principle of perfectibility, derived from the opposition between constancy and flux if not from the Incarnation, apply *across* the types or races of man as it applied *within* a particular order or type? Although from classical times through St. Augustine and into the early nineteenth century the idea of evolution had continually recurred as a solution to these questions, it was as constantly rejected as no real solution. God's goodness, the creation of man, the Fall, and the hope of human perfectibility as contrasted with the apparent experience of moral and spiritual degeneration did not lie well with evolutionism. Then, as now, there was the question of history.

Fixed in the Incarnation, an intervention of God for and on behalf of man in time, history and the chain of being could accommodate each other. But evolution raised grave difficulties. It could be nailed neither to time nor to the historical experience. Besides, to the medieval mind and imagination evolutionism was not sufficiently holistic: it would have to be broken down into evolutionisms of different kinds, based upon different criteria. This in itself was unsatisfactory. In the event, the keys which finally effected a transition from or a transformation of the great chain of being into evolutionary theory seem to have been "survival of the fittest" and "natural selection"—political projections on the screen of science— wedded to a vast increase in technological capability and awareness. Even then, God had to be supposed to have died, and His place taken by

Nature: an event most riotously signaled by the French Revolution. Still, for most of the eighteenth century the great chain of being was a major assumption of learned and unlearned alike. If, in Tillyard's words, "the eighteenth century inherited the idea of the chain of being, but, crassly trying to rationalize a glorious product of the imagination, ended by making it ridiculous and unacceptable in any form" (Tillyard, 1942, p. 26), many of the features of the chain of being are clearly discernible in evolutionary theory. Each in its context appears as an externalized and intellectualized myth providing a general framework for the rational and objective. Held in the constraints of a particular technology, theology, and awareness of time, the chain drew its boundaries around the possibilities, continuities, and discontinuities of experience. To that extent static, it could not have survived the industrial, technological and theological revolutions of the eighteenth and nineteenth centuries. These developments required a construct that would specifically contain the possibilities of varied and changing social experiences going with new social mobilities. Some such general framework has always been necessary to civilization that has never been a theocracy and has always addressed itself as much to physical as to metaphysical problems. Evolution seems to have filled the bill because, on the whole, a quite new technological capacity was unearthing a conception of time — and so of continuities and discontinuities in human relationships — inconceivable to previous generations.

To the annoyance of some the connotations of the word "theory" in "evolutionary theory" still have much in common with the "metaphor" and "supposal" which described the great chain. That is, evolution is still regarded by many as an unproven working hypothesis, as much a "supposal" or "metaphor" as the chain itself. The hierarchy of forms characteristic of the chain is present in evolution, so is the notion of no gap or no vacuum in the types. Indeed, it was just this notion that led to the search for, and the eventual "discovery" of, the missing link between man and the apes: Piltdown man, a forgery only recently proven to be such (see p. 102). Instead of the chain's single scale of criteria by which all objects in creation could be related, however, evolution has had diverse criteria as has seemed appropriate to the circumstances: the pragmatic approach. Biological criteria for people and animals, technological criteria where cultures were concerned, a nice mix of eclecticisms for modes of thought. "Nature" or the "Law of Nature" have taken the place of the Divine purpose and order; and "natural selection" and "survival of the fittest" are still regarded by some as viable solutions to the moral problems, begotten of the Fall, sin, and the hope of perfectibility. But the sleight of hand which identified a simpler or less well developed or primitive form with an earlier or more ancient form — thus translating a typology directly into a chronological series — though inevitably also derived from the chain of being, seems more closely related to another stream of operations: the exegesis of the sacred scriptures.

The main problem in this context so far as it concerns us here was monogenesis versus polygenesis. If all men were indeed of Adamic stock through Noah and his progeny, then the encounter with strange and primitive peoples must and did lead to several primary questions. Were the strangers men of Adamic stock or, referring to the chain of being, an intermediate species? If they were men of Adamic stock, how did they get where they were? What accounting was there of their history and present condition? The scriptures; the authority of the written word as it appeared in works by scholars, poets, travelers, chroniclers, fabulists and mythologists; and the assumptions of the time provided the basic data. Imagination did the rest. Later on in the seventeenth century Bishop Ussher's date for the creation in 4004 B.C. provided a much needed limitation for those who concerned themselves with how much space could be traversed in how much time, and the rate at which changes in custom and belief could occur. Today, though there is of course much more data, and that very much more certainly authenticated, the same questions are asked and the same imaginative impulse is invoked in attempting to answer them.

On the other hand, if the Creator had decided not on one unique creation of man but on several such creative acts in different places on the earth's surface — why should He not? — further questions arose. How many creative acts? What different kinds of men? What sort of definition of man might contain or subsume the difficulties inherent in several — but unknown — numbers of geneses? How should relations be ordered between them? Without written authorities to rely on, however, the histories of such peoples could and did become an exercise in persuasive imagination simply. Today, monogenesis, from which is derived what used to be called the "psychic unity of mankind," is an implicit assumption. It imposes a certain discipline in relation to the definition of man and in unraveling the histories of various kinds of men. But it is by no means unchallenged (Coon, 1962), and like diffusionism in relation to evolutionism, polygenesis is, as it always has been, a convenient way out of the operational and intellectual discipline imposed by monogenesis.

Ultimately, the decision between monogenesis and polygenesis must, because of the implications, be a moral one. If at least from the early

Renaissance through to the late eighteenth or early nineteenth century the encounter with primitive peoples had to be intellectually evaluated in terms of the scriptures and the great chain of being, the problems of monogenesis and polygenesis could hardly be discussed without adverting to the Fall and the idea of perfectibility. On the one hand, the Fall was seen as an historical event charting man's all-time low from which, albeit with occasional setbacks, he was, with the help of revealed religion, gradually raising himself to a peak of perfection still far out of sight. On the other hand, the historical record seemed to show, despite periodic upsurges, a gradual but certain decline and degeneration from which there was no escape. On both hands, improvement and decline were gauged not by reference to technological competence, biological adaptation, political forms, or sexual prowess, but by reference to moral and spiritual stature. Within terms of the implications of the three sets of dichotomies (monogenesis and polygenesis, the Fall and perfectibility, moral or spiritual measurement and technological or other measurement), and depending on the humor of the observer or writer and the audience he addressed, a nonliterate people could be thought of as either "noble" or "pristine" or "unspoiled," or as "rude" or "savage" or "degenerate." Both views persisted in roughly equal balance through to the early years of the nineteenth century despite the rationalist and positivist attitudes of the later eighteenth century. And each had its vocal proponents. In the heyday of nineteenth century evolutionism, however, when the political business of imperial expansion and colonization had become less haphazard and more a serious and self-conscious competitive enterprise, the primitive as noble was only rarely encountered in texts which were taken to be contributions to learning. He was usually depraved, superstitious, degenerate, or benighted when not simply comic. Nevertheless, though it did not emerge as preponderant until after the first quarter of this century, the opposite view, authentic to Christian belief and emerging mainly in aborigines protection societies and much of missionary work, persisted in many quarters.

Though the problems we have identified seem intrinsic to the Christian or European intellectual tradition, discussion of them was not confined to learned academies. On the contrary, since in the Christian tradition a "thinking about" always was, and still is, a futile vanity unless directly related to a "doing about," there was always a lively interchange between "doers" and "thinkers," and as often as not the "thinkers" were themselves "doers." The realization of this conjunction is, indeed, the basis of what in anthropology is called the "fieldwork tradition": the professional requirement of studying a culture at first hand through a technique of participant observation. Further, "thinking about" or "accounting for" a primitive people was always closely related to what should be done about the peoples encountered. Before the discovery of the Americas the problem was almost wholly intellectual. It is true that during the several crusades the problem was serious and practical. Yet since the encounter there was with peoples who shared a common heritage in the ancient world, and who in any case could deploy equivalent or greater powers of physical coercion, for the most part principle was forced to give way to expediency. A similar situation existed with the lone traveler, explorer, merchant, or missionary.

With the discovery of the Americas however, Europeans were faced with a situation in which they could do more or less as they wished. The white man had shouldered his burden. "Thinking about" and "doing about" at once became locked in the very serious relationship between morality and policies of permissiveness or enforcement. Within a few years of the first Spanish attempts to settle the Americas, Bartolomé de las Casas, a Dominican monk and missionary, disgusted at the way in which his compatriots were treating the Indians, had already begun his campaign for more humane and responsible attitudes and policies toward the native Indians, a campaign which was to culminate in the great debate at Valladolid in 1550–1551.

In this debate, which had been warming up for some years, Juan Gines de Sepúlveda, a great Aristotelian scholar, adumbrated the Aristotelian position on natural slavery—a position already implicitly adopted by most administrators and settlers in the Americas—and developed the argument that it was both necessary and in accordance with natural law to make war on the Indians in order to subjugate them, protect them from their own vices and depravities, and so create a situation in which it could become possible to educate and convert them. While both De Sepúlveda and Las Casas were seriously and sincerely concerned with how colonization could be made to accord with both law and reason, De Sepúlveda, as so many since his time, took his stand on what today we would call the best expert and scientific authority. Las Casas, like his many spiritual descendants to this day, stood on what is, virtually, traditional teaching on the lesson of the Incarnation. To De Sepúlveda's closely reasoned and authoritative arguments, Las Casas replied: "Mankind is one, and all men are alike in that which concerns their creation and all natural things, and no one is born enlightened.... The law of nations and natural law apply to Christian and gentile alike, and to all people of any sect, law, condition, or colour without any distinction whatsover" (Hanke, 1959, pp. 112–113).

If the idiom is somewhat different, the principles at issue in the debate at Valladolid continue to be contested today. However scientific or objective or learned or closely argued a particular "accounting for" may be, the moral implications are always susceptible to challenge. Though the see-saw of which view to adopt and implement in particular circumstances seems always to have been closely related to political exigencies and aspirations, the tension derives from the notion that a rational and ordered world should also be governed by that morality which can subsume numbers of differing normative moralities.

In relation to all the problems identified, whether we speak of the definition of man, or of the notion of an intermediate or transitional species, or no gap or vacuum in the natural order, or perfectibility, or origin, or history, or morality versus rationality and political expedience, the Australian Aborigines have served as a test case. Nor is it entirely surprising that they should have been cast in this role. They existed, have survived, and have always been accessible. Brought into the European ambience at a time when Reason was in the ascendant and scientific research was becoming a requirement of one professing to be educated, attention centered on them rather than on others. Of their rivals the Hottentots of southern Africa, regarded at first as nonhuman because their chatter was thought to be incomprehensible, monkey-like rather than articulate and manlike, soon disappeared from the scene as a functioning culture. Surviving individuals attracted the attention of biologists as the nineteenth century began to give way to the twentieth. But on the cultural side there was little opportunity to do very much. The Bushmen of the Kalahari, relatives of the Hottentots, have never been easily accessible, and it is only very recently that they have received any attention. Though some Caribs still survive, the Spaniards destroyed their traditional culture. The Patagonians, like the Veddas of Ceylon, some southern Indian hunting groups, and the forest dwellers of the Malaysian archipelago could only be encountered and studied on the basis of an expensive and highly organized expedition.

In Australia, however, the Aborigines were not only accessible, but, because of the pattern and density of European settlement, it was, as it still is, possible to maintain relatively cheaply a continuing interest in them. There they were, walking the streets of Sydney or Melbourne or Adelaide, begging at the back door, wandering across the pastures of a sheep station, hovering in the vicinity when a paterfamilias took his family on a picnic or to the races. How did they manage, these leftovers from the Stone Age as the experts had dubbed them? Where did they fit in the scheme of things? Were they men like "We," or a species intermediate between man and animal?

2   WHAT KIND OF MAN?

The passion for order, for classification and placement within a significant context, is not simply a scientific pursuit. It belongs more importantly to the eye which has been trained by a particular kind of upbringing and culture to select, reject, and pattern. Whatever the *a priori* choice for defining man, his differing physical attributes leap at once to the eye and so to the mind. The visual impact of bearing, facial features, skin color and apparel mesh into series of learned and received cultural correlations some of which are barely at the level of consciousness. When Abbie, for example, writes that ". . . neither white nor coloured has any warrant to read more into colour differences than differences of colour" (Abbie, 1969, p. 28) he must be presumed to be voicing some sort of personal ideal. In fact, physical aspect always evokes cultural correlations. The interplay that immediately ensues forms the basis for future relations. On one level certain predispositions may be confirmed or denied; at other levels problems are posed. We might ask, for example: If man, in what sense man? To whom or what most closely related? Why thus? Immediately and inevitably — it could not be otherwise — the questions must be referred to our heritage of assumptions. We plunge into problems of history, origins, present conditions, moral implications, and the conduct of relations. Once immersed in these problems the physical or biological features under consideration generally recede in significance.

Physical appearance is usually the first veil to be drawn aside. But this has not been the case with Australian Aborigines. Few people have received such continuously detailed treatment of their physical characteristics as they. Indeed, for no other people have physical and biological characteristics entered so widely and importantly into cultural considerations. Partly, this has been due to the fact that the Aborigines have been accessible. They require European medical treatment, and doctors who treat them keep records and publish them. Specialists in hospitals as well as academics tend to use their vacations for research among the Aborigines. More important, however, lacking an explicit cultural record as to history and origins, physical characteristics might provide the necessary clues. Nevertheless, lurking behind these considerations has been the question of the missing link, the transitional species.

For William Dampier, the Aborigines were "... the miserablest people in the world. Hodmadods (Hottentots), though nasty people, yet for wealth are Gentlemen to these: who have no houses, and skin garments, Sheep, Poultry, Fruits, etc. as Hodmadods have: ... And setting aside their Human Shape, they differ little from Brutes. They are tall, strait-bodied, and thin .... have great Bottle-Noses, pretty full Lips and wide Mouths .... They are long-visaged, and of very unpleasing Aspect .... The colour of their Skins ... is coal-black ... They have no sort of Cloaths, but a piece of the Rhind of a tree tied like a girdle about their Waists ... They have no houses, but lie in the open ... without covering ... Whether they cohabit one Man to one Woman, or promiscuously, I know not: but they do live in Companies, 20 or 30 Men, Women and Children ... Their only Food is a small sort of Fish, which they get by making Wares of Stone across little Coves or Branches of the Sea ..." (1906: (1) p. 453).

We may note in passing that in order to say something about Australians Dampier finds it necessary to give them placement: their "Human Shape," their brutishness, their skin color, their manner of life, their technological capacity. He compares them with the Hottentots and, implicitly, with his own culture. Abbie, who quotes Dampier at length, considers that the buccaneer "possessed the true spirit of scientific inquiry ... he gave a reasonably accurate account of the Aborigines ..." (Abbie, 1969, p. 21). But if Abbie places more weight on Dampier's descriptions of Aboriginal life than he does on the impressions which the Aborigines' physical aspect made on him, Mulvaney, who seems to lay stress on the last, and who quotes from the same passage, writes that it "epitomizes the contempt felt for primitive peoples by many seventeenth century Europeans" (Mulvaney, 1958, p. 135). Captain Cook, as we have seen, prompted no doubt by the more learned Banks, was, unlike Dampier, more disposed to rhapsodize over the "noble savage" — precisely *because* they went more or less naked and had little material equipment. Cook saw them as "dark brown," which has pleasant evocations; and Abbie corrects Dampier's "coal-black" — devilish and benighted? — to "chocolate" — pleasant, sweet? Angas, on the other hand, whose paintings of Aborigines and their equipment are far from contemptuous, says, "The true colour of their skins is so disguised by dirt or ochre and clay as to be hardly distinguishable .... Their eyes are universally of a dark reddish hazel, with black lashes, and deep overhanging brows: and the white being often tinged with yellow, a degree of savageness is imparted to their appearance .... Their heads are not wanting in the perceptive faculties, though in the reflective they are deficient: sight and hearing for instance are enjoyed in much greater perfection by the New Hollander, than even by the New

Zealander; the former can trace the footsteps of their enemies over any distance, and in places which would not afford the slightest indication to the eye of a European or even a New Zealander, thus shewing that the more perceptive faculties are always more perfect in savages and some animals than in civilized man, and the greater the advance towards intelligence and the refinements of civilization, the less perfect are the indications of the unaided senses" (Angas, 1846, Plate XXXV).

Dampier, Cook, Abbie, Mulvaney, and Angas—the way in which a "person seen" differs from a "person perceived" needs no further illustration. The impact of the encounter may trigger quite different pieces of cultural background and attitude. Hence, yet again, the need for the objective intellectual construct which can provide a rational account of what the Aborigines are, or are like; and which, because of the changes which take place when the dialectic inherent in the encounter (p. 84) is engaged, should be designed to accommodate those changes.

While no anthropologist today would write as Angas did, the temptation to do so or think so in private if not publicly remains (see Malinowski, 1967). Many laymen still speak the same way. For the idea of the savage exerts a strange fascination. There in the flesh is the Caliban in each of us, the wild thing which generations of forebears have hidden away. If he calls to be let out he must be the more forcefully restrained. Thus, though the more noted authors of general works on Australian Aborigines, Elkin, for example, or R. M. and C. H. Berndt, or Abbie, include chapters on physical characteristics in their books, it is, on the whole, in order to stop the reader from making all too easy, and often false, correlations between physical characteristics and culture. Caliban must be turned into Prospero, and Ariel left to his whimsy. If, in earlier times, few authors of works on other peoples did not feel obliged to include a section on physical characteristics, by the thirties of this century, say, photographs were doing the job more adequately. But this has not sufficed for Australian Aborigines. Leaving aside the fact that Aborigines are accessible, are there, can be photographed, described, measured, injected, sampled and so on at relatively small expense, we have to ask whether or not there are more deep-seated reasons for this interest, why the legitimate interests of physical anthropologists or human biologists should, in Australia, so often be connected with cultural affairs, whereas for other peoples in other parts of the world they are not.

From the earliest beginnings until the present day Australian Aborigines have confronted students with a series of apparent discontinuities which somehow have to be accounted for or rationalized. To what other kinds of men are these Aborigines most closely related? At the cultural level there were, and there remain, all sorts of gaps. Though it is true that between the Aborigines of mainland Australia and their nearest neighbors to the north, the New Guinea cultivators, there are, through the Torres Straits, gradations of cultural features, it is the final discontinuity that has attracted most attention. Though parallels of particular and separable features of Australian cultures can be found among this or that people elsewhere in the world, the totality of complexes, continuous among Australians themselves, remain distinctive of them. The boomerang, for example, popularly thought to be peculiar to Australians, occurs in a variety of forms in South India and the Americas; the spear-thrower is a part of the traditional material equipment of the Eskimos; marriage class systems may be found in parts of Melanesia; the complex known as totemism occurs in different forms all over the world. But it would be a rash and silly man indeed who would read particular connections into such parallels as these. Taken as wholes, Aboriginal cultures remain peculiar to themselves.

Considering the evidence provided by living and known historical cultures, the traditional question, How did they come to be thus? can only be answered by a variety of imaginative conjectures. On the other hand, bringing the cultural and biological levels together, the immense acceleration in archaeological research in Australia over the past twenty-five years is beginning to construct the outlines of what may have occurred over the last ten or fifteen thousand years. Yet until this effort is matched in Melanesia and the Malaysian archipelago, as one half of the picture begins to clear the other half remains as obscure as before. Moreover, though it is as yet inconclusive, the attempt to correlate the evidence of artifacts, the physical characteristics of the living, and what can be gleaned from vegetal remains in association with the bones of men and animals long dead and buried under earth, will, it is thought, fill out the picture in the course of time. But again, this needs a matching effort among peoples who lack the resources and that tradition and attitude which, stemming from the European cultural heritage, perceives such work as necessary.

Ever since 1795, when Blumenbach grouped Australians within the varieties of the human race, attempts have been made to relate Australians to other peoples on a basis of physical, anatomical, or biological features. All such efforts have foundered on one or another score, and each has yielded to fresh constructions which, in turn, have not been found satisfactory. The difficulty has always been that, even though

Australians have now been found to be differentiated among themselves, in relation to other peoples they have always constituted a homogeneous stock more like each other than they are like other peoples. The fact of discontinuities in the present necessarily leads into a search for continuities in or through the past. This is one of the foundations of evolutionary theory. In the sixties of the last century T. H. Huxley was remarking on the similarities between Neanderthal and Australian skulls. In a few years some scientists were claiming the two kinds of skull to be identical. Though such claims were later discounted, it should be noted that if valid the "fit" would be neat: Australians could be considered as Neanderthal survivors (and therefore submen), or as having developed independently from Europeans and others from a common Neanderthal stock. If today the form of argument remains much the same, the tentative conclusions differ, and it is realized that the problem is very much more complicated than our great-grandfathers thought. While the mounting archaeological evidence suggests that Australians, though representative of modern man, are, like ourselves, the survivors of a very ancient type of man — but cut off on their island continent for many thousands of years, and developing and evolving between themselves in isolation from the rest of the world — the continuities are still missing. One day, perhaps, somewhere in Java it may be, archaeologists will find the skulls and bones which will be identified as "Australoid" (Mulvaney, 1966, p. 305). Even then, it will require many more finds before the final link in the chain is forged.

The conclusion that in Australia evolution probably took an independent course has led, in recent years, to a rapid growth in environmental studies. To what extent, and in what particular ways, has the Aborigine been the creature of his physical environment? The answer, unexpected by those who have regarded Aborigines as some sort of "earlier" or subhuman type of man reacting to the exigencies of environmental change, but in line with the expectations of those for whom man is man wherever he may be, seems to be that the environment has been the artifact of man. That is, the changes in Australian natural and physical environments seem not so much due to climatic changes and the like — for these features seem to have remained pretty well constant over the time period concerned — but to the ways in which the Aborigine has exploited the resources of his environment (see Bowler *et al.*, 1970, *cit* pp. 52–60; Mulvaney and Golson, 1971). If this answer receives further confirmation, then much that has been taken for granted in relation to "early" or "primitive" man will have to come under fresh scrutiny. Nor is it any too early to do so. If we accept that Australians, and so other preliterate peoples, were as much — or almost as much — masters in their environment as we used to think we were in ours, then we are faced not so much with nature or natural selection related to a bleak environmentalism as with the regularities and quirks of man's initiatory creative powers. The working assumption that the features of an organism are adaptations toward exterior pressures may have to be qualified. Although evolutionism is sufficiently eclectic to cope with this for the time being, the reorientation of principle involved may well lead into new and more fruitful perceptions.

Was Angas' bushman in truth any more or less expert at his job than, say, a London Cockney, a Sydneysider, or someone from the Bronx? For Angas, as for many another, it would seem that expertise in the bush was somehow more animal, and expertise in the slum jungles of a modern city more in accord with the refinements of civilization. Does a civilized man, a white man for example, who becomes an expert in bushcraft then become more intelligent, or more like an animal? Or is he, like the Aborigine, simply using his creative intelligence to master his environment?

Ultimately, these questions pose the problem of giving some rational account of the differences between "We" and "They." But it might be short-circuited by asking whether differences in physical type give rise to differences in cultural potential. From the Middle Ages through into the nineteenth century the general assumption — made explicit on both sides of the debate at Valladolid — was that all types of men were teachable. If some individuals did not respond as brightly as others, this had no correlation with specific racial type or stock or skin color, but was to be encountered everywhere among all peoples. As Voltaire pointed out in *L'Ingenu*, teach, or in our idiom, acculturate a Huron and he will become as or more wise or knowledgeable than his teachers. In the nineteenth century, however, the great increase in biological knowledge went hand in hand with a variety of racial theories. For many, relative intelligence or stupidity became not the attributes of particular individuals everywhere, but qualities inhering in physical or biological stocks. And this last could be combined with the quite different notion of a given superiority through divine choice, a superiority which, of itself, did not deny stupidity in the ingroup or qualities of intelligence in outsiders.

Expressed in political terms, these questions were some of the overt issues of the American Civil War. Growing in momentum between the wars in anthropological circles, not until the fifties did it become more generally accepted that the correlation between cultural potential and physical stock was a canard, a piece of racist political propaganda; and that, while qualities of intelligence and stupidity seemed to be about correspondingly distributed through varieties of racial stock, they could only express themselves through and within a given cultural ambience. Yet this was developed into the notion of "cultural relativity," a position so flaccid intellectually and morally that it has always been vulnerable to pointed attack. Scientifically rather than intellectually the possibility or conviction of a correlation between physical stock and cultural potential has never died. It emerged with frightening force in Nazi Germany during the thirties. Now, albeit with less explicit political conviction – though the implications remain – the recent great advances in biological and ethno-logical science have brought the question to the forefront again. Is our being indelibly biologically programmed? If so, in what way?

Between the wars, stemming mainly from the work of Malinowski, Boas, Margaret Mead, and Ruth Benedict, the assumption among anthro-pologists that human beings were wholly and entirely children of their cultures grew into dogma. It was a dogma wholly consistent with liberal political aspirations: that all men were teachable, that education was the key to harmonious political relations, that if all were taught to be good there could be no evil. It was also a dogma in political opposition to what was happening in Germany. On both hands, however, the investigatory issues involved were sidestepped. What, if any, cultural proclivities are transmitted biologically? What, if any, effect does culture have on the transmission of genes? Are there any biological features that have tended to make particular cultures what they are rather than anything else? Students of culture, social and cultural anthropologists in particular, tend to dodge these questions. At the back of their minds is the dilemma be-tween science the arbiter and their own (not always explicit) political and moral ideals. Uneasily aware that science and scientists are prone to become the cooperators and victims of political and economic interests, so long as they themselves remain the beneficiaries of these circum-stances the question is conveniently shelved. In a politically liberal ambi-ence it is always necessary to be reminded that biological and ethological formulations *cannot* evade the moral issues. But what if the tables were turned? Suppose that – as in Nazi Germany – decisive political power came into the hands of those who based their policies on the discovery by some biological Galileo that cultural capacities and proclivities were determined by biological descent?

As in Galileo's time, a first reaction of many anthropologists and others might be to deny the truth on grounds of faith, and then marshal the intellectual arguments either to support their contention, or to deny the relevance of the truth. Alternatively, since one anthropological skill lies in showing how and in what ways peoples of other cultures suppress or head off unpleasant or inconvenient kinds of truth, it may become possible to apply this knowledge. But it is one thing to know *post hoc*, quite another to apply or recreate the circumstances at some future date. Nor have anthropologists shown themselves to be particularly adept at applying what knowledge they have. Yet what is so frightening about the truths which biological science may discover? Engaging the dialectic the question "Are they men?" is answered by the facts of articulate language and moral awareness. Superior or inferior men? The response cannot be other than "Inferior in some respects, superior in others. Let us learn their skills and insights and teach them our own." But at that scientific level which disengages the dialectic people tend to become specimens. This is what frightens. Specimens are things, things to be played with or tortured to find out what will happen.

All this may seem remote from the questions encountered in studying Australian Aborigines. It is not. If as scientists we ask "What is man?" we are bound to answer the whole question. Man has being at more than one level. He is, for example, spiritual, moral, and cultural as well as animal. He initiates as well as responds. If we accept the statement that Aboriginal culture "had become so stabilized that it could no longer suffer any fundamental change" (Birket-Smith, 1957/60, p. 51) and also accept the fact that Aborigines, only a few months away from a traditional life in the desert, have learned how to repair and cannibalize abandoned motor cars into serviceable vehicles, where does this put the cultural proclivities of biological descent, and what are we to say of population groups whose cultures do change? Is it possible that, like Voltaire's Huron, as Aborigines become familiar with our ways of life they will have as much potential in our environment as we ourselves?

3 RATIONAL DECEPTIONS

The gradual transformation through the eighteenth century of the chain of being, an explicitly imaginative and intellectual supposal, into evolutionism, a supposedly scientific theory, was more or less completed by the middle of the nineteenth century. Though many features of the chain of being dropped from sight, a main mode of argument within the construct survived. Since, as premise, there could be no gaps, no missing links, it was possible from a consideration of known appearances to postulate logically and intellectually—and even whimsically—a typological series. This, on the whole, was what was understood by the maxim of "no gaps": no gaps in the intellectual construct. Through the sixteenth and seventeenth centuries, however, as Europeans expanded overseas, reality began to imitate art. Intellectual categories began filling up with newly discovered people and things, and these, in turn, began to qualify and change the categories. Eventually, as new peoples, customs, usages, and things crowded onto the scene, the old intellectual categories became overburdened. They could not contain the growing volume of empirical reality, had to be refurbished. The process of doing so—rationalizing the chain of being—began in and continued through the eighteenth century. From postulating a logical or intellectual series, and then happening upon an empirical reality which fitted or qualified the category, students began positively to look for the reality which intellect and imagination had supposed might or ought to be there.

In the earlier years of the century this search was largely concerned with and confined to matching the discoveries of customs and beliefs in the opening new worlds with classical mythology and the usages and customs described by the ancients. Nor is it too bold an assertion to say that this building up of a body of comparative anthropology or mythology, naive though it was, laid the basis for that knowledge of classical mythology which, later in the century, was to become the mark of the educated person. Not simply a matter of knowing the literature of the Greeks and Romans, their customs, usages, and mythologies became relevant because of the living parallels that were being found. Though a sociologist might remark of this polite minuet—a movement from the present to what was old and past, then back to the present and to what was new—that it was an attempt in a time of technological change to transform the existential present into an integral part of the continuum from past into future or old into new, the activity of searching, or making a new discovery, seems to have become a value in itself. It was this passion for discovery which, combined with the growth of an enabling technology, led into science and evolutionary theory. It entailed a continuous, positive, and active interplay between intellect and imagination on the one hand, and—as interest in the classics began to wane before the onset of so much that was exciting and new—the empirical evidence and the techniques for dealing with it on the other. But, such was the ardor of the search, it could also entail on the parts of particular individuals certain blind spots in relation to the morality and motives of the procedures involved.

The discovery of the Piltdown skull is a good example. Since, intel-

lectually, it was possible to imagine or think of a type intermediate between man and the apes, it was appropriate not simply to wait for the
empirical instance to appear, but to go looking for it in likely places. For
more agile minds in a hurry, however, it became absolutely necessary to
find the evidence. Nevertheless, although the skull that was "found"
was presumed genuine — it was improper to question the probity and
integrity of a scientiest — it puzzled two or three generations of scientists.
As the empirical realization of a logical probability it was an offence to
the intellect. A juxtaposition of opposed features rather than the meld or
mediation between them that it should have been, the skull was too human
in one part, too ape-like in the other. The empirical discovery was an
intellectual absurdity. How could the problem be resolved without
invoking human weakness?

The ring held tight until 1955 (Weiner, 1955). We now know that the
skull was indeed a forgery, perpetrated to "prove" a theory as well as,
sadly, to achieve a certain fame and status within a highly prestigious
field of scientific investigation. Yet it is not difficult to imagine a situation
in which, given legitimate motives, data more ephemeral than a skull —
words, for example — may be so perceived and construed as to constitute
not so much a forgery as a falsification that, in all sincerity, integrity — or
simple naivete — is nonetheless a falsification. When, moving from the
tangible evidence of a skull, we take the same process of argument into
the arena of the social or cultural, the danger of mistakes is multiplied.

With this in mind, we may approach the question of paternity among
Australian Aborigines. Given an evolutionary framework, and the
presence of patrilineal and matrilineal forms of descent, it was possible
to say that, because the mother must be known, and the physiological
father not so certainly known, matriliny must have preceded patriliny. So
that matriliny was, therefore, an earlier, more primitive, or more ancient
form. Further, given that in patrilineal forms the principle of fatherhood
is acknowledged, and that in patrilineal societies there were and are rules
which attempt to ensure that physiological fatherhood should coincide
with social fatherhood, it would follow that in earlier matrilineal times
neither the principle nor the fact of fatherhood would be relevant.
From this it seemed to follow that there must have been a time when
marriage was unknown, when promiscuity reigned, when neither the
fact nor the principle of fatherhood were known let alone recognized.

Now, although today we know this line of reasoning to be false, not
only the mode of argument but its particulars continue into the present.
Whether or not in the dim reaches of prehistory matriliny prevailed

universally is impossible to show. Still, even though we now know that patriliny can change into matriliny, and that matrilineal forms are more closely correlated with constant warfare with outsiders, expansion over territory, capricious and uncertain rainfall, or economic circumstances requiring a mobile male population, the notion that matriliny might or should have preceded patriliny in the evolutionary scale is flattering to male egos, satisfying, and deeply ingrained in our present attitudes. Again, though a state of general and regular promiscuity has not been found, as the intellect moves along a posited scale of biocultural evolution the notion of promiscuity at some time in the past seems plausible and logical. As we have seen, to Dampier the empirical existence of promiscuity was already a possibility. Similarly, it would seem that there must have been a time, or stage, when paternity was neither acknowledged nor postulated. Thus, despite the widespread existence among Australian Aborigines of patrilineal forms and features, reports that they were ignorant of the male role in conception and procreation seemed to put the seal on Australians as a transitional species.

Before examining the Australian evidence it is as well to take a look at ourselves. We feel ourselves on pretty firm ground when we assert that before conception can take place the female ovum must be fertilized by male semen either through sexual union or by artificial insemination – or by any other process, purposeful or fortuitous, that results in male semen penetrating to, and fertilizing, the ovum. But these firm grounds begin to slip away when we ask why conception should take place at some times and not at others. Leaving aside barrenness, impotence, incompatibility and such – when conception does not occur – and confining ourselves to a situation where conception is possible, we have to explain a particular conception by some third factor: chance, statistical probability, virility, fecundity, beer and steak before sexual union, true love, uninhibited sexual union, favorable (but unknown) environmental circumstances in the womb – the choice of one or a combination of "third factors" is legion. Traditional Christianity provided a simple answer: Divine intervention. And there are still Christians today who are taught that the presumed biological father is not the "real" father but a foster father: the real father is God. Still, given that our general assumption and belief is that semen and ovum must come together, but that for conception to take place some third factor – a single feature or combination of features must be present, traditional Christianity yet admitted of a single exception: the Virgin Mary who, howsoever biologically fertilized, conceived by the Holy Spirit and gave birth.

Although some anthropologists have tended to confuse the Immaculate Conception and parthenogenesis, those who have argued the Australian case might have found themselves quite at home with the early fathers of the Church. On the one hand experience, intellect, and reason were recruited to make more palatable and acceptable to reason and experience a fact of revelation which contradicted ordinary experience. On the other hand experience, intellect, and reason have been recruited to explain why some Australians appeared to believe that semen was not necessary to conception. To state the issue more bluntly, if oversimply, while we generally hold that semen is ordinarily essential to a mix that requires some third factor for conception to occur, some Australian groups, apparently certain of the nature and potency of that third factor — a creative spirit or essence essential to the making of man as distinct from an animal — appeared to believe as an orthodoxy that semen was not necessary for conception. Given this, what was and is the anthropological problem?

For an evolutionist it was, on the whole, sufficient that the discovery had been made, that an empirical instance of a logical possibility had, apparently, been found. The dogma of fashionable scientific method rather than the skepticism of science was maintained. A diffusionist, on the other hand, had to decide, first, whether the "fact" was an instance of simple ignorance or rather one of social dogmatics. Then, since the ignorance or dogma was by no means common to all Australian groups, he would have to explain why neighbors had not enlightened the ignorant, or why some neighbors had accepted the dogma and others had rejected it. For the functionalist it was a question of showing how the particular instance of ignorance or dogma was consistent with other kinds of ignorance or dogmas. This procedure could lead into the argument — as distinct from the acceptance of an existential fact — that because it existed it was not only inevitable that it should exist, but that, given the other features, it was virtually impossible for it not to exist. For the structuralist the vital evidence is, and was, what is said in particular situations and contexts: the dogma in relation to the variety of modes of communicating experience. Something very like this position, for all the modernity of structuralism as an approach to ethnographic materials, was essentially that of Andrew Lang (1905) and Carveth Read (1918). What is being communicated when someone says what he does say? Given that a statement is a process of definition achieved by exclusion/inclusion, what, in an objective sense, is really being said when an Aborigine asserts that semen is not necessary to conception? A natural scientist, naive or ignorant of the kinds of problems found and tackled by anthropologists, might want to know what the *facts* were. This is the crux. In culture, where so much turns on the ambiguities of the word "believe," the "facts" usually turn out to be words, coded statements about the perception and meaning of experience.

The first general indication that Australians did not make a direct connection between coition and pregnancy occurred in 1899 with the publication of *The Native Tribes of Central Australia* by Spencer and Gillen. For convenience, however, we may take departure from W. E. Roth's report (Roth, 1903, p. 22) in 1903, of the Tully river people in Queensland: "Although sexual connection as a cause of conception is not recognized among the Tully River blacks so far as they themselves are concerned, it is admitted as true for all animals: — indeed this idea confirms them in their belief of superiority over the brute creation. A woman begets children because (a) she has been sitting over the fire on which she has roasted a particular species of black bream, which must have been given to her by the prospective father, (b) she has gone ahunting and caught a certain kind of bullfrog, (c) some men may have told her to be in an interesting condition, or (d) she may dream of having the child put inside her."

In an earlier manuscript (Roth, 1900), Roth was very much less emphatic. He wrote then (p. 53) that "Children are not necessarily due to copulation: indeed the cause is only *slightly* [my emphasis] recognized. On the other hand, a woman begets children because . . . etc., etc."

Further on, after saying that twins and triplets are a punishment inflicted on a woman by a mother-in-law for not getting firewood, he says: "It is only fair to state however that occasionally, twins will be accounted for by her having sexual connection with two different people." So that there was some kind of a sea-change as Roth reflected on his data and prepared it for final publication. However, going to the published source, aside from the fact that a woman does not "beget" children, and the ambiguity of (c), this is the kind of evidence which, much amplified and refined in later reports, and supported by Malinowski's material from the Trobriands, has led some anthropologists to assert — in spite of the fact that it is generally conceded that both Aborigines and Trobrianders always knew how animals mated and bred — that Aborigines "had no idea of the true relation between sexual intercourse and conception" (Kaberry, 1939, p. 312). Ashley-Montagu (1937) concluded that although Aborigines considered intercourse to have some connection with pregnancy, "in Australia practically universally according to orthodox belief, pregnancy is regarded as causally unconnected with intercourse" (p. 207). "Causally?" What a mound of ambiguity lies there!

When, further on (p. 307), Ashley-Montagu goes on to point out that "in Australia the concepts of 'motherhood' and 'fatherhood' are viewed as of an essentially non-biological, exclusively 'social' nature" he is saying nothing very special about Aboriginals — except, perhaps, for that word "exclusively." Which happens not to be the case. Much earlier in the general discussion, in a letter to his friend and mentor, R. R. Marett, Baldwin Spencer unwittingly demonstrated the point at issue. Having ranged himself on the side of those who considered Australians were ignorant of the connection between intercourse and pregnancy, he went on to say, "We, of course are well aware that of two women, one of whom is married, and the other is not, the former is the only one who can bear children . . ." (Marett and Penniman, 1932, p. 156).

If from Spencer's statement and our tales of gooseberry bushes, storks and the like it were to be concluded that we were ignorant of the "true relation between sexual intercourse and conception" *because* we related pregnancy to a legal contract or religious ceremony combined with the effects of the properties of certain animals or vegetables (compare Roth, *above*), we might delude ourselves into thinking the whole business rather silly. But this it is not. Given the distinction between subject and object, between what is experienced and what is simply observed or noted, medieval and Renaissance scholars were concerned that, consistent with divine revelation, words should reveal the truth of things. Through the nineteenth century and into the present, as we have become preoccupied with the things of scientific technology and discovery, words have tended to become much as things. Indeed, so many things have come into our cognizance during the last century and a half that our words — which articulate our thoughts about things, about our experience with things and each other — no longer do the jobs we want them to do. A "belief" is not a thing. It is a statement about things, about experiences, about the relations between experience and things. Devalued in relation to the immense variety of experiences begotten of many different social contexts, our words cannot have the precision they once did. Nevertheless, we begin to see sense when Meggitt (1962, pp. 272–273) says of the Walbiri that their explicit views on conception depend upon context. On ritual occasions men refer to the spirit entities known as *guruwari* as the significant factor. On other occasions they refer to both the *guruwari* and sexual intercourse. The women, who are not so involved in ritual, emphasize copulation. Older men regard copulation and *guruwari* as necessary. But since a child is thought to be formed from semen, and semen is closely associated with the *guruwari*, the latter are regarded as more important. Others maintain that the child is formed of intermingled blood and semen, vivified by the *guruwari*. For women, on the other hand, the action of the *guruwari* is secondary, and sexual intercourse is the significant preliminary to childbirth.

Roth's report, treated by many, including Spencer who had himself experienced and investigated the matter in central Australia, as "simply a fact" (Marett and Penniman, 1932, p. 156), has become a hydra. Which head is real or most significant for the purpose? Dixon, a linguist, after pointing out that Roth made his remarks on the Tully river people on the basis of at most a month's stay in the general area and without advantage of the language, has recently written, ". . . there is a verb *bulmbinya* 'to be the male progenitor of,' that has clear reference to the particular act of copulation that induced a conception" (Dixon, 1969). He goes on to draw a distinction between what he calls a "basic level of belief" and a "mystic level of belief," which last is "rather like, in Leach's words, a species of religious dogma; the truth which it expresses does not relate to the ordinary matter-of-fact world of everyday things, but to metaphysics." A far cry from the crudities of middle evolutionism, or Ashley-Montagu's (1937, p. 227) "adventitious rationalization calculated to explain the superiority of man over animals," Dixon's evidence shows the problem to be close kin to the "double-truth" of medieval theological philosophers. Man becomes a more rounded phenomenon, an articulate thinker as well as a biological and technological animal. The intellectual flat-earther is temporarily routed.

When Leach (1966, p. 46) poses the problem as one of *descent* [*sic*], the relationship between the "here-now" and the "other," he is echoing St. Paul on the meaning of the Incarnation, and of course a multitude of medieval scholars who sought, by a rational use of the intellect, to mediate between the lived experience of the "here-now" and two kinds of "otherness": the truths of revelation in relation to the experience of the many "here-nows" of past generations on the one hand, and the relationship as it might be developed by future generations on the other. Using the Jewish biosocial notion of descent (membership determined by mother, placement determined by genitor and/or pater) as a metaphor to indicate spiritual, moral, and intellectual continuity with the relevances of the events of the New Testament, St. Paul made it possible to speak of spiritual, moral, and intellectual heirs. Leach adumbrates and details the same principle with different material. He concludes his essay (*loc. cit.*)

with, "All I am saying is that social distance in time and space and generation is very frequently and very readily dovetailed in with a distinction between the living and the dead . . . The relationship between the here-now and the other can also be represented in other ways, for example as one of class status and power—the gods are perfect and powerful, men are imperfect and impotent; or as one of normality and abnormality—hence the supernatural births and immortality of divine beings."

Whatever one may think of Leach's conclusion—especially that "hence"—it is apparent that for him the question of paternity among Australian Aborigines is more significantly one concerned with the relations between social dogmatics, societal groups and categories, and the continuities and discontinuities of social experience. Spencer, a biologist, must have known that an unmarried woman could bear a child. But in his letter to Marett he could not prevent himself from reiterating a dogma of middle-class morality. Without such dogmas, where would or could a man stand? More generally, the issue Leach raises concerns the different kinds of questions that may be asked of the data. It is entirely legitimate to ask of other peoples whether they are ignorant of, or know about, the movements of particular heavenly bodies, the tracks of animals, or where water may be found. But it will not do to use the same criteria of "ignorance" and "knowledge" in relation to social dogmatics. If the question is not "What do they know?" but "How do they know and communicate what they think they know for what apparent purposes?" then we move to a quite different level of discourse. We become conscious of the fact that many of the truths which we take to be self-evident are matters of faith and dogma. Comparing dogma with dogma enables one to express a preference for one rather than the other. But having done that we have to ask how and why any people anywhere should adopt a particular dogma rather than another.

What is entailed, therefore, is not simply the commonsense observation that we, like Australians, can and do quite sincerely and with commitment make contradictory statements in different situations and contexts. Nor is it merely a question of attempting to find out what it is in particular situations that causes or enables us to respond in different ways or contradict ourselves. We might perhaps try to unravel the implications of the hypothesis that all human beings living in society find it necessary to know and feel themselves part of a continuum; and that, particularly in situations involving conception and birth—the creation of otherness in a new generation—some means must be found of bridging the gulfs between the present and past and future. The fact that such an interpretive statement might be posited on almost any series of features in social life—whether it be planting trees or the minuet referred to above (p. 102)—adds rather than detracts from its significance. It becomes a valid generalization or insight whose varieties may be explored. It is possible, too, to shift our ground a little and invert the problem. What is it we do when we use our capacity for making the selfsame statement refer to quite different series of experiences as occasion seems to demand? By juggling the words, by bringing different varieties of experience and image into relation with each other, we communicate in multiple codes of understanding. We begin, that is, to pose questions of communication and understanding in relation to experience. We reopen, within a much broader framework, a medieval problem.

"I am inclined to think," wrote Spencer (*idem*, p. 159) after arguing that the circumstances of traditional Australian life could hardly do otherwise than lead them into missing the connection between copulation and childbirth, "that the first savage, living under the social conditions of the Australians, who discovered the relationship between connexion and procreation, was an intelligent man." Thus obliquely have anthropologists and others always asked the peoples they studied to teach them what they themselves had forgotten. It is this reach into our own human roots, perhaps, that is responsible for our present ambivalent attitudes toward the meaning of "primitive." Spencer learned much, and left to future generations the benefit of his learning. Working as he did an ambience of buoyant confidence in the future, within an evolutionary framework combined with what was to become known as functionalism, he was led into setting the Aborigines apart as primitive and transitional on the one hand, and as somewhat like ourselves on the other. He worked out and confirmed the creative thought as well as the political biases of his time. For later generations the more difficult task refers not so much to the Aborigines themselves as to unraveling the data from its theoretical framework. If self-doubt has made Australians non- or preliterate rather than primitive, the process of learning and relearning ourselves through otherness goes on nonetheless. We too will make mistakes. As the philosophy of language, fed by the relatively new science of linguistics, has grown, developed and fired the imaginations of scholars in all fields, so anthropologists have begun to find in Australian life the kind of materials that will work out and confirm what is new and creative as well as mistaken within the general field of how we come to know and communicate and understand what we know. What has been largely ignored in the question of paternity in Australia is the significance of the fact that, before the arrival of Europeans with their animals, the Aborigines were almost unique in the animal world.

In an environment of marsupials, monotremes, insects, reptiles, and plants, man and his close companions, the dog and the rat, were virtually alone in the way they reproduced themselves. Even at the level of the animal, therefore, man was distinct and separate. Yet there have been few ethnographers who have not laid stress on the essential union and at oneness of Aborigines with the features of their environment. This was achieved, clearly, by the dogmas relating to creation. The ancestral and creative beings of the dreamtime created the world and all things in it, and at their own volition could have being, or manifest themselves as, the parts of their creation. Further, though creation occurred, it goes on occurring in a steady continuum. The creative stuff entered, as it now continues to enter, a womb and became a baby. This central dogma could and did, moreover, generate a series of confirmatory observances. For example, with an upright posture, forepaws used like hands, with head movements and ears so human, kangaroos are charmingly manlike. As has been pointed out, the females are subject to postpartum conception: to all outward appearances the dogma that semen was not always neces- sary to conception and birth would be confirmed. Indeed, it was once "widely believed by [European] laymen in Australia that the young kangaroo was born on the teat, presumably by a process of budding off" (Sharman and Pilton, 1964, p. 144). Further, male kangaroos (as well as emus) are equipped with bifid penises, a feature or property that becomes assimilated to man in the rite and operation of subincision.

In this and a variety of other and additional ways, Aboriginal rites rein- forced the dogma of an essential unity in the face of variety and difference. What to ourselves in some moods seems separate and distinct—and may indeed have appeared quite as separate and distinct in the secret ponder- ings of many an Aborigine—was so transformed that it could be per- ceived as a unity. In much the same way as the Piltdown skull was meant to bridge the gap between intellectual and empirical worlds—and Dixon bridges the gap between intellectual and scientific modes of dis- course with his "*species* of religious dogma"—Aborigines became an integral part of the world in which they lived. The existence of an incest prohibition should have warned us that the problem required more complex answers than "ignorance" could provide. The birth of a child was not the result of random copulation: it manifested and embodied the ordering and purposes of those who had created and continue to create all things. Nothing was thought of as existentially "so." All things and beings, including man with his distinctive moral awareness, were purposefully interconnected in the intricate designs of the ancestral beings of the dreamtime.

Let us now cast back to Roth and Ashley-Montagu. They interpreted Australian thought about paternity as *separating* them from animal life, as explaining the distinction between man and animal, as revealing the superiority of man over animal. They did not perceive the obverse, that man in Australia *was* different, that dogmas about paternity revealed the interconnectedness of things, made man a part of the whole. Nor did they perceive that the environment in which man thrives, acts, has being, exercises his animal, cultural, moral and spiritual faculties, is everywhere constructed of dogmas, of statements about himself and his being. They are the stuff by which man, morally aware, transforms existential being into a world of causalities and relevance, comes to know something of himself. This means that so long as the word, what is said, comprises a part of the evidence, intellectual perceptions of relevance have to precede techniques of scientific investigation. It also means that all man does is a "statement about" his being, that man and his environment are in a continuing state of recreation, that the product of this engagement — reality — is in continuing flux. One tends to forget that scientific techniques belong very firmly to our own perceptions of relevance, and that the essence of studying other cultures is that we are brought into contact with quite different perceptions of relevance and reality. Not until the relevances are fixed or approximated may the automaticisms of technique proceed and bear fruit.

4   SCIENCE, MORALITY, AND INTELLECTUAL PERCEPTION

Though, as one anthropologist has pointed out, "Too often we identify 'primitive man' with contemporary nonliterate peoples when the only legitimate use of the phrase 'primitive man' is when it is applied to prehistoric man" (Ashley-Montagu, 1968, p. 4), to whatever sector of Australian life the mind addresses itself, the word primitive begins to form. Despite censorship and suppression — some anthropologists prohibit the use of the word in their classes and seminars — the substantial meanings of primitive are there whatever the fashionable synonyms in favor. Whether it is painting or carving or sculpture, or religious life or cult, or myth or symbolism or language, or procuring food, or eating or cooking, or forms of social organization, or the ways in which the people approach and encounter one another, the contrast between what we do

and what Australians do — as distinct from the contrast between ourselves
and Australians — must evoke, first, the distinction, then a label to give
that distinction some placement. Do preliterate or nonliterate do the job?
Scarcely. Trouble begins only when attempts are made to give "primitive"
precise (but changing) scientific values. Primitive is a term of everyday
language. It is but a word which, as we have learned, shifts in its values as
we draw upon different experiences and contexts, as we make fleeting
comparisons, or come to anchor to discuss a defined and particular
question. Still, the use of "primitive" invites us to reflect on what kinds
of questions in what modes of discourse we can usefully ask and use in
relation to other cultures.

It is possible to use the vocabulary of scientific technology when describing an artifact — though few anthropologists have in fact managed to
do more than attempt to be precise with ordinary language. It is possible,
too, in the study of culture, to use a variety of techniques of analysis
made available by science, to be systematic, to cling close to skepticism.
But the difficulties of translating the concepts of one culture into those
of another are such that the kinds of precision associated with the natural
and physical sciences are rarely possible in social or cultural anthropology.
Hence the slow and nearly always implicit search for a sociological language or metalanguage capable of comprehending varieties of different
cultures within a single set of terms. Which, in a rather different idiom, is
precisely a search for that intellectual construct which will save all the
data more economically and elegantly. Even bereft of their technology
and technique, the natural and physical sciences are as demanding as the
puritan ethic which bore them. If the more spectacular advances have
required imagination, the latter would go for little were it not for the
thousands of less imaginative men and women who have applied themselves as hard and long at their multitudes of small but important problems as their forebears, long before Luther and Protestantism, labored
in their fields or counting houses, or wrestled with their letters and con-
sciences. No such scale of effort has been available for anthropology. Nor
is it necessarily appropriate that it should have been. The study of nonhuman or nonmoral phenomena tends to disengage the dialectic that is
necessary to the study of cultures and peoples.

In a sense, because nothing within the European cultural tradition
seems to occur without its counter, the more scientific techniques are
used for the study of nonmoral phenomena the more necessary it becomes to investigate other cultures without these techniques. If European
culture is to retain its authenticity and resilience, the engagement of the

participatory values through the study of other cultures becomes essential. Recent increases in mystical and other activities expressing the participatory values — as often as not derived from outside the European ambience — reveal that in the culture as a whole the dialectic is being engaged in a traditional way. But whether professional anthropologists, whose subject was born of this very engagement, will follow this lead, or tempt fate in a single-minded emphasis on science, remains to be seen.

During the eighteenth century the substance of what was to become anthropology, particularly social or cultural anthropology, contained a very wide spectrum of intellectual interests derived from a long tradition of scholarship and intellectual inquiry. Though a partial break in this tradition seems to have occurred with the European industrial and technological revolutions, it is precisely that industrial life, and the ways in which it contains our lives and thoughts, that on the one hand screen us from the past and on the other impel some to rediscover the tradition. During the nineteenth century and into the first half of this century, the range and variety of effective intellectual interests in anthropology narrowed considerably. There were always missionaries, like Bishop Codrington, who, having been educated in a traditional way in philosophy and theology, brought to the subject a wider and deeper intellectual understanding than those who in fact obtained control over the development of the subject. For though particular individuals could always continue their researches where and how they willed, recognition and status and acceptability in the subject within the wider world of learning tended to depend on which side of a dichotomy between scientific and intellectual inquiry one was ranged. In England and America, whether or not the work actually done justified the claim, it became almost obligatory to preface a piece of research with some remarks on the inductive and comparative methods joined to the ritual obeisance to scientific inquiry. Those who worked with their intellects rather than on their collections of "facts" were relegated to a limbo where their tiresome ideas could be rendered harmless to the then fashionable scientific dogmatics. In continental Europe, however, the simplicisms of what purported to be scientific inquiry never seriously rivaled intellectual inquiry: science and intellect went hand in hand. While it must surely be conceded that good research entails adequate evidence and an intellectual address that can appreciate the relevances of the evidence, the polarization between scientific inquiry on the one hand and intellectual problem and address on the other remains a difficulty hard to resolve.

In part, the difficulty stems from the sort of people who, in the nineteenth century, embraced anthropology. On the one hand there were the doctors, trained in biology, who were determined to bring to the study of culture the methods being developed by biological science. On the other hand were the lawyers, historians, classicists and others who, as often as not, prostituted their own professional techniques of inquiry by attempting to adopt those in which they were ill-tutored. Bemused by the naive and piecemeal comparative method of the time, and by the shibboleth of inductive reasoning, even Sherlock Holmes' success with the historian's method of deductive logic helped along by scientific technology passed them by. The great investigator was, after all, an amateur always poised to show up the professional. If the serious and scientific nature of the subject was to be protected against the exaggerations of the overimaginative, or the activities of intellectual pelicans, an approved and orthodox method was necessary. Then, too, partly as a result of the shift to scientific inquiry, the ethnographic material was perceived as a multitude of facts waiting to be collected before they disappeared for ever with the onset of civilization. In their hurry and anxiety they forgot or ignored what their forebears had done in the eighteenth century. For then, (as we shall see in more detail in Chapter 5), there had been attempts (for example, Père Lafitau, 1724) to describe other cultures as integrated wholes. Beliefs and dogmas, customs, usages, and features of social organization were seen as interdependent parts, as systems whose principles of interrelationship were to be teased out of the material. Studies such as Lafitau's, counterpointed by, for example, Pope's *Essay on Man* or Swift's *Gulliver's Travels*, represented the spirit of intellectual problem and endeavor. It seems to have been taken for granted that the basic stuff to be investigated or explained always comprised two quite different orders of evidence in indissoluble union: word and deed.

Nevertheless, Anglo-American anthropology adopted the model of an eighteenth-century pastime: the collection and display, first in private houses and later in museums, of curios, artifacts, insects, stuffed animals, bones, and plants. Such inventories of the world's stock of things were invaluable for, and well suited to, the construction of typological or evolutionary series. Nor have such collections been any the less valuable to the development of cultural studies in other frameworks. Yet it was on the whole unfortunate that the methods and cast of mind appropriate for arranging and relating things in a collection should have been carried into an enterprise requiring a quite different use of intellectual qualities. Features of social life such as marriage, exogamy, incest, descent, kinship, social organization, religion and so on — specific categories — became as so many "things," separable chunks of custom or usage or belief which could be arranged, rearranged, and compared with one another. This, indeed, was what passed for "comparative method." In such a context, necessarily technologically biased, Australian Aborigines could hardly appear as other than primitive. What passed for science or, more properly, scientific technique, became the master instead of the servant of intellectual perceptions and problems.

It is hardly surprising that the development of anthropology has been characterized by different kinds of confusion over science as a mode of thought, science as a set of techniques or a method intimately bound to the technological competence, and intellectual perceptions. Interplay and analogizing from one mode of discourse or understanding or perceptions of relations has been constant. Given the overriding aspiration to be scientific, different ways of organizing and finding relevance in the ethnographic material have gone along with different notions of what was thought to be characteristic, essential, and distinctive of science as a mode of investigation and/or explanation. Still, whether we now think of them as being scientific or not, whether we think of evolutionism or neo-evolutionism, marxism, diffusionism, functionalism or structuralism, there is no doubt that once a particular mode of organizing the data is adopted, be it psychological, sociological or biological, diachronic or synchronic or a way of trying to reconcile the diachrony with the synchrony, it stimulates research and opens up new avenues of understanding and explanation. Without these "theoretical frameworks" anthropology becomes something else. On the other hand, inspection seems to show that formulating a new theoretical framework which leads into different kinds of understanding arises not from the technique of a given orthodoxy but from hard application to the ethnography joined to a widening of contexts of relevance. Like all creative acts, new theory arises from the perception of relationship where none or a different one had hitherto been thought to exist. Scientific technique certainly aids the intellectual perception, but its main use lies in working out the implications of the perception.

Without some preexisting notion of how things are or might be it is difficult to conceive how one might react to the strange or unknown otherwise than by turning away or ignoring it. Indeed, it is said that when Captain Cook landed in Australia, the Aborigines who were there "saw" neither his ship nor his crew (Moorehead, 1966, p. 104). Their perceptions and modes of understanding were quite unable to accommodate the strange phenomenon. Suppose oneself, like Roth, encountered some quite strange usage, custom or belief—What would one do? Some might shrug their shoulders and stock it away for a philosophical anecdote over the port. Others might try to "explain" it. But to do so they would have to use some kind of framework of reference, some points of mutual understanding which would enable them to communicate either its strangeness or its intelligibility. Adumbrated and systematized, this is what theoretical frameworks are. New theory arises when old theory cannot accommodate the strange, the illogical, that which won't fit. The formulation of new theory, that is, depends on that intellectual grasp which, from a thorough researching of the material, can perceive widening contexts of relevance and new kinds of significance. Which is but to say that as the strange culture is absorbed into our own being, so we understand it better and widen our own horizons. As in the eighteenth century and before, and now with accelerating impetus, what was strange and "out there" in relation to the European heritage is being absorbed and becoming a part of ourselves. As the process continues Aborigines become less and less "other" and "primitive" and more and more like ourselves. Later generations tend to forget that those who commenced the dialectical engagement with otherness could not but view the total situation quite differently.

The partial break in tradition occasioned by the industrial revolution requires some emphasis. The eighteenth century was a culmination of medieval and Renaissance thought as well as the springboard of a technology capable of taking a man to the moon. In those days primitive or nonliterate peoples were both "noble" and "savage": a juxtaposition that, in the context of smoking mills in arcady, social upheavals and the accompanying output of satire, commentary and utopianism, accurately expressed the themes of paradise lost and the hope of a new paradise to be won. Having crossed the Rubicon of industrialization, however, the nineteenth century ushered in a quite new phase of imperial expansion. The "noble" dropped out. The dominant and myriad political tasks entailed in catering for the growing populations clustered round their machines required that the simpler peoples be not noble but savage, the primitive and wasteful occupiers of lands that could be more fruitfully husbanded and exploited by those who did not doubt for a moment—on doctrinal grounds, scientific or otherwise—that they, the ablest and fittest, should and would survive to inhabit the earth. The simpler peoples became both "other" and "enemy," the epitome of that which had been overcome, suppressed, or excised within ourselves.

The Hottentots disappeared, the Tasmanians were destroyed, the North American Indians were fought to a standstill and all but destroyed.

Australian Aborigines were harried and hunted or given temporary shelter in prisons. Science and its derivative as well as sustaining technology had all but flung loose from the participatory values. But the end of the First World War made Europeans pause. The expansionary drive had exhausted itself. Though the epithet "noble" did not return, many of the attitudes underlying such a compliment, freely given, did. Reacting from the disintegrative effects of the war, "integration," "interconnectedness," and "interrelatedness" were as much viable political aspirations as they were tools of sociological analysis. Australian Aborigines began to seem more like ourselves.

After the Second World War the participatory values received further impetus and wider acceptance, being incorporated into political and economic programs. The "dying race" began to multiply and merge into a new population. Work *with* as well as *on* Aborigines found a home and center in the Australian Institute of Aboriginal Studies. And as its activities reveal, Aboriginal prehistory, history, and ways of life have become worth knowing for their own sakes—for the ways in which they can expand everyone's knowledge of what is possible in human affairs—and not simply to prove or disprove a transitory theory of the nature of man and his origins (see, for example, Mulvaney, 1971b).

The eighteenth century was a period of intellectual doubt and skepticism mingled with strident certainties. In those days scholars really wanted to know about man's origins and nature. By the middle of the nineteenth century, however, professionalism, careerism and considerations of status had begun to make for a subtle but significant difference in outlook. The certainties of a given orthodoxy and obedience to what passed for scientific technique became, in anthropology, more important than intellectual perception. Scholars became less interested in finding out and more interested in promoting particular techniques and methods. Now, after a century and a half of scientific technique, and having vastly expanded the store of ethnographic knowledge, some anthropologists are beginning to question their intellectual premises. If professionalism and careerism are even more in evidence than they were in the nineteenth century, the old orthodoxies have more or less exhausted themselves, the new ones are too numerous to command more than a narrow consensus, the field has become more and more open to specialized and mechanical techniques. Nonetheless, there are those who seek the intellectual perceptions which might illuminate an atmosphere of doubt and skepticism. This of necessity breeds gimmicks. Still, instead of looking for instances or examples on which to pin labels—the classical procedure of museologists—are now asking, What is happening—in the organism, in the cultural environment? What is or might be being communicated, offered, rejected at which level in what context in relation to whom and what? What kinds of events and statements seem to "determine" or "explain" a particular situation in relation to whom?

As we begin to falter in our own certainties of being, identity, and purpose, so we seek to renew conviction by reaching again not only into the lives of others, but into that otherness which will explain them and ourselves to ourselves.

CHAPTER 4

Organization Man

1 FIXING THE PURPOSES

The nature, attributes, properties, and conditions of being of angels were, for medieval scholars, no idle concern. Messengers of God, angels were given by revelation as well as encountered, seen, and experienced. Sometimes appearing as aerial spherical bodies, sometimes assuming human shape, angels were not simply a theological convenience. They were frequently seen and encountered by all sorts and conditions of men and women. Today, though the idiom has changed to one of science fiction, much the same phenomenon, perhaps, has been experienced with the sighting of flying saucers or, to use scientific terminology, Unidentified Flying Objects. Nevertheless, given that angels existed, that humans frequently saw or experienced beings that might be angels, the orderly and mathematical medieval mind was forced into making them intelligible. Angels could be good or bad—Lucifer was a fallen angel—and they formed a hierarchy. The higher in the scale and nearer to God an angel was, the further from earth was his natural habitat. Not sexed, for they did not breed, angels were nevertheless referred to in the masculine gender. They formed a series between man and God, were spirit intelligences, had mass, could manifest themselves in corporeal form. Some argued that only those angels lower in the scale could take corporeal form; some felt that the lowest angels were corporeal if not quite in the same way as man; others thought otherwise. The series of links in the chain of being was their guide. But if spirit with mass, how much mass? How many angels could stand on the point of a needle? Since, mathematically, a point had no mass, but could only be determined by the intersection of two lines without mass, the point of a needle provided the limiting case: the smallest conceivable mass upon which another or several masses might be placed. The data was ordered, the problem posed. But alas! The solution eluded them. Were the premises wrong, the reasoning faulty, or must the solution hang on the discovery of more empirical evidence?

The wealth and complexity of the data on Aboriginal social organization tends to obscure the fact that thinking about it has much in common with medieval thought about angels. To make angels intelligible it was necessary to go, first, to the encounter: man's experience of angels. Second, relating this experience to other kinds of experience fixed what appeared to be the intrinsic properties of angels and also rationalized the encounter in the terms that ordered other kinds of experience. Third, the resultant was referred to that intellectual construct which, grounded in faith, revealed a rationally objective view: in this case the chain of being. A "fit" was obtained through an effective interplay between the three stages. Still, the process left the angelologists with an unsolved problem: how many could stand in what sort of space? On the other hand, this did not deter angelologists from continuing to investigate angels in the same terms that had yielded the impasse. By continuing to explore the "middle ground," by cooperating with the will of God, by an unshakeable faith in God, a solution would in time be found. Considering social organization, the unsolved problems are What is it for? Whence does it arise? Why *this* organization and not some other?

Defining man as an orderly creature, we find a certain orderliness – but we cannot do this without ascribing purpose. Order for what – eating, physical survival, reproduction, nurturing the young, the management of power, worship . . . ? For all of these, certainly. But if the notion of social organization is to have any precision there must be one assumed principal or primary purpose from which the others can be derived. An organization without purpose becomes its contrary: chaos. To find this principal or primary purpose we can, as a first approximation, either choose one that is explicit, but appropriate, or we can seek some underlying feature or principle which may be taken to subsume the variety of purposes overtly discernible – the requirements of the genetic code, the evolutionary purpose, environmental necessity, the divine purpose . . . . But on these matters anthropologists tend to reach the end of the line, groping uncertainly for guideposts. So they explore the middle ground, engaging in an interplay between the encounter, rationalizing the experience in terms that appear to order other kinds of experience, and referring the result to a variety of theoretical frameworks or interrelated assumptions about the nature of things.

Most of the exploration of this middle ground is a process of implicit or explicit comparisons. In earlier days often crude and naive, but growing more and more sophisticated and fruitful over the years, comparison is the social or cultural anthropologist's meat and drink. The object of doing so — if not merely for its own sake alone — is not only to discover the permutations of same or different principle underlying otherwise different and similar activities and vice versa, but to discover the principles upon which fruitful and valid comparisons may be made. In the eighteenth century, following the lead of Montesquieu and St. Simon, this process of making comparisons had the specific purpose of providing the bases on which a perfect society, wholly in accord with natural law, could be built. Derived from Plato's *Republic*, though anthropologists no longer explicitly adhere to this view, it is still very much alive in the way, implicitly if not explicitly, they often tend to idealize the peoples they study. Product of the utopianism inherent in anthropology, whether the people under investigation are idealized or otherwise the very process of doing fieldwork, ordering the data and writing a monograph yields the kinds of harmony sought by both Plato and St. Simon. Through a continuing process of making comparisons and searching for the logical fit, the futilities, contingencies, and regularities of social life, adventitiously preserved in experience, in memory, in notebooks, in recorded texts, become a more or less ordered and harmonious whole. Even if an author did not idealize the people he wrote about, the harmonies of his logic might lead a reader to suppose that he did. Problems relating to what kind of taxonomy to adopt, what level of abstraction from the concrete reality it is useful to think of the operation of particular combinations of principles, what rationally objective and explicit theoretical framework (or explicit criterion of comparison) to use, have all been more or less overcome. If, in spite of all this, it be held that, as comparative sociologists, anthropologists have not advanced very far, it is less from lack of imagination and application than from the inherent difficulties involved.

Up until the nineteenth century comparison, centered on religious belief, forms of worship, governmental institutions, and marriage, tended to be haphazard if always, implicitly, set against conditions at home. Though some authors — Thomas More, Swift, and Lafitau, for example — wrote of systems, of interlocking customs, institutions and ways of doing and saying things, on the whole the accounts of other forms of society, whether imagined or existing, permeated the intellectual world in a piecemeal way. With the adoption of evolutionary theory, however, a means was provided of combining relations in time and space within a general framework. But the notion of whole social orders composed of a variety of interrelated systems was either absent or held in abeyance. As we have seen, attention was centered on discrete institutional chunks, customs or usages thought of as things to be collected and arranged, as in a museum, within the covers of a book or journal. Though these chunks of custom were thought to correspond in a general way with European customs and institutions, the taxonomy—the adoption of terms such as exogamy, endogamy, magic, taboo, totemism, *mana*, animism, animatism and so on—tended to work against just this correspondence. The differences between "We" and "They" became emphasized.

The abandonment of nineteenth-century evolutionism in favor of a variety of interpretations of structure-functionalism ushered in a period of ordered confusion. For though there was common ground in the ideas of system, pattern and interrelatedness, and a general adherence as to the categories of system, pattern and interrelatedness, an inspection of different cultures showed that apparently similar institutions seemed to be geared to quite different systems and purposes. Thus, although witchcraft and sorcery in Africa appear, on the surface, to be quite different from, and not comparable with, witchcraft and sorcery in England or the United States, it could be held that underlying the different cultural expressions there was a similar set of relations: the kinds of relations typical of any relatively small and closed group of persons whose interactions were informed by political rivalry and economic competition for status. On the other hand, comparability begins to shift or disappear if we think of witchcraft and sorcery as defined by "a belief in supernatural agencies" or "a mode of accounting for accident" or a "means of combatting relative deprivation." Or again, despite doubts and contrary criticisms, totemism has been considered a primitive or early or embryonic mode of organizing religious life, or of coordinating religious and social life. But regard totemism as a form of cult within the larger religious framework, or as a mode of classifying within a unitary scheme the interrelations of individuals, groups, meterological phenomena, and natural species, then either "totemism" becomes meaningless, or we must accept changes in meaning with changes of definition derived from differences in comparative reference.

Such fluidities of meaning are and have been characteristic of social or cultural anthropology. Sustained fieldwork has gradually corroded the reality of an inherited taxonomy. Chunks of custom have been broken down into constituent sets of relations. Nevertheless, although it has always been appreciated that to describe and analyze the interrelatedness of social life there must be a corresponding interrelatedness in the ideas and concepts used to describe and analyze them, the old taxonomy, adapted to quite another outlook, has continued in use. Inevitably, meanings change, become confused as alternative explanatory or theoretical frameworks divide up the nineteenth-century chunks in different ways and compete for a consensus. On the other hand, as anthropology has become more professional, so anthropologists have been forced to familiarize themselves with the ethnographies of particular peoples, and have specialized in particular kinds of problem. This has given them a tool which their great-grandfathers lacked. For though anthropologists still spend much of their time debating the relative merits of particular theories or models at the expense of the ethnographic material available, resorting more and more to the things people actually do and say in a variety of contexts and places has begun to break the barriers of an outdated taxonomy. From this process, perhaps, a more useful taxonomy may be developed. Until then, however, anthropologists have to carry with them varieties of bases of comparison and interpretation.

Given these circumstances, social organization emerges as a patchwork of systems with overlapping fields of relevance. There is no single guiding point of reference. Just as angelology would always have been completely nonsensical without the notion of a Godhead, despite the encounters and experiences, so what is posited of social organization must find ground in some assumption of purpose, or in some more or less specific apprehensions as to why anything is what it is or appears to be. Moreover, since none of man's thinking and doing can be of any effect without organization, and this organization must in some way implement not only what he is thinking and doing but why things are done or thought at all, investigation and analysis must always involve an interactional quadrille between the assumptions of the investigator and investigated and the respective purposes posited on the parts of a particular organization. Thus if it be held that the primary theme of man's existence is his survival as a species rather than, say, a concern for the truth, or the development of his potential as man, or the survival of his particular culture, then perceptions of the forms of social organization will differ accordingly.

Existentially and in relation to the resources of the environment, Australians were organized much as other hunter-gatherer groups: family groups in a rhythm of dispersal and aggregation. Ontologically, however, the case is quite different. Aboriginals refer their activities and interactions to a variety of sets of rules and conventions — subsumed as marriage regulations, kinship, section, subsection, cult and ritual systems — which do not have their analogue anywhere. Why should they have such a complexity of rules? Australian Aborigines are quarrelsome and litigious — Is this because they have so many complex rules? Or do they have such rules in order to control their quarrelsomeness? Religion and ritual play such a large part in Aboriginal life that accounts of them often make it seem as though Aborigines were the puppets of their rules. Yet this they are not. Interleaved in the account of ritual activities is the evidence which shows that they are also the occasions for the flexibilities of political action. Further, just as an actor remembers his lines, the plot, and the thrust and nuances of his character in the context of the whole by containing them in the movements and gestures he has drilled himself into making on stage, so is Aboriginal ritual a "memory bank" of all that they consider worthwhile. If ritual can be said to have many purposes, which of them cannot be derived from the others?

If Aborigines happen to be fishing we can investigate the ways in which the activity is being carried out and report on an organization for fishing. Further experience, however, may reveal that the fishing was directed toward a ritual occasion in which prestige and status were at issue. If we now want to subsume the variety of activities in general terms we have to decide on the priorities. Is nourishing the body with food prior to nourishing the mind, soul, or emotions? Would there be any point to food if there were not, first, worship, status, prestige — and the ritual in which to preserve the relevance of food? In a protohistorical or evolutionary framework, food seems to come first. Yet since the food quest is organized, and foods are selected and treated in particular ways, the relevances of food are surely logically prior.

As with other topics and problems in anthropology, the question of social organization can never be static or simple. Different anthropologists ascribe differing priorities of importance and purpose. And each ascription competes in elegance and economy of effort with others. By choosing the middle ground it is possible to avoid for a while the implications of "purpose" and "beginning-and-end" points by the use of a variety of models of restricted scope which are also confined to selected universes of discourse. We may leave the ultimate questions until later. We can, as we have over the past century and a half, persevere in scientific technique rather than intellectual perception. Through these techniques great advances have been made. In suggesting that the use of scientific technique has been at the expense of intellectual effort, the appeal is not to the romantic and cosmic but to simple efficiency. For despite the rigor of science and technique social organization remains, according to one writer, "a plethora of highly diverse, contradictory, intractable, and often downright bad material . . . , Anyone who has attempted to impart to students some sense of a relatively self-contained and more or less consistent body of information on this subject is painfully aware of the fact that the eclecticism of social organization is exceeded only by its pretension to significance" (Tyler, 1969, p. 728).

If part of the problem arises from confusing separate universes of discourse, and leaping from preliminary questions to ultimate causes, these are precisely the passions which brought anthropology into being as a profession, which still recruit, hold, and sustain the student whether young or mature. Fieldwork and reflection bring detail and technique to the fore. Initial passions then reassert themselves. What had seemed to be problems of simple ethnographic information turn out to involve questions of fundamental importance in relation to the ways in which we do or should perceive ourselves, others, and the world about us. Particularly is this so when anthropologists fix their gaze on Australian Aborigines. More tortuously than the medieval angelologist — because there is so much more data for the mind to seize and tangle — intellectual perceptions, scientific techniques, and the participatory values weave their possibilities within a prison of competing premises.

2   CRITERIA OF COMPARISON

William Dampier's observation of Australians, "Whether they cohabit one Man to one Woman, or promiscuously, I know not . . ." indicates that he was thinking of promiscuity in relation only to marriage and the regulation of sexual access. But even if sexual promiscuity tends to imply general promiscuity, the word itself can also mean no explicit forms of order or social organization. Dampier's honestly expressed ignorance on the matter was generally shared by others who came in contact with, or who thought about Australian Aborigines until the second half of the nineteenth century. By then, however, it was almost too late. For those Australians who were accessible, traditional life had changed. Almost from the beginning, therefore, a process of working things out on the basis of *information about* social organization has been substituted for finding out by observation. Moreover, apart from escaped convicts, bushmen, and bushrangers who, if they might have lived with Aboriginal groups for longer or shorter periods, have not left us their memoirs, few Europeans could have survived the rigors of traditional nomadic life. Besides, until the demand for systematizing the ethnographic materials of anthropology began to make it necessary to professionalize the subject, such inquiries as were made into Australian life were broad and general and did not necessarily require a close study of what Australians actually did.

For Captain Cook, with a host of other things to do, it was more or less sufficient to describe Australian life in a general way, identify them as noble savages in a state of nature, and remark on their freedom from the cares and responsibilities of civilized life. There were those such as James Dawson, and later, Daisy Bates, who, while they collected odd customs and usages, were overridingly concerned with helping the Australians in their relations with settlers. There were others like Richard Sadleir or Elie Reclus who were concerned, in the case of the former, to show from the evidence of language that Australians had descended from a higher state of existence rather than risen from a lower, and, in the case of the latter, to encourage the study of Australians in order to reveal the original condition of mankind. (Bates, 1938; Dawson, 1881; Reclus, 1895; Sadleir, 1883.) But it was not until Fison, Howitt, Spencer and Gillen, Mathew, Roth, and Mathews put pen to paper that what had become, virtually, a collection of isolated customs and usages, could be seen as capable of being articulated into a more or less coherent whole.

That a total coherence remains an as yet unrealized ideal is beside the point. It is in the nature of things. Between the way in which people actually pursue their affairs, the native or "homemade" model of the way in which the people say they do or ought to go about their business, the attempts to construct a statistical or logically consistent version by means of which activities and statements about them might be the more economically understood by others, and the attempt to transform the verbal logic not simply into a mathematical notation but into the logic of mathematics, lies a host of pitfalls in the relevance of perceptions. The virtues and vices of different modes of interrelating the raw data depend on the congruence of the mode with the questions being asked and the kinds of answers required. As we have seen in the case of paternity, data providing the answer "ignorant" can be shown to be consistent, contradictory, and finally transformed into revealing something quite different. This may occur unwittingly with each of the many pieces of data which require to be interrelated when dealing with social organization. Still, with every attempt to order or rationalize the data several different kinds of general question are being asked at the same time: What do or did they do? What guides or guided them in their doing? How best may this doing and guiding be made intelligible? What concepts or languages do we use so as to make Australians comparable with others? What is there in it for us — intellectually, morally, politically, emotionally? Or, from what sorts of universal propositions or themes may we derive the features of Australian life, and how do these features qualify the propositions?

It is generally accepted that around 1788 when white settlement in Australia began, there were about 300,000 Australians distributed among between 400 and 700 tribes averaging between 500 and 600 persons each (R. M. and C. H. Berndt, 1964, p. 28). Yet it is difficult not to hesitate over what may be meant by a "tribe." In general, we derive the meaning of tribe by contrast and comparison with what we mean by nation-state. That is, a tribe is a group of people without a centrally organized government, judiciary, executive, police force, and army. More positively, we think of a tribe as a group of people who speak the same language or dialect; who regard a particular portion of land as their own even though rights of exploitation, economic or religious, may be subdivided among individuals or sections of the group; who think of themselves as forming a unity as against others; who give themselves a name to express this unity; amongst whom intermarriage is possible; who are as though kin, or who can address each other in terms of the kin idiom. Yet none of these criteria are necessarily exclusive. Others may speak the same language or dialect; religious and economic rights to land might be interdigitated with the rights of others whom we might think of as belonging to a different tribe; sections of different tribes may coalesce into a unity, temporarily or for longer periods; not all Australian so-called tribes have a name for themselves; marriage frequently crosses what we may think of as tribal boundaries, so that most of the members of a "tribe" will have kinsfolk in other "tribes." If we add to these criteria that whereby we distinguish feud (intratribal) from war (intertribal), or an inevitable resort to force (intertribal) as against a customary resort to other, more peaceful procedures (intratribal), we are in no better shape.

Nevertheless, not simply because we have the word "tribe" and want to use it, but because it is convenient to recognize and label a collection of people who have more in common among themselves than they have with others, tribe is adequate enough. It identifies, gives placement on a map. But it is still an imposition on the Australian situation. The coherence it might suggest has little correspondence with the realities of Australian life over the past fifty years or so, and whether or not there ever were groups of Australians *organized* into specific and particular tribes one or two centuries ago we do not know. Either we can use tribe as a simple convenience, roughly but not exclusively fulfilling the conditions rehearsed above, not think of the tribe at all, or resort to something like Unspecified Larger Groups: ULGs.

The resort to ULGs would have its advantages. For it would then be more obvious that a varied assortment of inclusive characteristics was not a specification. We would be forced to think not of size but of relations. To do this, however, it is necessary to build up a series of smaller sets which can be included in a hierarchy of sets. Far better known than the tribe, because more frequently experienced, seen and contacted by Europeans, is the group known as the "horde." Though horde is passing into desuetude (on account of its pejorative connotations) in favor of "local group," neither is adequate, and "band" or "mob" (a layman's colloquialism) might be more suitable. What is denoted is a group of persons usually composed of a core of patrikinsmen together with their wives and children and, perhaps, one or two families or unmarried men who were, preferably, not affines. Averaging from fifteen to thirty persons all told, though it might be as large as fifty, this was the group which habitually camped together, hunted, foraged, and traveled as a more or less coherent unit. The members had a common interest in exploiting the resources of a particular tract of land—which might very well be interdigitated with other tracts of land belonging to others—and for the core of patrikinsmen at least there were the common interests of conserving and maintaining resources by rituals, and of knowing the land and its features in relation to a stock of mythological lore. Keeping to the general pattern of nomadic life, rhythms of concentration and dispersal, some nights would see the whole group gathered together, most others would find them scattered in coupled family groups and the like. Much depended on the availability of food and water. From time to time some members of the group would camp with some members of another local group—to gather news, chat, hunt or forage together. At other times, as the seasons changed, two or more local groups would meet and camp together for ceremonial purposes, to perform particular rituals, to settle disputes, feast together, initiate, or make part-payments on a variety of transactional arrangements. Indeed, the notion of the tribe in Australia really arises from the fact that some local groups met and interacted with each other more frequently than each met and interacted with other groups. But since they would have to speak the same dialect or language to do so effectively, it is to this kind of collectivity that the designation "tribe" refers.

Though the membership of a horde or local group tended to fluctuate, it was the fundamental and basic unit of Australian life. It shaped the nursery environment and fostered the kind of interpersonal relationships that are possible only with a group of this size. It was, on the whole, an exogamous group whose members interacted together more frequently than they did with others. Membership was not enforced, and individuals or families that wanted to do so could wander off and live by themselves or join another group. Relationships would seem to have been affectionate, though it may be presumed there were some rivalries or hostilities or envies. Within this ambience the adults taught their children hunting and foraging lore, trained them in technological techniques, and communicated to them a knowledge, experience, and awareness of the country which, together with the myths that interrelated the features of the physical environment and so gave them relevance, formed the basic equipment necessary to face the world of the larger society. Yet if it is too strong to assert that no European has actually lived and traveled with such a group through an annual cycle, the record of his adventures is hard to find.

That we know anything at all about the local group is due to the fact that Europeans have encountered and interviewed the members of such groups either by the wayside, or in their camps, or when some have come into a government or mission or sheep station or some other convenient point of contact. With the advent of the motor vehicle, moreover, it has been possible to seek out Aboriginal camps, stay with them for a while, and accompany them on short hunting and foraging trips. So that although nothing can quite make good the lack of knowledge and insight which could have come from a sustained study through participatory observation, there is the evidence of some hundreds of accidental or prearranged encounters. Where, as must be the case, direct evidence is lacking, imagination, intellection, and a knowledge of hunting and gathering peoples elsewhere can go some way toward closing the gap. Nevertheless, since it is possible to obtain a great deal of information on kinship terminologies, marriage rules, moiety systems, section and totemic systems, life cycles, myths and rituals from sustained conversations and interviews, or by attending ceremonial occasions, anthropological attention has tended to concentrate on these more formal aspects of Australian life at the expense of those insights which might have been gained from a participation in the daily life of hunting, foraging, and making do. It is rather like unraveling the complexities of European life by being able to attend official banquets, the opening of a legislative assembly, church services, christenings, weddings, and funerals but being unable to see the daily round and family life of workmen, typists, businessmen, and others. Still, precisely these formal aspects provide the intellectual challenge. They yield homemade categories and explanations of activities which an investigator can transform into sets of relations that seem to him to have comparative value or be in some way more meaningful than the kinds of explanation received from respondents.

Given that it is possible to transform the rules and conventions by which a people order their interrelationships into a more or less economic statement or description of the way things are in relation to an explanatory framework, two questions remain. Does the transformation contain a hidden assumption retranslating the statement into a supposal based on particular purpose? Why are interrelationships ordered in such a way? Though the second does not necessarily bear on the first, in the history of anthropology it has almost invariably done so. If we say in answer to the second question that interrelationships are so arranged in order, by a careful selection of attitudes appropriate to particular relationships, to discriminate between each other; or alternatively, in order to exploit and allocate the resources of the environment in an appropriate way; or again, in order to make love and procreate; or again, to defend themselves and kill enemies; or any one of a dozen other ends and means to yet further ends, we simply create alternative supposals of purpose derived from those interrelated assumptions about the nature of social life which anthropologists are bound to build into their theoretical or explanatory frameworks. Yet the two main dimensions of Australian life — concentrated together for relatively short periods, and alone or with a companion in the vast stretches of the Australian environment — have no analogue in our own lives. Seeing, encountering, and experiencing Aborigines in their phases of togetherness inevitably brings them closer, invites us to think of their own explicit grounds of being as not so very distant from our own. But what of those long periods alone with scarce a word spoken — Does the mind stop functioning?

If we assume that whatever is garnered in the wild must somehow feed back into the ceremonial situation of togetherness, is the synthesis all that we need? We know that Australian forms of social organization are permeated by duality. Is this, as has been held (Lévi-Strauss, 1962b) the reflection of a characteristic of the human mind — for settled peoples without this marked dichotomy of being are also permeated by duality — or may it be, in the Australian case, more closely related to their two dimensions of life? If the latter, then, since in prehistory all men were hunter-gatherers, is this characteristic of the human mind something we have failed to outgrow through ages under quite different conditions of existence, or is it a characteristic that enabled our ancestors to be successful hunter-gatherers, cultivators, and townsfolk? Does a journey to the moon correspond with an Aborigine's quest for food when he too stretches his technology to the breaking point? Finally, what of this duality in relation to that triadic conversation which we have suggested is characteristic of European thought?

3 THE LOGICAL AND EMPIRICAL

Life may have been hard within the Australian local group, but it was simple. Man was the prey only of himself. Given wit and an inherited store of knowledge, the environment yielded its resources, nourishing the mind as well as the body. What might have been an eternal struggle between man and his environment was transformed by the ancestral beings of the dreamtime into a legacy of alliance and union. Drought and dearth could bring death, but since the ancestral beings intended creation for man, and death itself was but a new beginning, the Aborigine's realization of his lot was confidence, invention, and dignity in temporary failure. When faced with his fellow man, the Aborigine transformed what might have been a confrontation between the irresistible and the immovable into manageable relationships: one part of that definition of man which goes to moral awareness. Having rather more resonances than Captain Cook may have considered, the Australian local group was a natural group: a core of closely knit kinsfolk, genealogically linked; brothers whose wives bore children to whom they were all, equally, as father. Individuals and, perhaps, their families joined themselves to this core. As a collection of animal beings such a group could have maintained itself by mating among themselves—as baboons and other troop animals do. But the Australian local group was not composed of animals—ever: it was an exogamous group.

Once we admit explicit rules of exogamy, and so rules of incest and marriage, all of which are derived from moral awareness, we are forced to think of the local group as derived from or realizing a more general category of moral awareness. That is, however "natural" the local group might appear to be, its existence as a cooperative and exploitative unit must be derived from a more inclusive category. Thus, rather than enter a protohistorical or evolutionary framework and think of the local group as groping outward to find some means of regulating relationships between itself and other local groups, it seems more useful and logically consistent to think of it sociologically: as derived from the more inclusive categories. As soon as we do so we have to think of the local group as derived from, and realizing in particular circumstances the import of kinship system, marriage rules, section and subsection systems, totemic systems, rituals and mythology—categories which are not by any means coextensive with the "tribe." In this light we begin to perceive the significance of the local group as an interactional group. For though the categories mentioned connote a variety of kinds of groupings of persons engaged in particular activities and interactional relations, they realize themselves as concrete groups only intermittently if at all. The organizational *categories* rather than the *groups* that are organized describe the limits of Aboriginal awareness, and particular kinds of groupings are subservient to this awareness. In this light, too, the two dimensions of Aboriginal life appear as derived from the total awareness rather than from environmental conditions.

Australian man's uniqueness in, and so separation from, the natural environment as mammal, rational and morally aware goes along with the perception and articulate thought which, through the ancestral beings, created a legacy of alliance with the natural environment. Consistently, Australian forms of social organization reveal two primary and interrelated themes: first, the interdigital and crosscutting nature of classificatory schemes as they relate to humans, and as humans relate to features of the environment. No category which groups people together for particular purposes contains persons exclusively of that group and no other; and each category groups together those who, in other situations, will be differently grouped. Rivalry is balanced by cooperation, opposition by complementarity. There is no group of persons whose relations with the features of the natural environment are precisely the same, each category contains those whose particular relationships with, and responsibilities for, particular features of the environment are different. The second theme, concomitant with the first, is that modes of classification move toward the unique, identify the particular. If every single thing in experience were expressly unique, communication would require too large a vocabulary and too complicated a syntax to be possible. On the other hand, given a limited number of things to be classified, in this case persons, it is possible so to arrange matters that, in relation to a totality of classificatory schemes each individual becomes, and may be perceived as, unique. In short, a sufficient number of modes of classification on the one hand stimulates—even demands and demonstrates—

perceptions of a complete integration and union of the self with otherness, and on the other hand points to the individual as unique and separate from all else. At all levels of Aboriginal organization categories of sameness, aggregation and cooperation are accompanied by others which, in evoking situations of rivalry and opposition, revealed uniqueness in being.

If we consider a hypothetical linguistic "unit" comprising, say, some twelve or fourteen local groups, the language or dialect barrier would have enforced a rough social horizon. But only a rough one. While the members of some local groups would have interacted more often and more significantly with colinguals, other local groups within the linguistic unit would have interacted as often with the members of local groups from another linguistic "unit." Bilingualism was common, territories associated with local groups were not necessarily mutually exclusive blocks of land but reached out and interpenetrated each other. The land itself was, in a sense, free for all. The territory associated with a local group comprised a set of resources and religious responsibilities whose placements in space were interdigitated with those of other local groups. In traveling from one place to another members of local groups were bound to encounter one another. Yet even if we take a propensity to journey long distances outside and beyond the "tribal" borders—to attend particular rituals and ceremonies, to follow out the travels of an ancestral being, or to acquire valuable stuffs—into account, the number of persons with whom a man or woman interacted in a lifetime could hardly have exceeded one thousand, and averaged very much less than that—say, five hundred. Not, in European terms, a large interactional scope. Further, no Australian could interact with another in a peaceful and ordered way outside the categories of kinship, and, where strangers were involved, little significant interaction could take place until section or subsection membership and kin category had been established. Since, however, section membership was limited to four possibilities, subsection normally to sixteen, and the kin categories ranged from twelve to twenty-five or so, the permutations of possible basic behavior patterns was sharply reduced.

Yet "kin" categories may be misleading. Extending outside and beyond the local group, these categories, long assumed by investigators to be based upon real or putative consanguineal relations, could differentiate the generations, sexes, lineals, collaterals, and affines as well as other, more particularized relationships. But since these jobs could be, and were done by other systems of classification, what have been called the "kin" categories really seem to have distinguished and grouped together, on an interpersonal level, those from whom Ego had certain expectations, to whom he or she had particular obligations, or whom he or she had to avoid, or joke with. For though these "kin" categories could or might spell out a consanguineal genealogical tree, the fact that persons who were definitely not on such a tree had to be designated within the "kin" idiom shows that, whatever their origins, the "kin" categories were as much expectational as consanguineal or genealogical categories. Indeed, relative positions on a kinship chart could be changed irrespective of genealogical relationship. A "kin" relationship was a personal relationship, and the latter was an expectational relationship of a designated type, connoting particular kinds of mutual obligation. Since, too, marriage rules — and so by implication large segments of the rules relating to incest and exogamy — seem to have been determined by the "kin" categories rather than by section or subsection systems (but see *below* pp. 140–143), the "kin" idiom as a set of expectational categories connoting claims to property and mutual rights and obligations would seem to be logically prior to marriage rules and hence to genealogy. That is, marriage rules — as distinct from matings — and genealogy could be derived from the "kin"idiom.

From a protohistorical, evolutionary, extensionist, or genetic viewpoint, however, the opposite view must prevail. Man was first aware of his mother and designated her; then he was aware of close kin and designated them; then he moved out to choose a mate and designated her and the relationship he had with her — and so on. But how did he do this? Empirical reality seems to move from the center to the circumference, to demand that the smaller grow into the larger. Thought and logic move in the opposite direction. Was that frail creature who crossed the threshold to become man more aware of his thought, which demands that the smaller be derived from the larger, the less inclusive from the more inclusive, than he was of his puny animality, his physiological development? Or did the thought come with the act, encompassing and informing the latter?

While protohistorical, extensionist, or genetic assumptions have led into what may be mistaken perceptions as to the nature of the "kin" categories, they and the sociological view are at one in appreciating that membership of the local group neither exhausted the full range of genealogical relationships available nor realized the variety of expectations which society afforded. The design of social relations demanded a larger horizon than the local group, and the latter was but a part of a larger design. "Society" is a set or system of articulated categories, not necessarily congruent with a group of people. The fact that we can derive a "society" from an individual shows, paradoxically, that the latter is derived from the former.

At the level of the local group, for most of the time in an annual cycle, a person habitually interacted and cooperated with only about thirty others. An appreciation and recognition of individuality or personal identity were fostered by the close interpersonal relationships of day-to-day life. The land and its rocks and hillocks, its valleys and pools, animals, plants, birds, and insects revealed themselves to the eye and in myths in all their splendid variety. The gaze that searched the clear night sky struck with brilliants, and which could conceive of his ancestors as in those lights, might reach for the horizon in vain. Yet the effect on Australians of this seemingly boundless world in which they had being, has barely been studied. Like other hunters and gatherers, they ordered it, projecting from the organizational categories to make it an immense arena of relevance. Subsistence, traveling, camping arrangements, ritual, and ceremony raised each man to a position of command and service. By measuring space not in miles or days but in terms of the social categories which related him to his fellows, social and physical spaces became mnemonics of each other: the land came under control, giving to him what he asked of it through rituals and the ancestral beings who made it. Though the self was subordinated to group and category — to the extent of rarely using a personal name — and basic expectations in interpersonal relationships were determined by relative position in a system of comparatively few "kin" categories, particular relationships with the features of the physical environment added to the variety of modes of social classification served to define unique identities. These modes of social classification we may now consider in more detail.

The descent groups of shallow depth within the local group could extend into clans whose members were dispersed in different local groups. Generally exogamous, the Australian clan was not necessarily a descent group genealogically based, but a group whose common descent referred to an ancestral being of the dreamtime, or one or a group of ancestral beings whose common association with particular tracts of land was also enjoyed by those who regarded themselves as their descendants. While membership entailed a common stock of knowledge in the shape of myths, and cooperation in the performance of rituals, it did not necessarily include day-to-day economic cooperation for subsistence. Moiety systems might divide people into two or four ways, depending whether a patrilineal, or matrilineal, or both kinds of moiety were recognized. They formed opposed but complementary categories for ceremonial and ritual purposes, distinguished affines, and were yet another category of exogamy: membership was determined by descent. When local groups met and made camp together it was necessary so to order the spatial arrangement of family hearths and windbreaks that kin who had to avoid each other — most importantly the spouse and mother-in-law — need not encounter each other. This could be done effectively by arranging the camp in relation to patrilineal moieties. Section and subsection systems might separate and distinguish from four to sixteen classes or types of person, each class consisting of grouped categories of kin. They distinguished generation levels, spouses, affines, those in avoidance or restraint relationships and a series of other relationships such as circumcisor and circumcised. They also grouped together those whom an Ego might marry. But since this was an inclusive rather than an exclusive category, marriage partners were determined by the kinship categories themselves rather than by the section or subsection categories. Neighboring peoples could match their respective systems and, in spite of a different nomenclature in relation to the total system, it was possible to discover corresponding sections or subsections: a process which served as a first approximation when trying to determine the position of a stranger or visitor within the categories of the kin idiom. While this, together with the fact that in recent years members of different linguistic groups have been interacting more frequently, takes us some way toward understanding why it is that Australian peoples tend to adopt the more complex systems of neighbors rather than vice versa, it is certainly not the whole story. The various totemic systems could distinguish males from females, males among themselves and females among themselves, descent groups, children from one or other parent, one cult group from another, the concomitants of one life cycle from another. At the same time, through these totemic systems each individual was brought into a vital relationship with the features of his physical environment on the one hand, and the ancestral beings who created them on the other.

Though it would be unusual to find a local group divided within itself in *all* of the ways mentioned, few were not so divided in most or all of them. Still, the cooperative solidarity of the local group was hardly impaired. For the local group was a category for habitual food-gathering, hunting, traveling, and camping where the other systems of categories brought together and ordered the activities of the members of other local groups both within and outside the confines of the linguistic unit. Bounded only by the categories, society was finite only in the sense that the range of activities of an individual must be finite and had different ranges of finiteness in relation to particular individuals. Moreover, it is at least questionable whether an articulation of the variety of systems included in the total organizational design could designate the terms of a permanent and fixed set of interrelations. Each system connoted a formal cycle through the generations which, depending on the available population, relative fecundity, deaths from sickness or particular exigencies, and "wrong" marriages, need not always be "in phase" with other cycles. In such circumstances temporary or more permanent qualifications of the rules and conventions must seem always to have been an inherent possibility. But whether such changes were random, depended on outside events, or were implied in the systems themselves, they can certainly be subsumed in a more or less ordered political process. Yet so firmly ensconced is the assumption that Aborigines are and have been the slaves of their rules and systems, and so absorbing the intellectual challenge of working out the implications of the rules, the politics of the situation have gone more or less unsung.

It might be difficult to show conclusively that differences in interpersonal relationships within or outside the local group were rooted in the fact that, sociocentrically, the individual was or could be defined by a unique constellation of common categories. But, assuming it, between this sociocentric definition of the individual, the cyclic nature of the systems, and that appreciation of individuality which must have arisen from varieties of experience with others, there must have been a significant interplay. This interplay can point to no other than a political process whereby some sought to preserve or expand particular interests against those who competed. From this a small jump leads into the suggestion that if the several parts of a total social organization can appear to be designed for particular purposes such as, for example, the production and distribution of food and artifacts, or the determination of relative status, or the maintenance of order, or the pursuit of war, or whatever it might be, the totality may usefully be seen, at one level of analysis, as designed to define the individual. Identity, or the nature of particular being, springs out of the details of social organization and the truths which devolve from the exercise of political initiatives by some and their acceptance by others.

Where identity is in doubt the indications are that the social organization is awry; and where the social organization is awry the nature of particular being is in doubt. No one knows who or what they are, or what roles to perform. Increasing interactions with strangers who, hitherto, had been encountered only rarely or intermittently, certainly could produce this kind of alienation and engender a willingness on the part of Aborigines to adopt more complex categories of social organization rather than simplify. The question of choice where circumstances are relatively fluid and interests at issue is what the political process is all about. Yet, to reemphasize the point, the ontological and so political implications for the people acting out the intricacies of Aboriginal organization detail have attracted less attention than the logical implications of the systems themselves. Though it would be impossible to derive the rules implicit in what is happening without consulting Aborigines as to why it *is* happening, the question of how the explicit rules-systems should work has tended to become divorced from how the people make them work. Consequently, deriving rules from what happens tends to become lost in the purport of the explicit rationalizations. The complexities of these rules have attracted an attention which the Aborigines themselves have not. Few of those who have written about Aboriginal life have succeeded in communicating a convincing awareness of what it is like to live within the terms of such systems. Most usually we are offered either the complexities of disembodied rules or systems, or the vignette of care-free people bound only by nature's bounty, cheerful and generous. Perhaps the gap between they and us—leading such different lives—is too wide to bridge. On the other hand, it may be because between the being of Australians and the analysis and description of the systems which contain their being there is little correspondence of purposes,

As an example we may turn very briefly to what has become known as the "Murngin controversy." The issues as seen by Warner, whose publications started the controversy, are: the substantive nature of Murngin asymmetrical marriage; the subsection system and its significance for regulating marriage and descent; the way the kinship system and the subsection system are interrelated; the way the nuclear families of orientation and procreation relate to the kinship system and the social structure system; the nature of the unilineal local organization; the relation of the clans and other territorial groupings to the kinship system line of descent and the subsection system. (Warner, 1958, pp. xv–xvi.)

To consider each of these issues in detail would be more appropriate to a learned journal and need not detain us here. On the other hand, we may very shortly examine the kinds of assumptions adopted in order to reconcile the Murngin asymmetric rule of matrilateral cross-cousin marriage—although alternative marriages are possible—with a symmetrical subsection system. For whether marriage is primarily determined by kinship position, or subsection membership, or both in interaction, since marriage links both kinship and subsection systems one would expect some kind of logical fit or consistency between them. Indeed, other Australian peoples with subsection systems have symmetric marriage rules: matrilateral (Ego marries mother's brother's daughter or MBD) *and* patrilateral (Ego marries father's sister's daughter or FZD) marriage. One kind of symmetry is consistent with the other. Why do the Murngin have what appears to be an unworkable or unwieldy relationship between kinship and subsection systems, and how do they make it work?

The last is an empirical question and need not concern us. Perhaps they shift and make do. At the same time, we ought to note that an asymmetric rule of this kind is nicely suited to expansion, interaction with neighbors, and political activity generally. Commentaries on the Murngin rarely take these features into account. Instead, it is assumed that the Murngin are rigidly governed by their rules, and — in the face of comparative experience — that these rules must be sufficiently interconsistent to work harmoniously. Thus the problem of showing how the rules do or should work has become dependent on differing and competing assumptions about the nature and purpose of a social order, and the modes of analysis adequate to these assumptions. In the light of this, perhaps, we may be able to appreciate how slow and complex the process of anthropological investigation can be.

The people in question live in northeastern Arnhem Land. Warner, who first studied them intensively (Warner, 1937), called them Murngin but admitted that the name was not satisfactory. R. M. Berndt (1955), who studied them much later, reported that "murngin" was a clan name, and that the collective name for all the clans together, by which the people called themselves, was Wulamba. Whether the difference of name reflects a changing social order, the result of political activity, rather than an investigatory correction seems uncertain. Probably a bit of both. Still, the descendants of the people Warner studied are there, dispersed in local groups of the kind already described, each local group being bisected into generation levels and divided into at least three subsections by the subsection system. There are clans — people with a putative ancestor in common — each clan being distributed among the local groups as descent groups of shallow depth. There are systems of inheritance and succession whereby property, privileges, claims, and obligations are handed down the generations; and there is a set or system of terms, twenty-two in number, called the "kinship" categories. Assuming that a social organization continually recreates a particular kind of social order through time, what is the most satisfactory and elegant way of describing the articulation or interrelationships of the systems which make up the social organization?

Now though much of the controversy has been due simply to misunderstandings and a lack of consistency and uniformity in notating and interrelating the subsection categories (Barnes, 1967, pp. 9–26) and in handling the "kin" categories in relation to whether they are patri- or matri-determined (Maddock, 1970), the core of the controversy, the asymmetry, remains. Again, although with Maddock's article (*above*) the datum of MBD marriage disappears in favor of a marriage between Ego and the mother's mother's brother's daughter's daughter (MMBDD), and the Murngin (or Wulamba) are not now as exceptional as they had seemed to be, the asymmetry is still there, and so is the problem of what it is all for.

First, let us take the problem of assumptions in attempting to articulate subsections with kinship categories as they relate to marriage and inheritance. If the kinship categories are regarded as consanguineal terms, extensions virtually of the family environment of parents and children, then descent becomes basic to analysis, and marriages must be viewed as arrangements between clans or descent groups. The "submerged" or implicit lines of descent which may be contained in the subsection systems, matrilineal moieties for example, attain an importance in their own right although they are derived from or implied in the explicit categories (cf. Dumont, 1966). Further, what is explicit in other systems becomes residual to the primacy of descent. Thus, by tying the important inheritance relationship between Ego and his MMB— whose daughter's daughter is Ego's marriage partner—to an "oblique" line of descent (R. M. Berndt, 1955), a mode of transmitting tradition and an organization down the generations becomes an extension of the kind of transmission encountered within the family environment rather than something quite different, a mode of transmitting tradition that is, quite precisely, *outside* the family environment. Cultural transmission is surely broader than, and prior to, descent, which is merely one mode of transmission among others. But why should there be a subsection system to clarify what is already entailed in a supposed descent system?

Moving from descent to marriage, if the "kin" categories are regarded not as necessarily denoting consanguineals but as marking out suitable marriage partners and exchange relationships (which may include consanguineals in particular relationships), then descent becomes derivative and the subsection system becomes a further elaboration of reciprocal exchange obligations, avoidances, claims, and duties whilst still allowing clans and descent groups to act as corporate groups, participating in marriages and exchanges. On both views, however, the rule of asymmetric marriage requires either that the "kin" system as such extend beyond the linguistic group, be "open-ended," only tangentially articulated to the subsection system—and there is no reason why it should not be—or that it form a closed circle. This might include, on a descent basis, clans organized as wife-givers and wife-takers, each clan giving to one (or some) clan(s) and taking from others or one congruent and consistent with the subsection system. But here, unfortunately, the ethnographic evidence is confused or lacking and, as Barnes (1967, p. 9), remarks "Whatever the rules of the [marriage] system may be, only intensive research into recent marriage negotiations can elucidate the hierarchy of rules and preferences and the mechanisms for resolving conflicting claims."

According priority or primacy to descent, or marriage, referring these variously to cultural transmission, nurturing the young, or the management of social relations, contains an implicit notion as to what social organization is for: to maintain itself. A third view or set of assumptions about the nature of society, its organization, and how to describe it, takes departure from the subsection system. Adopting the position that "structure or complementarity is necessarily logically and historically prior to substance and individuality" (Dumont 1966, p. 238), this view deliberately eschews descent as a primary concept or building block, and, regarding the subsection system as the broadest delineation of society—to be a member of society, temporarily or permanently, placement in the subsection system has to be allocated—sees the subsection system as, specifically, an intermarriage system. Some ingenuity is required to contain the rather confused evidence on alternative marriages (see Barnes, 1967, pp. 22–24), but it can be done if "regular" and "alternate" marriage arrangements are allowed to alternate down the generations (Dumont, 1966). The kinship system becomes subsidiary, a denotation of particular persons within the categories of the subsection system.

Inasmuch as a subsection category contains persons additional to those whom an Ego may marry, the "kin" categories presumably distinguish relationships of complementarity other than or in addition to those implied in marriage. Good enough—if the model is a transformation of the ethnographic evidence. For although there is no need for the model simply to reflect the people's activities and thoughts, the process of converting the raw data into an abstract formulation of relations should not be vitiated by internal contradictions. But if the people themselves are as confused about their own rules as they appear to be (Barnes, 1967, p. 26), the model is unlikely to be tested for consistency against the ethnographic evidence. Indeed, the fact that there has been an "adjustment movement" (R. M. Berndt, 1962) in Arnhem land, in which the people over whom the "Murngin controversy" has raged have participated, indicates a social organization that is awry, and that the first symbolic statements in the search for a new identity — and so for a new kind of social organization that will contain or secrete that identity — have been made. In which case the ethnographic evidence that might have solved the controversy is probably no longer available.

Finally, a fourth view: that the "kin" categories are a mode of social classification which, in ordering sets of expectations or claims and obligations, not only provides a primary frame of reference for ordering the universe, but also, in so doing, may designate consanguines, and determines marriage partners in terms wider than those connoted by consanguineal relationship. Stemming from, let us say, Hocart (1936/70) who pointed out that by translating "kin" terms into European consanguineal categories the relevance of the terms was at once narrowed and wholly misconstrued, this viewpoint would take the "kin" categories as a wider frame of reference than the subsection categories. It follows that if marriage is in part determined by the subsection categories, the prior reference is to the "kin" categories — which order the universe as well as consanguineals. Since in fact relationships expressible in the "kin" categories extend outside the dialect group, the asymmetric rule of marriage is, at least in part, accounted for. Thinking of society not as a determinable chunk of people congruent with a series of systems arranged in a conceptual hierarchy, but as an abstraction connoting the activities and ideas inherent in sets or systems of interrelated categories (which may be arranged in a logical hierarchy) by which people order their lives and understand themselves, the subsection system appears as a mode of grouping the "kin" categories in particular combinations.

In this view the subsections remain a means of organizing a variety of relationships of complementarity, marriage being one of them. Indeed, it ties in with the fact that in indirect address people refer to one another by subsection names, and that a visitor or stranger is first identified by section or subsection category (his relationship of generalized complementarity) and only later, when more is known about him, by a kinship category. The last is both wider and more inclusive in that it orders the universe, and at the same time more specific in that it denotes a particular kind of complementarity. Still, such a view is one that has been long contested in anthropology. It turns on the competing values of a sociological truth against what appears to be a truth of protohistorical or evolutionary development.

There has been scant treatment here of the tortuous technicalities of the "Murngin controversy." It would have been beside the point to have done so. The controversy continues, the list of contributors grows larger and larger, most of the participants are agreed that it presents an intellectual challenge, and that it is this intellectual challenge which has moved them into making a contribution. Yet to quote Barnes (1967, p. 46) again, ". . . this challenge was met not by seeking for more empirical data to elucidate those matters on which Warner was obscure or silent. Instead, various writers put forward their own suggestions about the way the system worked. This was done in such a slap-dash fashion that confusion was increased rather than diminished. Concepts changed their meaning, inconsistent interpretations were put forward simultaneously, and far too often criticism was direct at showing where others had erred rather than determining where they might have been right." Even so, supposing that writers had not been "slap-dash," that Barnes had no ground for making his criticisms on their modes of execution, that each writer had been able to go to the field and check the data for himself — Would the problem have been solved?

The appeal for more or better empirical evidence brings us back to angelology. Perhaps, in relation to the premises, the empirical evidence was never there, or at least not available in a form in which its relevance could be appreciated.

In raising some of the more general issues of the controversy the primary concern has been the nature of the intellectual challenge rather than a solution to the problem. What has emerged from the short review is the way in which problems arise not so much from faults in a particular line of reasoning — though these of course have played their parts — as from the assumptions that are made about the nature and significance of the evidence. The smoke of argument has tended to conceal the fact that, in taking up the challenge posed by the existence of apparently inconsistent sets of rules and conventions, the peoples of Arnhem Land have been a battleground for competing assumptions about the nature, origins, and purposes of society. In such a context truths grounded in notions of linear time — protohistorical, evolutionary, developmental, genetic, or extensionist views — are pitted against the logic of the categories, sociological truths, which are independent of linear time. Yet both are dependent upon, and feed back into, varieties of ontological assumptions. Which returns us to the question of identity, what it is to be an Aborigine, have being in an Aboriginal culture.

In general, questions of identity (see C. H. Berndt, 1961) have not been of much explicit concern to anthropologists. The nature of both particular and collective being has, to a great extent, simply emerged from the "fit" or relationship between lives that are lived and the articulation of the framework of concepts used to contain and describe them. But because activities are purposeful, analytic concepts have to conform to them in some measure to contain them. The purposes which make the activities relevant also clothe the analysis with force and conviction. It is the business of an anthropologist to discover purposes, explicit and implicit, arrange them in a hierarchy of dependency, and achieve a fit. But in doing so he has to employ, if he can, categories which are not only appropriate to the circumstances being described, but which have a common currency of meaning in the subject. The hierarchy of purposes is the problem. For though with successive abstractions and transformations particular purposes become subsumed in generalized relations, these last depend upon how the hierarchy of purposes was organized. That is, upon initial assumptions. It follows from this that the as yet unrealized ambition of anthropologists to develop a sociological language—a system of categories from whose stock it would be possible to analyze or describe any form of society—must itself depend on the nature of these initial assumptions. Just as the superficial simplicities of Aboriginal life excited the imagination of those who sought man's, and so our own, origin, so its more lately discovered complexities have become a field in which different kinds of assumptions compete with one another in the development of a sociological language.

Further, because Australian communities are small, with a restricted range of interactions, and their forms of organization imply intricate cyclic rhythms, they provide the opportunity to attempt to translate or transform the language of experience, perception, intuition, and empirical observation—all imbued with implied or explicit purpose—into the *a priori* language of mathematics—in which relations are paramount, purpose irrelevant, and empirical content nil.

4 MATHEMATICS, OBJECTIVITY, AND SOCIOLOGICAL LANGUAGE

Movement into the language of mathematics is an intellectual act analogous to the normal anthropological task of participating in a strange culture, understanding it, translating into a European language the terms in which the people of that culture understand themselves, and then executing a transformation which brings that culture within the embrace of the rationally objective. But it is more difficult and hazardous. If translation distorts, and transformation yields intellectual clarity at the expense of a multifaceted empirical reality, at least the result seems relevant: ideally an ontological statement valid for both "They" and "We." Mathematics entails not only a transformation of the data, but a real transformation in our own habitual modes of intellection. Which makes for difficulties of communication between professionals and the public at large. Social and cultural anthropology, the novel, history, utopian writing, science fiction, and political ideology are aspects of one another. The reach into another world remains firmly tied to an idiom of understanding born of current social circumstances, dreams, and fantasies. Whether or not to cut the relationship with these other genres — if indeed it is possible — has been a continuing dilemma. If other cultures share in our reality, analyses of them are often acts of perception and controlled imagination which may disappear like dreams when the dreamer awakes. Only the memory of an experience remains.

Australian Aborigines exist, do things, organize themselves in a variety of ways to do these things. What anthropologists should make of the fact of Aboriginal existence — or any other people's existence — is and always has been a source of on-going debate intrinsic to that European reach for otherness which has always taken it for granted that *something*, aside from political manipulation, should be made or thought of other kinds of existence and being. Just as, now, we long to bring beings from outer space into our reality, so that we may share their reality, so have Europeans related to other cultures. Yet what should be done or thought when different realities are brought into relationship is not necessarily obvious. Other civilizations, our equals or superiors in intellection, have not considered the problem worth pursuing. Sporadic and simple description have sufficed: realities have been ethnocentrically fixed. Still, if within anthropology and the European ambience there has been general agreement about intellectual standards and what, at a particular point in time, constitute problems, most ethnographers have made their own choice and gone their own way. Bred in the bone, the common ancestry with other literary and philosophical genres reveals itself. No great events turn on the choice that is made. A successful response to otherness has sufficed. Whether or not such a response should continue to be adequate to a discipline composed of professionals is part of the debate. Practiced at making translations and transformations on a relatively simple cultural level, anthropologists are now being challenged to make that transformation of their own thought which, in the *a priori* terms of mathematics, will yield a mode of describing and thinking about any kind of culture anywhere. But to appreciate whether transcending the past in such a way would entail too great a price, some discussion of context is a necessary preliminary.

Behind genetic, protohistorical, and evolutionist theories about the nature of man and society or culture is the assumption contained in Dryden's line, ". . . mighty things from small beginnings grow." Building on the smaller to achieve the larger, working from what appears simple to what seems more complex, and from what seems to be chronologically prior to what seems to be later, this process always, if only implicitly, carries with it a notion of the nature of developmental processes. It is clearly a part of extensionist assumptions whether or not the analysis is purportedly diachronic or synchronic. Also implicit is the idea of man as essentially a "loner," a single individual forever compromising his true nature by stifling himself in community, but nonetheless doomed to entangle himself in progressively more and more highly organized communities. Hence his longing to break free of community ties and be alone with himself. Quite clear and open in the social contract theories of the eighteenth century, and an explicit axiom or even fetish in the building of North America, whence it has come down to us through de Tocqueville as "individualism," it has its ethnological projection in what may be called "gorilla" theory. For the gorilla, though it has some social life, is essentially a loner: Shane riding into the sunset, alone with his horse, after experiencing the corruption of community life; an appropriate myth for the great European and particularly American migrations and expansions of the eighteenth and nineteenth centuries. Man was casting off the restraints of corrupt communities to build new utopias in which he could realize himself as he actually was, a loner with minimum community needs.

The opposite view may be dubbed "baboon" theory. A primate like ourselves and the gorilla, the baboon is a troop and social animal. The first assumption to be made about baboons is not that two or three baboons gathered together and decided in the interests of survival, safety and an ordered life to form a troop, but that they always were to be found in troops. If ever there was a time when they were not to be found in troops, they were probably not baboons. In this view man appears as the child of circumstance, culture, and the social order, inevitably and thoroughly locked to his fellows, injuring himself and others in the attempt to be unique and divest himself of community responsibilities. John Donne's "No man is an island, entire of itself . . . Any man's death diminishes me, because I am involved in Mankind . . ." seems appropriate. Nevertheless, history and social experience show that because or in spite of his social or cultural conditioning, man, or men, feel called upon to assert themselves over or against their fellows. Either way, as well as objectively, individual and community are joined in dialectical engagement. The tension produced is fundamental to the European or Western tradition, a powerful impetus in its intellectual endeavors. The question of how far man's initiatives are a product only of the circumstances of community life is continually posed.

Within this dialectic the two kinds of approach we have mentioned differ widely in their appreciations of the nature, condition, and predicament of man. The first, gorilla theory, is clearly dominated by Genesis. First an environment and animals, then a man, then woman, then desire or sexual intercourse, then moral awareness, then marriage, then family, then the extension into kinship, then a band, then a larger and more explicitly political community — and so on to more complicated forms of community life as the population grew and exploitation of material resources became more specialized and complex. Assimilated to the great chain of being (though in a sense opposed to it since the harmonies predicated by the chain proceeded from that which encompassed all to those progressively smaller entities which contained less) these perceptions of growth from smaller to larger, or from the relatively undifferentiated to the more differentiated, were essential to evolutionism whether biological or social. It was in an intellectual atmosphere dominated by this approach that most of the concepts or analytic tools of anthropology were coined and developed in the nineteenth century. They carry its imprint, are loaded with the assumptions that produced them. As we have seen, the whole notion of "primitive," which might have been useful, descriptive and without any necessary pejorative connotations, became imbued with the concomitants of this kind of developmental approach. As we shall see (Chapter 5), though "totemism" begins as phenomenological, connoting a particular kind of relationship between persons and flora or fauna, it swiftly became thought of as an intermediate type or stage between a condition without religion and a condition with religion. So fixed, and becoming particularly attached to Australian life, little could be done with it.

Much the same may be said in varying degrees of those other terms which were used to describe and analyze that which we were not, but once were or might have been. Tylor's "survivals," drawn from the same stock of assumptions, provided confirmatory evidence. But, as we have seen, when diachronic approaches were abandoned in favor of synchronic studies the same terms were used. They entered the new perspective with their traditional loads of meaning, and much that was implicit in diachronic reasoning remained active in synchronic. The adroit use of passive forms, which indicated man's subservience to culture and society and obscured his initiatives (baboon), could not strip extensionist arguments of their developmental assumptions (gorilla). Despite more and more urgent claims that anthropology was a science — very necessary for the financial support that was needed if anthropologists were to do the work they envisaged as necessary before primitive or simple peoples disappeared from the earth — terms indigenous to a particular culture began to be used more and more often as organizing concepts. This was, of course, a part of the classic process of absorbing another culture, and it revealed anthropologists as concerned with understanding how others understood themselves, rather than with how the totality might be understood. But it meant that the more general stock of concepts had to be remembered as having different meanings in different cultures. Though this growing atomization of the subject and the increasing numbers of particularist monographs caused concern and alarm, each fresh recommendation as to what might be done merely increased the rate of atomization. An approach whose assumptions and concepts connoted sets of relations which could be used to describe any society anywhere was wholly lacking. Anthropologists still described particular forms of otherness, still employed genetic or extensionist modes of argument and assumptions, could not see their way to a sociological language.

The point being made does not turn on what concepts are appropriate to diachronic studies as opposed to synchronic. If the great chain of being seemed inappropriate, Marxism, sired by Hegel out of utopian romanticism, an authentic nineteenth-century product with an impeccable pedigree, had already shown that "baboon" and "gorilla" theories could be subsumed, transcended, or at least held in both hands. Roughly resolving the conceptual opposition between the diachrony on the one hand, and the synchrony on the other, history could be thought of in terms of sociological relations, which, turning on economic criteria of objectivity and causality, were contained in the competition and struggle for the command of material resources. Still, as a transcultural or sociological language marxism has rarely set well on the conditions of primitive or simple peoples. Its concepts and relations seemed too firmly attached to particular historical and cultural conditions. Gorilla theorists could not accept the maxim that "it is not the consciousness of men that determines their existence, but on the contrary, their social existence which determines their consciousness." If cultural determinists, or baboon theorists, could agree with the maxim, they tended to jib at the political implications for themselves and their science. Even though, through Mao, the Chinese perceived that the sets of relations posited by marxism could and did refer, in China, to groups and categories of people quite different from those they had connoted in Europe, until simple peoples began to form an integral part of the European environment marxism has only infrequently been invoked as an analytical framework.

Are Russian theorists to be blamed for their opposition to Chinese marxism? Is there not something weird and incongruous in a sociology which, setting aside both baboon and gorilla, can indicate that groups as unlike each other as European factory workers and Chinese peasants are, so far as sets of relations go, equivalent to each other? People, the concrete realities of life, disappear in a film of abstractions. Things that seem clearly different become the same. But just this is involved in a sociological language. An adze or a digging stick corresponds with a caterpillar tractored earthmover. The negotiations of a Tiwi elder attempting to obtain another wife may be contained in the horse trading of a congressman seeking votes. Aboriginal forms of social organization become particular combinations and permutations of at least some of the relations contained in the social organization of an industrialized state. Insights of this kind, pushing ourselves into otherness and incorporating otherness into ourselves, are the very stuff of anthropology. They are the basis for making raw data communicable, acceptable, rational, and of comparative value. Early European travelers and missionaries attempted to make their observations of primitive life intelligible by setting them against more familiar kinds of otherness: their own rural customs, or quarryings of the Bible or the classics. The Victorians found intelligibility by hanging their reports on the evolutionary tree. The structure-functionalists have provided kaleidoscopes: the colored particles form different patterns according to twist or methodological approach. Sociological language takes the primary relations as given, and asks us to fill the slots with data. In a sense, the cake has been eaten.

Despite Mao's example, so far as a true sociological language is concerned marxism has one defect in common with other sociological or anthropological theories which contain a romantic or utopian impulse: assumptions about man's basic purposes in being are written into the theory. While analyses in the light of such theory can reveal these purposes in all their detail, all that can truly be claimed is that the theory can show the empirical projections of what has already been premised or assumed. As scientific formulations, which must allow of falsification, such theories fail. A critique can only attempt to show that other kinds of purposes attributed either to man, or built into an alternative theory, are a more elegant and economic interpretation of the data. A sociological language, using words, is bound to have some assumptions of purpose written into it — this is the way human beings use words. But the beauty of mathematics is that it deals in relations which are in themselves quite independent of purpose. If sets of relations could be transformed into mathematic terms then, hypothetically, any society could be described and so analyzed by a particular arrangement of terms drawn from a common stock. Moreover, since mathematical formulations can yield all possible relations, and empirical reality is likely to cluster in but a few of these, the possibility arises of being able to say why *these* and not *those*. But making the transformation is not simply one of technique or adaptation. It entails a quite new way of thinking about social life, a leap quite as awesome as that entailed in an Australian Aboriginal becoming a financial wizard.

Mathematical notation may be an economy, and the use of mathematical symbols rather than words or sentences does little harm once the idiom is familiar. But by so doing one is no more thinking in mathematical terms, than, say, transliterating Roman characters into Cyrillic or Arabic characters may be said to be a translation into Russian or Arabic. Mathematical terms are what they are or stand for: the relations expressed are not dependent on the experience or perception of social situation. Words, on the other hand, have chameleon values and, depending on emphasis, position, and context, carry varying loads of meaning. Still a literary genre, anthropology requires a careful use of words if accuracy of communication is not to be sacrificed. Particularly is this so when variants of "to be, make, do" are used to describe the relations and equivalences of simple peoples. The difference between "I" and "I *am*," or between "I: rain" — in apparently quite simple juxtaposition — and "I rain, I am rain, I make rain" is the whole difference between participation and separation. Yet these verbs are the principal tools by which Europeans understand themselves and, consequently, have to try to understand others. Because mathematics is suited to handling relations in numerical form, it is deceptively easy to assume that by quantifying certain kinds of data it then becomes possible to think mathematically. This is a kind of translation, not a transformation. Further, as was pointed out by Professor Flower in 1889 when congratulating Sir Edward Tylor on a paper dealing with the application of a rigid statistical method in relation to kinship behavior, "the value of such a method depended entirely upon the units of comparison being of equivalent value, and this . . . seemed to be a very great difficulty when dealing with groups of mankind" (Flower, 1889, pp. 270–271). That is, statistical techniques are dependent on the prior qualitative appreciation and logical or structural analysis, carry their moral and political loads, and may lend a spurious weight of truth to the inevitable distortions of cross-cultural translation. Mathematical logic, on the other hand, is independent of purpose and moral value.

Despite the very real perils (in anthropology) of correlating synonyms, or what is derived with its original, quantification has led not only into the construction of a variety of valuable statistical correlations and models, but has enabled critics to see just how far the construction of social systems out of the bits and pieces of observed behavior and texts recorded in a notebook can depend on inadvertent or clever use of language rather than logic. Further, although so much of anthropology as distinct from the more widely known branches of general sociology is concerned with the knitting together of qualitative rather than quantitative data, the latter is an essential framework for the former. At a simple level, a habitually interacting group of thirty persons has a different framework of action from a group of some thousands. Qualitative and quantitative may be in some senses opposed categories. But to think of them as necessarily independent of each other is an intellectual solecism. Accepting that qualitative analyses are a logical priority if quantification is to be made relevant, the use of the two modes in parallel provides mutual modification in an essential dialectic. Again, in attempting to probe the histories of peoples without written records, the use of statistical methods in relation to linguistic data, the variations in what is essentially a single set of "kin" terms, for example, is necessary and central rather than auxiliary and useful. All, of course, depends on what kinds of questions are being asked, what kinds of answers are being sought, and what kinds of data are suited to what methods, questions, and answers. Still, though it is possible to claim, for example, that a study of love and affection, constituting an implicit or explicit comparison of differing modes of expressing these qualities, is entirely legitimate, it would be wholly unreal to contend, further, that these qualities were quite independent of, say, a quantitative framework of choices. One loves what there is to love.

If the choice seems to be, broadly, between scientific and humane modes of study, only an obstinate and dogmatic committal to one rather than the other can obscure the view that both may work together within the terms of a continuing dialectic. If we accept that a particular kind of elegance or aesthetic becomes the test of theories which, in dealing with purpose and purposes, have purposes and assumptions of purpose written into them, it is still possible to transform that elegance into mathematical language. But it should be remembered that mathematical thinking will organize not the empirical evidence but the ways in which it is conceptualized. Since there are competing conceptualizations, there will be competing mathematical formulations. It is at this point that the dialectic starts, that mathematical thinking will help us reject or qualify particular kinds of conceptualization.

Consider now what anthropology involves. An investigator observes some activities, or is told about activities he has not observed. We may, referring to the diagram below, call this A. In order to find out about the

activities the investigator consults those who are participating in them, or he consults bystanders who know something about them. They explain what is happening. This is R_1, rationalizations on the action or events by the indigenous people, rationalizations that may interconnect with one another into what has been called a "homemade" model. Meanwhile, however, the investigator has noted the events, perceived them to some extent, and has attempted to understand them in the only terms he has available: his own. This is represented by R_2, a point of view represented by most of the early travelers and, indeed, by most travelers and tourists today. As consultations proceed, however, as the "homemade" models and the investigator's models of how and why people behave thus interact and modify each other, the position R_3 is reached. Still at the notebook or diary and reflective stage, R_3 represents a rationalization and abstraction of the interaction between R_1 and R_2. The more acute and perceptive of early travelers and sojourners, including missionaries and administrative officers, have often written or given accounts from this point. Still, because it often happens that at R_1 the interlocutor makes statements about hypothetical events, or about events said to be historical, or about events that the investigator has not seen and may never see, R_3 may have a very precarious anchorage in events actually observed. Fragments of concrete reality have been knitted together and transformed into sentences, statements which, whether reflective or apparently simply descriptive, make up a set of rationalizations relating and connecting events and activities. This becomes the data. After further thought and reflection, and consultation with colleagues as to how best the material may be ordered and presented so that, without loss of accuracy in relation to what has actually been observed or perceived, it may be made communicable in terms of concepts acceptable to colleagues, a monograph, R_4, is written: a rerationalization of the whole of the preceding process in terms of certain sets of more or less interrelated assumptions called theory — the rationally objective explanatory or comparative framework.

In their allusions to classical mythology, usages, and accounts as well as in their references to the scriptures and their own native rural customs, travelers and sojourners over the last four centuries seem to have been groping for R_4 or a standpoint much like it. They were piecing together bits of ethnography — which later professionals have been able to conflate in more abstract terms — in a search for the criteria by or through which another culture might be comprehended. But actually to reach R_4 rather than grope for it there must be either a firm *a priori* model of social relations — such as evolutionary theory — or a variety of models built up through the cumulative experience and knowledge of ethnographic materials should be available. This last has only become possible over the last sixty years or so with the development of the tradition of intensive fieldwork. To reach R_5, representing a sociological language capable of describing and analyzing with the use of a single set of inclusive terms the sets of relations in any culture or society, a further process of abstraction and rerationalization is required. R_6 represents the full transformation into mathematical language: *a priori* relations capable of containing all possible kinds of empirical relations.

Though, as auxiliaries to a main argument, mathematical techniques of various kinds may be employed anywhere along the route from R_2 to R_5, R_5 and R_6 are in the nature of substitutes for each other, the one being more, or less, elegant and economic in presentation than the other in particular circumstances. R_6 could be derived from R_5 and vice versa, the more elegant — which need not be the mathematical formulation (see, for example, Korn and Needham, 1970, pp. 393–420) — being the more acceptable. However, R_6 cannot be derived directly from A: R_1 and R_2 must precede. Though at R_1 and R_2 the rationalizations may be sober and considered rather than merely impressionistic, objectivity in any meaningful sense is not achieved until R_4. The test of objectivity goes not so much to the mode of observation as to the inconsistencies in the logic of the patterns of relations that interrelate the observations. It is the intellectual, rationally objective framework that provides objectivity, not the observer.

If we wait until R_4 before moving to R_6, the bits and pieces of what was seen or might have been seen or said by someone at some time have already become welded into a model: an economic representation in terms of sets of relations of what the whole might look like if it were possible to retrieve more than a few fragments of what is actually there. The appearance of the model, the sets of relations it models, is determined by the fragments themselves only if the logic that holds them together and shapes the model is molded from the implications inherent in the fragments. Otherwise, as was so often the case in nineteenth-century anthropology, the fragments simply decorate the logic or theory, the latter becoming independent of observations. Thus, though it is by no means impossible to move into R_6 from R_4, R_3 is perhaps a more convenient point. For here the fragments are beginning to make sense, and that because they are being fitted into a hierarchy of purposes stemming from initial and basic assumptions about the nature of society, the systems which compose it, and their aetiology. If this "sense" is now transformed into mathematical language, the latter may at least help to qualify or falsify the conceptual scheme. One has only to glance through *Kinship and Social Organization* (Buchler and Selby, 1968, pp. 151–163, 279–309) to see what can be done, particularly in relation to Australian Aboriginal culture. But what would we be doing if we could and did think of all the sets of relations inherent in culture as being "just so," in a mathematical harmony?

The working assumptions of both Greek and medieval thinkers centered on the idea of a harmony in affairs that was subject to mathematical law and that could only, ultimately, be rendered intelligible through mathematics. Still, this notion of an ordered flux subject to a stasis of immutable law was difficult to locate and identify at the level of people's interactions with each other. Plato's alternative and authoritarian State as developed in his *Republic* was precisely the attempt to demonstrate how interactions might be ordered in accordance with mathematical harmonies. With more color than the *Republic*, the great chain of being was, similarly, a rationally objective and *a priori* mode of ordering the world in mathematical terms: a factorial progression wedded to criteria of inclusion and exclusion. But it was qualified by the participatory values inherent in the Gospels and revelation. The hundreds of utopias which have followed the *Republic* have, again, set out to show how an ordered harmony of social relationships is possible. Satirical or otherwise, most have been centered on a harmony derived from mathematical logic, *a priori* thinking, and the authority of an idea realized in necessarily authoritarian political institutions. Given that the religious bases of many of these utopias have had to admit the participatory values, and so flux in relation to a rationally objective authority, democratic forms which have been realized have not long been harmonious. The idea of harmony and the praxis of democracy are antithetical.

Correspondingly, the history of European political institutions may be seen as a continuing dialectic between authoritarian and democratic forms of government. Though a kind of synthesis was achieved by the medieval Church which, formally at least, employed democratic procedures of election in its bestowal of authority, internally the dialectic was continuously engaged. In the political field authoritarian and democratic forms have tended to alternate rather than synthesize. Europeans have suffered, but have not for long been able to abide the political projections of the kind of thinking demonstrated in the *Republic*. Paradoxically, in the *Republic*, a remarkable example of rational objectivity, Plato seems to have advocated a complete subservience to, rather than active engagement of, participation in oneness. Anthropologists are involved in variations of the same paradox. Aspirations to a harmonious intellectual or analytical framework (and so to the kind of society that would fit the framework) are at odds with the active participatory values (which make that kind of society impossible).

The differences between twentieth-century anthropology and much of what went before have stemmed largely from the tradition of sustained and intensive fieldwork. The idea of a harmony in social relationships emerges in the basic assumption of equilibrium, in attempting to demonstrate pattern and consistent interdependencies, in the present thrust toward mathematical language. The shift from collecting pieces of dubious ethnography in order to illustrate an *a priori* formulation into a procedure of participant observation devoted to a particular people or problem has yielded not simply immeasurably more fragments with which to construct a model of the society being studied, but much better ones. The monograph that is written at R_4, though always a kind of utopia, a nowhere, has come closer and closer to being something somewhere. Imagination and perceptions providing an experience anchored in space and time have allowed us to talk about, and to some extent even understand, particular peoples in various parts of the world. The process has been one of continually testing particular assumptions of purpose in men's lives against logical elegance and consistency within a context of growing familiarity with the way in which ethnographic fragments probably or at least possibly fit together.

This process is now under heavy fire. A surfeit of more and more accurate particulars has obscured uniformities and discouraged synthetic analyses. But it has not quite killed eighteenth- and nineteenth-century dreams of a science of morality and society. The pendulum is swinging back. The ways in which things *probably* fit together must inevitably become ways in which things *should* fit together. Just as medieval scholars succeeded in containing a jumble of othernesses into *a priori* thinking, only to see it crumble under the impact of the Renaissance and the discovery of new things; and as the rationalism of the eighteenth century, having, as it were digested the Renaissance, gave way to a new wave of fresh discoveries which, in turn, were reordered by nineteenth-century *a priori* evolutionary science; so this *a priori* reasoning has been followed by yet another vast accession of ethnographic materials. Neo-evolutionism, neo-marxism, and mathematical formulations indicate a phase of reorganization, a process of looking for another and appropriate *a priori* mode of containing the data.

Within the next generation the increasing specialization and professionalism within anthropology seems bound to lead into mathematical or other kinds of *a priori* terminology which, though communicating accurately to colleagues, may not say anything very much to the public at large: a familiar feature of any specialized profession. Still, the response to this vision of the future on the parts of newcomers to the subject cannot be said to be informed with enthusiasm. Those who want to become anthropologists are moved not by that reach for otherness connoted by the passage from literary skills and perceptions to *a priori* reasoning, but by that more earthy and even romantic desire to incorporate and render intelligible another cultural experience. The traditional impetus to anthropology, its missionary and moral outlook, is still the dominant force. The fact that relations in society are informed by political activities linked to material, spiritual, and moral resources of almost infinite variety is what stirs the imagination. Systems without people seem sterile. So long as Australian Aborigines retain a distinctive way of life, so long as whatever it is that Aborigines eventually become they retain something of otherness, anthropologists will continue to be interested in them. But professionalism will demand its price, and, if history is any guide, systems rather than people will take the day. As the available varieties of otherness are washed with uniformity and become, outwardly at least, merged into a monoculture, so perhaps the challenge presented by systems will become more attractive. On the other hand, there is little indication that the central dialectic is losing any of its force. Europe is not yet a uniformity, the participatory values continue to engage the formulations of rational objectivity. Even if Aborigines were to disappear off the face of the earth their classic, historic condition will remain an otherness with a myriad problems awaiting solution. Research into and teaching from texts will provide the basis for empirical studies in other environments; and as their biological competences improve, anthropologists will address themselves more and more to the biological bases of man's symbolling faculties. Otherness is not simply strange people but a mode of understanding more much better.

CHAPTER 5

Religious Man

1 PHENOMENON AND ONTOLOGY

There is no culture from whose activities and categories of understanding it is not possible to infer an instruction to break free of moral constraints and soar, like a hawk, beyond and above the laocoon coils of given social relations. Instruction and ability to comply form essential parts of what is meant by "the spirit of man." They define man's essential quality. Central to the religious experience but often elusive in the rotes and rituals of religious organization, the instruction exhorts individuals to adhere to the normal norms of the social order and, by so doing, to learn how to transcend them appropriately in order to achieve, albeit temporarily, what may be conveniently called "spiritual" being. Implicit in this process is the possibility of revivifying or renewing the moral order, or of realizing a new moral order. Didactically explicit in the great world religions, the tension and dialectic between morality and spirituality is nowhere more marked than in the Christian tradition: it is continuously expressed as a tension between the given moral order and a new moral order to be realized in a new social order. The impulse to Plato's *Republic* and the workings attributed to the Holy Spirit have always gone hand in hand. Everywhere man reaches heights in successfully realizing the instruction. Failure results either in ignominy or in a variety of nonconformist activities that to a greater or lesser extent qualify or contravene the received tradition of normative morality. In other cultures under tight control, within the European tradition the instruction is open: ignominies, nonconformities, excess, wrongdoing, and immoralities are consequently more numerous and have to be suffered.

159

The safest and most sensible course in any cultural context lies in adherence to the moral norms, particularly to the prescribed ways of expressing those norms. Virtue resides in conformity, in adhering to the laws and norms which provide the standard by means of which significant departures may be recognized. Every culture has its ways and means of controlling nonconformity within particular limits, and of preventing those nonconformities which, exceeding the limits, become wrongdoings. Still, there is no culture which does not allow that particular kinds of non-conformity may in fact turn out to be transcensions of value not only to the particular individuals concerned but to the community at large. The perilous flight from moral to spiritual, from partial understanding to fuller understanding, from obedience to mastery, from alienation to an at oneness of inner and outer conditions, may be informal, formal, or even institutionalized as, for example, in the case of the shaman. All initiation rituals afford an initiand some brief experience of this flight, some glimpse of the nature of the transformation and transition involved. In common with other religions, traditional Christianity has always taken pains to instruct and inform those who would positively and self-consciously aspire to the spiritual condition. But it has only rarely been successful in controlling those same aspirations when they have emerged — collectively or individually but continuously in history and so often spontaneously — from that which inheres in itself: the impulse to realize not spirituality only but a new moral order.

The different manifestations or expressions of this tension between adherence to a law or set of rules, and transcending them in virtue of them, is explicit all through the New Testament. Situationally contained in the historical facts of the Roman hegemony and thrust toward univer-salism on the one hand, and Jewish exclusivism and adherence to the Mosaic law on the other, the burden of Christ's teaching, followed by Paul, was precisely the paradox contained in affirming the law and at the same time equally positively asserting that it was for each and everyone to transcend the law in the minutiae of daily events. Rather than leave it to specially gifted, receptive, and capable men — such as the prophets — to renew and revivify the law from time to time, it was for everyone, through the Holy Spirit, continually to attempt to comprehend, transcend and so revivify the law through all the vicissitudes of day-to-day living in a complex of given social relations. It was an enormous, almost impossible demand to make of ordinary human beings who, in order to survive and maintain their identity, must organize themselves according to a con-sensus of rules or precepts and adhere to them. Just this demand was

made of the Jewish communities of the time. Just this historical circumstance has been repeated with every instance of the European encounter
with other cultures. The latter, faced with a tradition imbued with
missionary purpose, are asked to give up their law, their distinctive
identity and solidarity against all others, in favor of a universalism based
upon a mode, open to all, of continuously transcending, revivifying, and
changing the laws which describe that universalism.

At the level of action, responses have varied from that of the Jews who,
though they rejected the demand, have nevertheless participated and in
many instances taken the lead in the developing European ambience, to
complete absorption or complete rejection. European reactions have been
as varied as the responses. Behind these reactions has lain a dilemma
which, derived from the tension mentioned, has expressed itself politically as well as in more purely intellectual, imaginative or exploratory pur-
suits. We have already come across one example in the great debate at
Valladolid: the orthodox, Aristotelian, even scientific phenomenological and organization-man view pitted against a perspective that
includes, both in relation to own and other cultures, a vision of the spirit,
power or principles that lies beneath or behind the varieties of external
forms. In first making the distinction, then the transition between a phenomenology and ontology, Las Casas was doing nothing less than, as a
Christian, was incumbent on him. De Sepúlveda, hardly less Christian
in one sense, put greater weight on the phenomena or outward forms and
came to different conclusions. Between them Las Casas and De Sepúlveda
enacted a continuing problem of the Church: to what extent may an organization, inevitably corrupting but necessary for ordered thought and
social relations, suffer varieties of different kinds of transcendence without disintegrating? The same choice is inherent in anthropological
work. To what extent may a body of scholars, professionally organized in
associations, institutes, and universities, suffer varieties of attempts to
grasp the ontology lying behind the external phenomena and yet remain
an ordered, empirical discipline with a consensus of aims and methods?

Early travelers tended to be phenomenonological. They described the
appearance of the people, the modes of livelihood, weddings, funerals,
and the rituals of worship. Often, too, they remarked on forms of political
organization. Only rarely, and then shortly, did they allow themselves an
entry into the ontology with such adjectives as "happy" or "gay" or
"contented" or "miserable." Traveling, always on the move, they had
little opportunity for that close acquaintance necessary to the perception
of an ontology. Part of the charm of Marco Polo's record is that he

developed an experienced tourist's eye, a sensitivity to the local scene which invited him to understand as well as describe what he saw. Going further, for the missionary who has always had to live with his people and his mistakes relating to their ontology, an undue concentration on the outward forms at the expense of the inward spirit or principle could only be disastrous.

Unlike a traveler, an anthropologist must try to go beyond the phenomena. Nevertheless, whether missionary, traveler, explorer or anthropologist or administrative officer, the distinction between phenomena and ontology, and moving between them, is neither simple nor, always, necessarily desirable. Still, some confusion results when it is not apparent to a reader that the writer is aware of such a distinction and movement, or when, as often happens, the writer insists he is investigating phenomena oblivious of the fact that he has made the transition to ontology. The works of two French missionaries, Sagard and Lafitau, illustrate the point. Gabriel Sagard was a brother in the Recollects, a strict and ascetic order. His account of the Hurons (Sagard, 1632; English translation, 1939), based on little more than a year of residence with them, is deservedly a classic in anthropological literature. We might expect of Sagard, perhaps, a serenely charitable address coupled with a strict adherence to Christian dogmatics, particularly the precepts of his Order. This expectation is borne out in his narrative. A well-educated, courageous, but admirably simple man, Sagard goes to the phenomena. He describes the country, its fauna and flora, the occupations of the people, their modes of livelihood, their feasts, dances, songs and ceremonies, their appearance, government, funerals, birth and initiation rituals. Where his susceptibilities as a European, Frenchman, Christian, and missionary are offended, he is forthright but charitable, critical and also appreciative. If he was aware of the problem of making the transition from one set of categories to another, he does not show that he knows how to resolve it. He commences many a chapter with a classical allusion—to Plato, Pliny, Cicero, Julius Caesar and others. Yet these allusions are simple starting points rather than comparisons, texts to be adumbrated rather than cultural contexts to be subsumed. Thus (p. 121): "We read that Caesar praised the Germans highly for having in their ancient savage life such continence as to consider it a very vile thing for a young man to have the company of a woman or girl before he was twenty years old. It is the reverse with the boys and young men of Canada, and especially with those of the Huron country ..." Or (p. 167): "Cicero has said, in speaking of the nature of the gods, that there is no people so savage, so brutal, or so barbarous that has not some instinctive notion about them." Then he goes on to discuss Huron deities. But it is difficult to find in his account those vital connections between discrete activities that reveal a penetration into the ontology. He had little sociological sense. He observes with his eyes, and his heart is open and receptive. He is, in his way, *sympathique*. Yet his intellect and perceptions seem imprisoned in the devout and well-educated lay-brother from a French province. A strict formalist in his own culture, he was unable to bring to his observations of another culture the intellectual agility required for continuous analogizing, comparison, and the perceiving of correspondence in principle and relationship underlying what he saw.

Apart from its sustained observational detail, Sagard's account hardly differs in general tone from Herodotus and many another phenomenologist both before and since Sagard wrote. His abilities to transcend a given phenomenon were, it seems, confined to the phenomena of his own native culture. Still, the capacity to observe strange phenomena and then transcend them in order to perceive the ontology in terms of the phenomena is only partly a question of historical period, of gradually, through a cumulative experience, developing an awareness of the relations lying behind the raw material of observation. A century earlier Las Casas had been going beyond the outward forms and penetrating the ontology — though not systematically. Two centuries were to pass before professional anthropologists succeeded in emulating Lafitau's achievement in 1724. The wonder is not that it took so long but, despite the professional systematics of this century, that it has happened at all. To reach beyond the phenomena of another culture and enter into its ontology without losing hold of one's own ontology and rationally objective framework of understanding is not easy.

De la Crequinière seems to have seen the problem. "Keep an inquiring mind, but remain steadfast in your own religion," he advised the traveler. "Carry a Bible to make comparisons. Tolerate and try to understand strange customs. Behave well. Do not fall in love — it is distracting. Do not gamble — confidence tricksters abound. Study history, languages, and geography" (De la Crequinière, 1705). Thus pithily the substance of today's advice to the fieldworker embarking on his first project.

Of the thousands of historians, satirists, novelists, tractarians, and ethnographers within the European ambience who have made the attempt to penetrate another social order, imaginatively or otherwise, perhaps only a few score may be said to have entirely succeeded. Yet significance should be attached not to the few who have succeeded but to the multitudes who have tried. It is the attempt that is important, the attempt to realize in a series of different projections that part of the New Testament message which demands that men affirm their laws (and so their cultural differences) and at the same time transcend them. This is precisely what Lafitau tried to do, not necessarily in his personal life but in that projection of his total personality or being which contained his ethnographic endeavors.

Lafitau's *Moeurs des Sauvages Ameriquains, comparees aux moeurs des premier temps* (1724) is the first full-scale ethnographic monograph. He considers the history and origins of (mainly) the Huron and Iroquois peoples, their forms of government, economy, cult and religious practices, family and marriage, warfare, medicine, language – the full range of their culture: an invaluable document. But what is important for our purposes here is not so much what he accomplished but what he said he wanted to accomplish. He insists that he is engaged on a serious work of scholarship based on his own empirical observations over a period of five years, and informed by his own quite considerable scholarly abilities and achievement. He himself is not an untutored traveler, nor is he a scholar attempting to make sense of the random anecdotes of untutored travelers. He certainly has the advantage of other accounts (he continues), but whereas most of these deal with artifacts, dress, subsistence activities and so on (the phenomena of culture), he is embarking on the examination of beliefs (ontology) and the actions that derive from them. Many accounts of savage or primitive peoples (he goes on) contain little to show that they have any religion. This is playing into the hands of the atheists who claim that religion was the invention of man for the maintenance of peace and order. If one cares to examine the customs of primitive peoples we come to perceive that behind what most authors present as a collection of isolated activities and strange beliefs there is a system of symbols and religious categories. Moreover, as and because our own religious categories form a system, we can describe the primitive system in terms of our own. The same argument and approach, Lafitau goes on, apply to political, economic and domestic relations, modes of burial, warfare, medicinal practice and the rest. In particular, language is not a vocabulary merely. A word list of equivalents is of small value. It is the structure of the language that is important. Nor, claims Lafitau, is all this merely an idle intellectual exercise. Comparing systems can throw light on the usages of the ancients, such as the orgies of Bacchus, the feasts of Isis and Osiris, and pharaonic marriage; help us to discern historical origins (and so historical processes); and provide us with insights into the relevance and meaning of our own ways and prejudices.

Although in the deed Lafitau does not quite measure his purposes, all the way through his book there are passages in the kind of language that was not to become standard usage until after the first quarter of the twentieth century. But there are also passages which could be found in any eighteenth- or nineteenth-century ethnography. Writing as he did at the very beginning of the Enlightenment, perhaps it is to be expected that those who read him only appreciated those parts which happened to fit with the general outlook and spirit of the period. On the other hand, since he is not often quoted or referred to, it may be that he was simply lost in the bustle of social and political changes, in the chameleon criteria of scholarly and scientific endeavor and ambition. Besides, positivist (in which is included scientific) modes of thought and investigation became dominant, and in such an atmosphere Lafitau would have seemed too speculative. Yet the tension we are considering was and is a tension, not to be resolved unilaterally. For while the world of scholarship, research, and investigation generally adhered to positivist views, going to the phenomena and insisting upon order and orthodoxy — and this particularly in relation to those topics and problems which we now think of as coming within the ambits of sociology and anthropology — opponents, though they were disorganized and differed among themselves, were not wanting.

Starting (say) with the French Revolution, the world of action, of possibly realizable social and political relations, has been notable for its plethora of attempts at transcendence. Whether we think of the romantics, the authors of utopias, the founding of a myriad enthusiastic and other religious sects and movements, or the many attempts to create new and ideal communities both in Europe and European extensions overseas — all attempts on one projection or another to transcend a present set of rules or orthodoxy — it becomes clear that the tension, corresponding to that between rational objectivity and participation in Oneness, was never more dynamic. Nor was it necessarily a tension between one class of person and another. It was truly collective, inherent in everybody. Positivist in their publications and scholarly lives, scholars and scientists did not necessarily preserve this address in their personal lives. The portentous voicing of strict adherence to moral precepts did not always square with what was actually done. All through the nineteenth century and into the present many Christian missionaries, particularly those who were Protestant and evangelical — who, if we did not know them better, surely might have been expected to go to what lay beyond and behind — stressed not the affirmation of principle or belief which might be expressed in a variety of culturally defined ways, but emphasized those externals — such as clothing, attendance at services, sexual probity, abstention from feasting, alcohol and smoking, a sober demeanor—in virtue of which the inward grace and belief would presently flower.

For a missionary in the field this was a very real operational problem— How best to realize the process involved in that classic demand? Notwithstanding the atheist or agnostic leanings or convictions of many scholars of the period, the intellectual projection of the same tension involved a like problem. With the founding of anthropological societies in Britain, France, and the United States within the same decade, scholars interested in comparative religion based their inquiries not, as Lafitau had proposed, on the attempt to find out what kinds of activity devolved from particular beliefs, but on the intuitive and wholly subjective assertion of what a belief might be after the description of overt or manifest activities. That is, belief was derived from activity. "If I were to act like that it could only be because I believed *in* such-and-such, or because I believed *that* such-and-such was so . . ." Reacting from the view that, whatever else it might be in addition, religion was, or ideally contained— as Lafitau had implied—the explicans of man's being and activity, for rather more than a century religious activities have been more or less arbitrarily defined and then "explained" as derived from the exigencies of feeding and survival in particular social, cultural, and physical environments. The necessary basis became superfluous superstructure. "True" religion was tacitly defined as a kind of introspection in private or gathered together, punctuated perhaps by an exhortation or homily. Ritual activities were lumped under magic and superstition. In such an atmosphere it became possible for churchmen as well as others to declare, particularly and for example in the case of Australian Aborigines, that religion did not exist among them.

If, on a scholarly and intellectual level, Cicero and Sagard's allusion to him were almost entirely ignored, it was surely the political ambience that, dominating intellectual or scientific views, led accurate observers and good scholars into asserting that if, for example, Australians had religion it was certainly not in any sense "true" religion; or that, since Australians were the "most primitive" of people, it was not logical to suppose that they could have any religion. Listen to Sir James Frazer: ". . . among the aborigines of Australia, the rudest savages as to whom we possess accurate information, magic is universally practiced, whereas religion, in the sense of a propitiation or reconciliation of the higher powers, seems to be nearly unknown . . . nobody dreams of propitiating gods by prayer and sacrifice" (J. G. Frazer, 1960, p. 72).

There is no need to dally with Frazer's absurd "definition" of religion.

What is important is that dehumanizing the "other" by such *a priori* definitions belongs more closely to bigotry and political exigency than to scientific or intellectual endeavor. So does the inverse or reverse: that "They" are more human than "We," that the other religion is more vivifying, useful, desirable, and in some way contains those very secrets of human being which we have somehow lost. Yet such political attitudes are inevitable. If both views seem equally silly, the story of the study of Aboriginal religion is nonetheless a microcosm of the process whereby the inversion has been realized (see Stanner, 1967). From "no religion" to "totemism" – an intermediate, primitive or embryonic form of religion. From totemism simply to a variety of different and complex kinds of totemism. From this to religion, and from the latter to a rather superior kind of religion. Yet this should not obscure the fact that the historical process involved in the change of attitude represents the acting out over time of the dialectic between "We" and "They" implied in the process of absorption. Moreover, not only has the course of this dialectic been determined by the European address to otherness, but this very address has been determined by a series of further dialectics. In the present context, the philosophical or intellectual problem posed by the Greeks – How far is the substance contained in the form? – had its action projection in the historical situation represented by Jesus' and St. Paul's relations with Jewish orthodoxy: that the form and letter of the law are subject to constant reinterpretation according to their spirit.

The early Church, faced with the task of organization, of giving form to certain kinds of consciousness, absorbed the dilemma. How determine the validity of the inward and invisible grace, the awareness of truth, when it is expressed independently of a given outward and manifest form? Habitually making the transition between form and content, the law and its spirit, the thing and its principle, often with disastrous results, Europeans have sought to adumbrate these terms of their being in relation to other cultures. If it is difficult not to overemphasize the form, the law, and the thing at the expense of the content, the spirit, and the principle, it is the dialectic that is important, not the choice between alternatives. The deeper a fieldworker delves the more he becomes aware that each piece of evidence can generate successive bifurcations of the nature phenomenon/ontology. This circumstance tends to enforce analysis of total semantic fields rather than search for simplicist causal relations. Against the flat screen of cause and effect, Aboriginal ideas on conception could only be placed on a continuum between "ignorant" and "not ignorant," whether the continuum was regarded synchronically or skewed through time so as to become an evolutionary series. The same ideas understood as a statement about the continuities of their conditions of being open a vast new field. Similarly, viewed as statements about the relevances of the sum of man's varieties of conditions of being, the rituals of religious life cease to be the childish inanities which many have made of them. They become, instead, the keys to an ontology in which we may the more clearly see ourselves.

2   RELIGIOUS LIFE

Between the attitude that denied the Australian Aborigines any religious life, and that which accords to them a flourishing and fully developed religion, lies the ascription of "totemism." It is to totemism that we now turn. First, however, some preliminaries. R. R. Marett once quoted a French senator as saying "... either one believes in a religion, and then everything in it appears natural; or one does not believe in it, and then everything in it appears absurd" (Marett, 1925, p. 204). Clearly, if we adhere to a definition or view of religion or the religious life that makes Australians appear absurd, we have only ourselves to blame if we fail to understand them and what they do. By the same token, if we adhere to a definition of religion that makes successive investigators of Aboriginal religion look absurd, then we can only fail to appreciate why, for over a century, anthropologists have asked the sorts of questions they have. We need a view if not a definition of religion that can bring us into some kind of contact with Australian Aborigines, which does not do marked injustice to our own views on the religious life, and which at the same time enables us to evaluate the endeavors of those who have struggled to make sense of the data available.

Does totemism represent an early or embryonic prereligious complex in man's cultural ancestry? Is it, on the other hand, an intermediate stage between no religion and religion? Does totemism contain the possibility of development and transformation into the great world religions? If the lineaments of totemism are discernible in developed religions, does this mean that the latter are simply survivals from the past, or that totemism is another word for religion? Accepting that totemism is articulated to the social order, how far are totemism and the social order necessary to each other? Does Australian totemism represent a universal way of thinking about things and people, or is it peculiar to the Aborigines? Permute the terms how one wills, questions and answers depend on the existence of totemism as a definable and separate complex of beliefs and activities. The question now being asked is, Is it such a definable complex? To answer it we have to ask, What is religion?

For anthropological purposes, remembering the words of the French senator, religion can only be inadequately defined when ethnocentrically viewed in terms of what we might believe or want its content to be. We should, rather, choose those terms which enable us to discover what its form and content are in particular cases. As a start we may reverse the oft-reiterated statement made of nonliterate peoples — that religion pervades or underlies their way of life — and say that "that which underlies or pervades any people's lives, or anybody's life, is what we mean by religion." Where the springs of thought and action are, there we find religion welling. As guideposts let us first take a leaf from Emile Durkheim who, in his *Les Formes Élémentaires de la Vie Religieuse* (1912), reemphasized that religion was concerned with cohesion, with the maintenance of the rules that regulate community life and bind men and women together into a society. Then, as Godfrey Lienhardt has indicated, however misled one may think them to be religions are, after all, concerned with truth, with the discovery and systematization of particular kinds of assumptions regarding the nature of man and his environment, and with guaranteeing the truth of these assumptions. "Tribal religions," he writes, "involve on the one hand a sense of human ignorance and weakness and on the other a means of guaranteeing the assumptions upon which are based a people's only means of dealing with the disabilities which follow from human ignorance and weakness. If there were no guarantee, for example, that a diviner was permitted an insight into the true grounds of an illness, there would be no means of dealing with that illness . . . . What for primitive peoples is truth often seems to us to be a fallacy based upon ignorance. But it is a concern for truth, as they see it, which often prevents them from accepting assumptions upon which our notions of truth are based, just as it is a concern for truth which prevents us from accepting what we see as their errors" (Lienhardt, 1956, p. 327).

Thus, whether we derive the word religion from *religare*, to bind or hold back, or from *relegere*, to collect together and so to recollect, ponder, think intensely about, both etymologies in relation to what we have learned from Durkheim and Lienhardt evoke the wider essentials of any religion: a set of rules which regulate community life; a series of assumptions about the nature of man, his society and the environment from which the rules derive their force; that thought which, grounded in experience, reveals itself in action and addresses itself articulately to the rules and assumptions in order either to confirm or change them. Given a continual interaction between experience, rules and assumptions, those categories which are capable of comprehending the total interaction, and which are also capable of guaranteeing the validity or worthwhileness of the interaction, indicate what is meant by religion.

It should be noted that purpose (maintaining, guaranteeing, discovering the truth) is, and finally must always be, written into any view or definition of religion. What is not so obvious, though it is implicit in purpose, is that causation or aetiology must also be written into any notion of religion as a coherent system. The point at which assumptions, rules, thought, experience, purpose, and causation meet and offer a sociological relevance is in the idea and fact of power—the effectiveness that influences, changes, or moves. In dealing with religion we are dealing with the experience of power, with rules, assumptions and thoughts about the nature of power, with the identification of varieties of kinds of powers, with the manifestations and effects of particular powers, the exercise and control of power, the ends and purposes of power, and, more particularly, with the ordering of powers considered to be peculiarly creative, beneficial, destructive, or dangerous. Mostly implicit in the series of conjectures which spring from man's thought, contemplation, and experience, or which may be revealed to him in a vision, dream or trance or state of possession or ecstasy, the existence of these powers is made less inexplicit by series of symbols which, in classifying them, identifies and orders them. Rules order the relationships between men and the identified powers, make the relevances of the symbols more explicit, and legitimize (or stigmatize) the powers they refer to. The assumptions, which must be taken to be articles of faith grounded in experience, affirm and guarantee the validity or otherwise of particular conjectures, and so reveal and guarantee the truth of things. Though changes in experience, assumptions, and rules about power are not always easy to trace and identify, it is clear that in a nonliterate society the content of a religion will change as experience broadens, assumptions change, and new rules are brought into force. In a literate society, however, where experience, assumptions, and rules are summarized and synthesized in authoritative written form, there is usually some lag between changes in the former and changes in the latter.

At the level of the animal, man is prey to impulses which are rooted in his animal nature. At the level of the cultural, man is given to symbolizing, communicates articulately, makes things. Aware of his animal nature and his cultural capacities, man is also a moral being. He discriminates between right and wrong, and he subjects himself to obligation. This he does whether he is inherently a "loner" or a social being. Conscious of his own powers over himself, others, and the natural world about him, man is the more acutely sensible of his weaknesses and of the powers to which he himself is subordinate. These powers, many of which an observer might well think of as corresponding or coinciding with man's inner fears or impulses or desires, and which often tally with the identifications and relations of psychological idioms, are generally if not always represented as exterior and external to man himself, and may take the form of a loose hierarchy. Sometimes minor powers are seen as refractions of, or as deriving from, a greater power, and at other times they appear as independent movers. Always, however, while the minor powers tend to be more accurately identified, they are legitimized or explained by greater powers which are generally but by no means always rather more vaguely defined. If it be true—on a view wholly determined by participation in Oneness—that "an inner view of our own selves reveals the internal and external character of all things," then articulate awareness and communication of what is revealed depend upon externalization, upon containment in some visible shape or form or symbol. Rational objectivity further demands that what is externalized be systematized by reference to a given set of rules.

If we think of the powers normally and normatively exercised by man as cultural and moral powers, and the powers represented as in some way exterior to man or as not wholly within his control as divine powers, then the interrelations of divine and moral and cultural powers fill out the field of religion. The difficulty in comparative religion has always been that culturally determined modes of classifying and identifying particular powers, especially when those powers are identified in terms of classes of multivalent symbols, only sometimes correspond, usually overlap, and very rarely coincide. At this point anthropological taxonomy founders. The loose use of "ghost," "spirit," "sprite," "imp" and so on tends to mislead rather than inform; it becomes necessary to resort to vernacular terms together with exegeses as to their meanings. Still, it is only by going backward in this way that we may, eventually, be able to move forward. Indigenous words and symbols have to be broken down into the component relations they connote or denote and then reassembled into more meaningful constellations, constellations with a common denominator of transcultural relevance.

The easy way in which nineteenth- and early twentieth-century anthropologists used a single word to cover all sorts of quite different kinds of relations has left anthropology with a burden from which it is still trying to disencumber itself. Nowhere has this process been more evident that in relation to the religious life of Australian Aborigines. Nevertheless, as a start in this process of breaking down and rebuilding, we can say that while moral powers are limited and defined by obligation, by the rules and conventions of a social order, and are necessarily subject to the limitations of time and space, divine powers, if not wholly free from particular allocations and spheres of influence, are not subject to enforceable obligation, and are not necessarily limited by time and space. In principle, divine powers are self-willed free-movers. When man acts self-willedly, nonmorally, in defiance of obligation, he usurps the divine prerogative. On the other hand, there are occasions, typically but not always identified as states of trance or possession, ecstasy and the like, when man, far from usurping the divine, is assumed into and is at one with, the divine. This is man at the level of the spiritual: the experience of harmony between interior personal feeling with outer conditions, the reconciliation of animal, cultural, and moral being in the self with the total environment, physical and social.

Accepting these four levels of being in man, the most common and sensible manifestations of the exercise of divine powers are to be found in meterological phenomena, in storms, thunder, lightning, earthquake, flood, or volcanic eruption. These exterior powers frequently have their analogues in, and through man's symboling capacities are brought into an interplay with, man's animal and moral condition. Storm and anger, for example, fructifying rain and semen, thunder and the male experience of orgasm, or earthquake and sexual union. Deemed to be more than usually immanent during physiological changes or metamorphoses, in the processes of procreation, birth, death, puberty, and sickness, divine powers are also usually thought of as attending the widening of moral powers: betrothal, marriage, and parenthood, for example, or changes of status and the assumption of office. The exploitation of environmental resources such as animal and vegetable foods, water, and mineral deposits often evokes the presence of divine powers; so do certain manufacturing and trading activities whose outcome is not wholly dependent on the skills and foresight of man. Not subject to enforceable obligation, the divine powers are nevertheless ordered and identified by the human mind. This order finds expression in institutional life, in a variety of rituals, ceremonies, and initiation rites which, though they sometimes obscure, may also lead men into an understanding of the interrelations of divine and moral powers, and an appreciation of the relations between their different levels of being. Ultimately and ideally, one may suppose, an enlightened participation in such rituals and ceremonies would lead into at least a brief experience of those harmonies characteristic of spiritual being. More than ordinarily evident in the emergency upon which men's fates hang, divine powers are yet always immanent, ever present, free-moving powers that cause, create, move, attack, destroy, bless, or yield their bounty. They are intimately bound up with the assumptions which sanction the three primary rules round which moral powers focus: the incest taboo, which orders an otherwise perhaps uncontrollable impulse to sexual activity in the interests of regulated sexual access, ordered marriage, and established economic and political relations; the restriction on killing or injuring without due cause; the variety of restrictions on the user of different kinds of property.

The field of religion does not, however, consist in simply identifying and interrelating the variety of powers of which man is cognizant. Nor is it exhausted by listing the symbols, myths, and ritual activities by means of which man seeks to catch, contain, and even imprison the characteristics and interrelations of these very elusive powers. These are but the framework for a continuing dialectic between the moral and divine, and animal and moral, and the moral and the spiritual in which the cultural capacities of symboling and articulate thought play the major mediating role. Though the regularities of an ordered moral life are accommodated to such regularities as may be perceived and recognized in the divine, the capriciousness and whimsy of the latter may at any time set these regularities at nought. Resolving the opposition between the animal and instinctual or self-willed and free-moving elements in oneself on the one hand, and subjection to a complex of obligations on the other, is a continuous process in which the former is not always held by the latter.

Since the spiritual represents an at-oneness with the divine, the moral is opposed to it and must be reconciled or transcended if the spiritual is to be achieved. It is achieved, if only momentarily, in the realization that there is more to man's being than flesh, bone, blood, and brain. Nourished on music, painting, carving; on stargazing and random thoughts which come unbidden; on the sexual act which, in reality or imaginatively or in symbolic form, opens the gates of consciousness; on exercises which erase desire and thoughts of obligation; on the attempt to focus on what is eternal despite an overwhelming experience of the transitory; the achievement of spiritual being is something that belongs to man, and so, of course, to the Australian Aborigines. Yet it is not always evident in the earlier literature that Aborigines were accorded just these human capacities. Aboriginal institutional life is so very unlike our own that it has never been easy to see in them expressions of the same fears, feelings, yearnings, stirrings, and passion for order, beauty, and form that we ourselves experience directly or vicariously through those who have brought them to our attention.

In every culture that we know anything about, as Durkheim reminded us, religious activities make for social cohesion and solidarity. It is a theme that has been much labored. But the more subtle features have long gone unnoticed. The cohesion and solidarity refer not simply to the existential "here-now" but to that wider context of being in which the animal moves into the human and becomes aware of his being in relation to a past with which he can have no firsthand acquaintance, and in relation to a space of which he thinks he does have some acquaintance. In extending the limitations of the time and space of the "here-now," and by inhabiting these extensions with ancestors, ghosts, spirits, creative beings and the like, religious occasions present individual and community with those landmarks, those mappings, by means of which the human mind can move beyond the confines of its animal prison. That wider context exists, is no idle imagining. Then again, cohesion and solidarity are but one side of the coin. As Victor Turner (1969) among others has shown, religious occasions point up the divisions and oppositions within a society, and reveal what it is dangerous or wrong to do as well as what is proper and appropriate in the circumstances. So that Durkheim's over-simple cohesion and solidarity become transformed into more subtle endpoints to be attained only by those further perceptions and activities which enable members of community to transcend their differences and divisions. Following through, it becomes clearer that religion or the religious occasion presents the individual with the gathered contexts of his being: he is invited to reflect on, or simply look at, and then integrate, all those separate and often contradictory activities and experiences which meet in himself, which can meet in no other in quite the same way, and which therefore give him his own solidarity, cohesion or identity, which make him himself. In this sense religion brings together into a coherent whole and presents to individual and community the sum total of experiential time-spaces available to the culture. Yet it is no exaggeration to say that these kinds of considerations have entered but peripherally into work on Australian Aborigines.

Between the many differentiated possibilities offered by a moneyed and literate environment capable of ordering millions into a coherent whole, and that of the Australian Aborigines, there is the widest of gulfs. But it is not unbridgeable. Of the many features that prevent us crossing the divide perhaps the most important is an inability to perceive that much the same cluster of related social representations that is projected by the behavior and speech of one or two Aborigines is in our highly differentiated society projected by the interactions of many more. If we accept the field of religion not as a series of more or less arbitrarily and eclectically selected institutions, but as the identification and ordering of powers in the world—and include in this animal, cultural, moral, and spiritual powers—it becomes apparent that all institutions permute and combine some if not all of these powers in different ways for different purposes in different situations. Each term in the series, "conception—birth—sickness—death" involves changes in physiological state, changes in animal being which trigger the moral sense and, through the symboling faculties, bring spiritual qualities in view. In Aboriginal culture as well as among ourselves each of these occasions is invested with ritual activities which, in pointing to a particular relation of powers, reveal the pertinent grounds of being and awareness. The terms "child—puberty—betrothal—marriage—parent—grandparent—mortuary rites" indicate not simply a series of statuses but increases in awareness, the transition from one set of rights and obligations to another, the transcension of a limited moral field in order to enter another. The movements are accompanied or signaled by ceremonials and rituals. Rather than view these occasions as discrete institutional complexes, anthropologists are beginning to see them as particular configurations of a more general semantic field. But again, this is a departure pioneered outside the Australian field, mainly by Turner (*op. cit*), and the treatment of Aboriginal materials within this kind of framework is only just beginning. When it becomes more general we shall, perhaps, appreciate with deeper insight just what was involved in the successive initiations into varieties of cult groups and their hierarchies which, traditionally, Aborigines underwent as they grew older and advanced in wisdom and awareness. If sacrifice, the central institutional act of transformation in many other religious systems, seems until recently (see Stanner, 1966) to have been undeveloped in traditional Aboriginal life, this seems to have been more because anthropologists have concentrated on the institution as the unit of analysis rather than on the elements whose permutations and combinations form different institutions. Concerned as it is with power, religious life at the level of the collective must secrete the political process. But little has as yet been done to extricate this process from its ritual contexts.

The essence of the anthropological enterprise is the continuous movement of mind and imagination from the terms of one culture to the terms of another — not in order to make all similar but, through an appropriate analytic or explanatory framework, to seek out the crucial varieties, differences, and permutations and combinations of the kinds of awareness of which man is capable. This, the preparedness to reach into the unknown and expand the available fields of awareness, defines the authenticity of anthropology.

3 TOTEMISM

The central feature of Aboriginal religious life is and has been the mirage or fact of totemism. Are the relations between man and the fauna or flora or meteorological phenomena or minerals or events or artifacts in the Aboriginal cultural environment of such a sort and quality that we can and should pick them out as distinctive, or do they represent a universal in human experience and modes of thought? The compromise between these two extremes, that totemism is a useful general category which in Australia receives a peculiarly dense and elaborate expression, has been the position most usually adopted. It has been a convenient compromise. But it is, nonetheless, an inertial evasion of the issue, the preservation of the hollow form of a nineteenth-century inheritance. The cross-currents of European thought have always been reflected in approaches to ethnographic material. The problems posed by the latter have always been precisely those being posed in the European intellectual and political environment. Ethnographic materials are seized upon to work out the problems. When the European problem has been temporarily resolved, the ethnographic problem melts away — only to be resurrected in relation to new problems in the European ambience.

Behind the taxonomic and phenomenological preoccupations of nineteenth-century anthropologists lay a more general issue continually restated in a variety of ways by historians, political and economic theorists, sociologists, scientists, essayists, novelists, and satirists. At one pole was man the loner, self-aware and in command of himself, his affairs and his future. Given a scientific knowledge of society or culture and the processes of social change, an ordered developmental progress could be effected by deliberate acts of will. At the opposite pole was man the member of society. The tracks of his thought and consciousness were predetermined by the social ambience; he was the prisoner of ineluctable social and cultural processes. Even if these processes were to be scientifically formulated man would remain the child of circumstance. This was the underlying issue posed by totemism in Australia.

Given that totemism existed, what were the relations between the phenomenon and the ontology it indicated? Did similar kinds of procedural forms secrete similar kinds of substance? How far could the substance of an address to the external world be said to spring from an interior condition, and how far could this interior condition be altered or transformed by a change in the orthodox forms which had hitherto expressed and preserved the address? These issues were, and still are, central to theories of social change and the historical or developmental process. Since, however, the rules of the discourse required empirical demonstration, an assertion that a change of form did not necessarily entail a change in inward substance had to be accompanied by a persuasive demonstration of the processes involved. This posed difficulties. For it entailed a transition from scientific to political levels. Yet the central problem of the phenomenon and the ontology remains, and the debate continues in terms of shifting points of view and changes in the units to be analyzed. The very fact that, for example, R. M. and C. H. Berndt (1964, pp. 189–196) can list individual totemism, sex totemism, moiety totemism, section and subsection totemism, clan totemism, conception totemism, birth totemism, dream totemism, and multiple totemism should lead us to suppose that totems and their significations formed a system, parts of which were combined and permuted in different ways in different situations. Although Lafitau had provided the clue, it has taken years of hard work and study to follow it up. As always, facts are begotten and generated by ideas, and it takes fresh ideas to see new relevances in the facts.

The earliest mention of what, in the European literature, was to become known as totemism is, apparently, by Lescarbot in 1609 as *Aoutem* ("Son daemon appelle Aoutem . . .") from the Ojibway (Lescarbot, 1609, p. 683). Over a hundred and fifty years later, Alexander Henry, describing an Algonquin funeral and the gifts bestowed on the corpse, reported that, "To these are added his badge, called in the Algonquin tonge, a *totem* [*sic*], and which is in the nature of an armorial bearing" (Henry, 1921). But totemism did not become a "problem" until toward the end of the third quarter of the nineteenth century when, as part of the process of sorting out and ordering the accumulating mass of ethnographic material, J. F M'Lennan made it into one. He seized on a couple of pages in an account by Long (1791, pp. 86–87), an eighteenth-century trader and interpreter who had worked among the Ojibway of North America, changed Long's "totam" to Henry's "totem," and hypothesized a phenomenological cluster that constituted an evolutionary phase. "We have found," he wrote (M'Lennan, 1869–1870) "that there are tribes of men (called primitive) now existing on the earth in the Totem stage, each named after some animal or plant, which is its symbol or ensign, and which by the tribesmen is religiously regarded; having kinship through mothers only, and exogamy as their marriage law . . . the tribesmen believe themselves to be descended from the Totem, and in every case to be nominally at least, of its breed and species. We have seen a relation existing between the tribesmen and their Totem . . . that might well grow into that of worshipper and god, leading to the establishment of religious ceremonials to allay the Totem's just anger, or secure his continued protection . . . . We have also seen that while the intellectual condition of men that accompanies Totemism is well established for all the lower races of men now existing, there is much evidence that the higher races had anciently been in a similar condition . . ."

The game was on. Although, as Long himself had pointed out, his observation was similar to one he might have made in the English countryside, M'Lennan seems to have been taken by the strange word, totam, and erected it into a distinct socio-religious phenomenon: identification with, and worship of, flora and fauna combined with matriliny and exogamy. Then, placing the phenomenon in any evolutionary context, he presented it as the framework of a particular mode of thought whose specificity was to be inferred from the phenomenon, and hazarded the opinion that what seemed to be the more familiar form of religion had grown out of this complex. Though he was not absolutely explicit as to whether the "intellectual condition" accompanying totemism was detachable from its organizational matrix, his language suggests that he believed it not to be. Like Marx and others writing at this time, M'Lennan, a lawyer, seems to have been holding the line that it was the forms of social existence which determined men's consciousness rather than vice versa.

On the whole, Sir Edward Tylor took an opposite view. For him, holding to the psychic unity of mankind, all religion had started in dream life and had given rise to what he called "animism" — the imputation of soul or spirit or life-stuff in all existents. Though he had had "much conversation on the philosophy of totems" (Tylor, 1899, p. 138) with M'Lennan while the latter was writing his paper, nearly thirty years were to pass before he stated his doubts explicitly (*loc. cit.*, pp. 138–48). In the light of his own contribution, to which totemism as a mode of thought simply was easily assimilable, it is not hard to see why he should protest "against the manner in which totems have been placed almost at the foundation of religion . . . Totemism has been exaggerated out of all proportion to its

real theological magnitude" (*loc. cit.*, p. 144). He dismissed the organizational relevances in a couple of lines. Yet is was just this idea of a specific
organizational matrix imprisoning a particular mode of thought that has
kept the problem alive. This the more especially on account of the difficulties of disentangling (a) the phenomena of organization; (b) the principles
or sets of relations which, lying behind the phenomena, form a system;
and (c) an ontology which must in some way relate to those principles.

Like Tylor, Frazer took the position that evolution was a continuing
and inclusive process whose developing parts were not necessarily inter-
dependent. Just as the genetic developmental process in the womb
paralleled or corresponded with the general evolutionary process, so
modes of thought—which Frazer distinguished as magical, religious, and
scientific—might be found represented in any developed cultural ambience, though they also represented protohistorical or evolutionary stages
of development. Modes of thought, in short, were not dependent on forms
of social organization. It was, indeed, a particularly strong position to
hold in relation to totemism. For at the phenomenological level it gradually became apparent that totems were not confined to animals and plants
but included meterological phenomena such as the rainbow, thunder, and
lightning; might be an artifact, such as an axe or hatchet, or a human
condition or event such as vomiting; could in fact be almost anything—
particularly where Australian Aborigines were concerned. The correlation between a totem and an exogamous matrilineal group did not hold.
Totems were attached to moieties, phratries, and clans, whether patrilineal or matrilineal, as well as to single individuals. There were cult totems, sex totems, conception totems, dream totems, and local totems.
Food taboos in relation to a totem were anything but consistent. So that,
originating in observations of North American Indians, totems and totemism of various kinds began to be discovered and identified all over the
world in every type of culture or society including industrialized society.
"All definitions of totemism," wrote Piddington (1950–1958, p. 204), "are
either so specific as to exclude a number of systems which are commonly
referred to as 'totemic' or so general as to include many phenomena
which cannot properly be referred to by this term." Yet this was precisely the problem: What *was* the "proper" use of the term? Neither in
Australia nor elsewhere could the varied phenomena that seemed to go
along with the minimal definition of an ascribed relationship between
social groups and objects in nature, animate or inanimate, be reduced to
any cluster of constants.

The failure to discover positive correlations at the phenomenological level led, as inevitably it must, into a variety of hypotheses concerning origins, possible developmental processes, and the imaginary historical events which could be recruited to explain inconsistency, variety, and anomaly. In this vein the topic quickly became an arena for the rival theories of Frazer, Andrew Lang, Robertson-Smith, Herbert Spencer, A. C. Haddon and many others. Though by 1910 Goldenweiser was contesting the validity of totemism as a concept subsuming particular and discrete phenomena such as clan organization, exogamy, and a peculiarly intimate relationship between persons organized into groups and their totems, as time passed he became less sure. By 1934 (Goldenweiser, 1934) he was attaching totemism to "sib systems," accounting for variations in terms of the resultants of different historical processes, and finding its attenuated fragments in romantic or emotional attitudes toward animals. Like Tylor who, unhappy though he was with M'Lennan's paper, could not deny the phenomenon. Goldenweiser, in terms rather similar to Tylor's, seems to have felt, in the end, that the phenomenon had to be explained. He did so, like many another, by resorting to particular but unknown historical circumstances. Though Lévi-Strauss (1963, p. 5) has recently recruited to his own purposes Lowie's conclusion in 1935 that he (Lowie) was "not convinced that all the acumen and erudition lavished on the subject has established the reality of the totemic phenomenon," it was precisely the reality of the phenomenon that *had* been established. The problem was, and remains, how to transcend the phenomenon and incorporate it into an explanatory framework.

M'Lennan posed and perhaps confused several issues, each of which he assimilated to an evolutionary framework. For him totemism signified a form of social organization which housed and incubated particular kinds of awareness of otherness—the environment, other men, causative powers. From his language it may be understood that, as a child is parted from its mother after incubation in the womb, so the social organization and the awarenesses it incubated could, in the course of time, part company. As with Goldenweiser and others who followed his (M'Lennan's) example, where the minimal relationship was found in association with different forms of social organization it could be explained as a "vestige" or "survival" from a former evolutionary stage, or as an historical development or "adhesion." Allowing that in the present context the word "awareness" subsumes what M'Lennan called "intellect" and "worship," he was not wholly explicit about either. Still, from the sentence "... the intellectual condition of men that accompanies Totemism is well established for all the lower races of men now existing . . ." it is clear that he is referring to a consensus that he can take for granted: irrational, prescientific, magical, or even random or unordered modes of thought. On "worship," in which "intellect" is inevitably subsumed to a greater or lesser extent, M'Lennan is a little more explicit though he, like many nineteenth-century anthropologists, used the word very loosely and generally. At any rate, identity with particular ancestral totems goes together with separation from others. In more modern terminology, totems were logico-symbolic categories providing the framework within which the self could distinguish itself and relate to otherness, whether this last was projected into nature, the field of social relations, or the cosmos at large. Totems were "worshiped" (peculiarly loved, respected, venerated, reverenced) because, presumably, they were ancestral, gave birth to the self, gave being, and might give or withhold rewards or punish. As the intellect developed, so runs the argument, attitudes of worship were extended and differentiated to include other things, signs or symbols. Nature gods and religious ceremonials developed. Polytheism became monotheism.

No apology need be made for a certain amount of "reading in," though a glance at M'Lennan's essay will show how little there has been. If only as a heuristic device, some attempt must be made to transcend the actual words of an essay which, written a century ago, might so easily be dismissed. It seems important to appreciate that the main elements of M'Lennan's essay—the phenomenon, the latter's organizational matrix, the associated mode of thought, developmental process, and the ontology—do not continually appear and reappear in varieties of permutations and combinations in essays and books on totemism because M'Lennan wrote about them, but because these questions were and are of significance within the European ambience, and could and still can be worked out and adumbrated in relation to totemism.

If this were not so, more respect would have been paid to the ethnographic evidence. Long had written: "One part of the religious superstition of the Savages, consists in each of them having his *totam*, or favourite spirit, which he believes watches over him. This *totam* they conceive assumes the shape of some beast or other, and therefore they never kill, hunt, or eat the animal whose form they think this *totam* bears . . . . The idea of destiny, or, if I may be allowed the phrase, '*Totamism*,' however strange, is not confined to the Savages . . ." (Long, *op, cit.*, pp. 86–87). The trader, that is, saw beyond the phenomenon into the ontology and perceived something like a universal. He seems to have been aware that the fleeting thought or reflection on life's meaning must be caught and imprisoned in a word, thing, form, or existent if it is not to be lost for ever. Life's pathways must be marked, man's destinies mapped, the continuities maintained. Nor could Tylor have been wholly unaware of this process. But he thought of "savages" as children — as incomplete humans (see Tylor, 1866) — and considered this hugely important saving of the thought as merely the childish imputation of life in existents. It did not seem to cross his mind that it was the thought that had life, a life which the existent could preserve and hold.

M'Lennan's opposite view, that existents — things, words, forms of social organization — maintained the life of the thought, was, one feels, rather more sensible. Yet his argument failed because he does not seem to have been wholly aware of the implications of what he was saying, and he attached the argument too rigidly to data that could not stand up. Eighty years later Lévi-Strauss felt bound to argue the advantages of deleting the word "totemism" from the anthropological vocabulary (Lévi-Strauss, 1963). Denying that totemism had any useful and distinct identity, he would have us assimilate the phenomenon to a general theory of cognition and its transformational processes — thus transcending both Tylor and M'Lennan. But he was only able to take this position on the basis of what had been happening over the intervening years. First, there has been a developing awareness of the nature of the phenomenon and its ontology through the accumulated experience of investigating it elsewhere as well as in Australia. Second, in those ninety years there have been a series of differentiations in our own thought and experience of ourselves which in this and other contexts has accelerated the process of assimilating and understanding varieties of otherness. Third, the tremendous developments in linguistics have not only led us back into a truly medieval appreciation of the word but enabled us to gallop well beyond.

Nevertheless, totemism remains a "problem" — of much the same kind as asking "How many Angels . . . ?" For while it is true that sustained fieldwork experience must, in time, qualify the intellect that addresses the material, dogmas die hard. Just as reality imitates art, so empirical data tends to be born of the questions asked by the intellect. If the questions are barren neither gooseberry bush nor stork nor cabbage patch will yield up its fruit.

As has already been suggested, for many of the earlier writers totemism, taboo, exogamy — even magic, science, and religion — were discrete things, concrete phenomena which people "had." Indeed, if there was to be a science of society, if the vagaries of subjective interpretation were to be avoided, it was necessary — temporarily at any rate — to abandon the gist of Montesquieu's "spirit of the laws" and first find and identify phenomena. It was a mechanical mode appropriate to a society dominated by a technology based on steam power, connecting rods, gears, and belt drives. Lévi-Straussian structuralism is no less appropriate to a technology based upon electronics. With the former model, activities and logical categories were treated as phenomena at equivalent levels. The latter demands that activities be transformed into logical categories of inclusion/exclusion. For Durkheim, expressing a transitional mode, the accent lay on the logical categories. But these went along with, if they did not depend on, a particular institutional framework or series of activities which articulated the variety of *groups* which composed a community.

Though Durkheim's use of "articulate" is ambiguous, he has been generally understood as meaning "jointed" or "connected" rather than "voiced" or "expressed." This indeed is how his treatment of totemism comes across. Given that Australians were primitive, that religion existed in order to articulate and weld into a coherent whole the separate and even mutually opposed parts and segments of a society, and that among Australian Aborigines this job of articulation was being done by totemism, totemism could be viewed as a primitive form of religion. Further, feeding back into and reinforcing the initial assumption, because the totemic phenomenon could be incorporated into a general theory of religion, the sociological relevance of religion became the clearer. Since totems, as logical categories, symbolized or stood for the parts or segments which composed the community, and the totems were "worshiped," what Australians were doing was worshiping their society, the logical categories and organizational forms that gave them identity, being, and purpose. As a general formulation about religion, the statement could hold for more developed religions elsewhere. Durkheim was probably aware that this was, precisely, the deeper relevance of what the Old Testament prophets meant by idolatry. But then, Australians were primitive and had often been called idolators. Besides, so much of religion everywhere could be called idolatrous in this sense. Further, however, Durkheim wrote at a time when established and orthodox religion in Europe was under heavy attack and had suffered severe defeats. Authoritative coroners had pronounced that God was dead. Yet if God was dead, why did religion persist? This was the question asked of Australian Aborigines. Was religion the opium of the masses, necessary for the dominant class to keep order, or could an increasingly sophisticated, literate, and industrialized European community well do without it? Again we are brought round to problems of European rather than Aboriginal concern.

For Simmel (1959, pp. 6–11) and others it was not organized religion that gave rise to religiosity or being religious, but man's religiosity that gives rise to organized religion. Paradoxically, marxism, based upon precisely the opposite view, was just then in the process of building just that intellectual framework which could – to paraphrase Simmel on religion – give man belonging, identity, and purpose; order his reactions to exterior nature and his fellow man; and give direction to the apparent vagaries and whimsies of fate. It was a problem vital to settle. Much hung in the balance. Was it possible for science to show, on the basis of empirical evidence, on which side men's faith should be pinned? Within this context Durkheim's solution was a compromise: religion kept things together, substance and form were mutually dependent. Environmental or evolutionary forces were responsible for shifting the equilibrium into a new key.

Although, for Freud (1913–1960), totemism was certainly more of a cluster of relations than a thing, it was still a definable complex which could be detached from a particular institutional framework. Inhering in all of us, totemism could be accounted for in terms of a protohistorical event whose significance is repeated in the process of each individual's psychological growth and development. It could then be incorporated into a psychology grounded in the interrelations of husband (father), wife (mother) and child – a basic but universal unit within varying social environments. It was a question of sexual drives, jealousy, killing, and guilt. Indeed, since no human being is without guilt, jealousy, or sexual drives, and few can assert that they have never experienced an impulse to kill, it may be that Freud had an answer. Such is the mythological elasticity of an evolutionist framework of thought. On the other hand, the direct experience of Australian totemism has been perceived to incorporate so very much more than Freud appears to have allowed for, that even if we accept the Freudian myth, in explaining so much it explains very little in particular. For Elkin (1964, p. 140), for example, totemism is "more than a mechanism for regulating marriage .... It is a view of nature and life, of the universe and man, which colours and influences the Aborigine's social groupings and mythologies, inspires their rituals and links them to the past. It unites them with nature's activities and species in a bond of mutual life-giving, and imparts confidence amidst the vicissitudes of life."

It may be of course that all this may be taken to derive from the sexual drive and its consequences: totems and totemism are the lens through which the energics generated by the triadic relationship are refracted into the wider community. On the other hand, at a particular sociological level and as Radcliffe-Brown (1952, pp. 117–132) in his first essay on totemism in 1929 would have it, since the first positive requirement for survival is success in the food quest, the totemic elaboration may be explained as a mode of ordering the exploitation and allocation of the food resources of the environment. If this seems reasonable enough in the Australian context — for totems must occur somewhere in the total environment — it fails to stand up in conditions where totemism is not as elaborate as in Australia. That is, it is insufficient as a general explanation. Indeed, this kind of positivist thought always founders when moved from the particular to the general. Listen again to Elkin. Totemism, he writes, is "our key to the understanding of the Aboriginal philosophy and the universe — a philosophy which regards man and nature as one corporate whole for social, ceremonial and religious purposes, a philosophy which from one aspect is preanimistic, but from another is animistic, a philosophy which is historical, being formed on the heroic acts of the past which provide the sanctions for the present, a philosophy which, indeed, passes into the realm of religion and provides that faith, hope and courage in the face of his daily needs which man must have if he is to persevere and persist, both as an individual and as a social being" (From Stanner, 1965, p. 224). If this, both on the interpretive level and for the Aborigine, seems to make of totemism a general portmanteau of everything and anything, at least it indicates that in Aboriginal culture totemism is not a particular thing but has the widest significance. As Stanner dryly remarks (*idem*): "In short, the problems of understanding Totemism are the problems of understanding religion anywhere." Which is what Durkheim had implied.

The relationship between totem and totemite might be indistinguishable from fetishism were it not for the fact that the former has always involved something more than an attachment, often amounting to an obsession, between an individual and some other thing. Kinship with, descent from, inheritance of, identity through, fate or destiny determined by, particular kinds of awareness achieved through, place in the cosmos given by — these are some of the features included in that "more." They are ascriptive features at the level of the collective. Though there are instances when totems may be chosen by individuals at their own volition, this only reemphasizes the question why a culture should provide totems to be chosen. Because, phenomenologically, the relationship between a totem and totemite has not been found to be associated with any constant cluster of organizational forms, it follows that the totemic relationship is not dependent on, and so may be detached from, a particular contextual matrix even though the latter must to some extent determine local expressions. This is why anthropologists have either (a) denied the reality of totemism as a phenomenon; or (b) confined themselves to local and particular interpretations and exegeses; or (c) attempted, either psychologically or sociologically, to assimilate the relationship to a universal in human affairs.

If totems, in our terms, fell into a recognizable phenomenological class — either flora or fauna or meteorological phenomena, for example — the task of explication would be made much easier. But they do not do this. In transcending the difficulty·by suggesting that totems form a class in that as logical categories the relations of difference between totems are homologues of the relations of difference in social relationships, Lévi-Strauss (*op. cit.*, pp. 72–90) plays an ace. Similarities are finite, differences are infinite. If the homologues are not at first apparent one has only to look harder and longer. If that fails a resort to mythical history can always explain the corruption of the present. (See Hiatt, 1969.) In declining the implied invitation to have faith, however, Stanner goes to an opposite extreme and is convinced that the totems of Australian Aborigines are "irreducibly arbitrary" (1965, p. 227).

For an anthropologist to say firmly that something is arbitrary is startling. He is, after all, concerned with discovering the systemic in the regularities of social life. The claim of arbitrariness is either very important or an escape hatch or simply giving it up. Stanner certainly does not mean that totemism is simply fetishism, subject to the whimsy of particular individuals. He insists, on the contrary, that totems are existents which refer to, or are signs of, matters of faith or axiom; and that while these matters of faith or axiom may be seen as forming systems which are of prime importance, the totems themselves are "arbitrary" and, presumably, of minor importance in themselves. That is, because totems and totemism explain and, in relation to the totemite, are not to be explained, the investigator is asked to explain totems or totemism, or render them intelligible, by finding out what it is they do explain. The task is to discover what are matters of faith or axiom and then show the parts played by totems within the relationship totem-totemite. Totems are universalized not as totems but as the media through which matters of faith and axiom, the articulate determinants of being, become known. Which is to place the whole weight on the ontology, the substance, and reject the form. To put the point more generally, at whatever level we press the relationship between substance and form, the former is more susceptible to system than the latter. Is this acceptable? To get at substance we have first to find the form. So soon as substance is discovered it becomes a form leading into further substance—and so on *ad infinitum*. If there is no discernible order in form, then the substance is surely as disordered. On the other hand, if one can perceive some order in the substance in spite of the disorder in the form, then the question is why the form should be seen as disordered. In short, arbitrariness will not do.

If totems are the media they are supposed to be, then they themselves should form some kind of system. They simply cannot be arbitrary. There are, or in history were, determinants of choice. Red for "stop" or "danger" and green for "go" or "safe" are not arbitrary. The selection emerges from our cultural history and may even be rooted in our biology. Indeed, the whole thrust of Lévi-Strauss' argument both in *Totemism* (1963) and in *The Savage Mind* (Lévi-Strauss, 1962b) was to show that there was order in the forms but that this order resulted from the very being and nature of man, particularly from the operations of his brain. Which, in principle, brings us back to M'Lennan and Tylor—with this difference: that for Tylor the operations of the human mind could be intuited from the axiom of the psychic unity of mankind, whereas for Lévi-Strauss the human mind, seated in the capacity or proclivity of the brain to make binary discriminations, may select and permute in infinite variety but must do so in an ordered way; and because this order derives from binary discriminations, it must be discoverable by an analysis based upon binary discriminations. Whimsy, chance and arbitrary are taboo.

Like a myth which, having dealt with a series of transformations, returns the listener to the opening scene at another level, let us travel back to Long's "guardian spirit" and "idea of destiny," to Henry's "armorial bearing," and finally to Lescarbot's Aoutem. As Lescarbot (1914, p. 101) heard it, the word was applied not to an animal or plant or meteorological phenomenon but to Jacques Cartier. What did Jacques Cartier mean or represent to the Ojibways? If we said that a totem can be a European we would lose all the force and flavor implied in the fact that a European was a totem.

4   MYTHOLOGIES

Looked at institutionally there are of course many aspects of traditional Australian religious life which have not been, and cannot be, considered here. For whether we think of sacred boards, sand drawings, increase rites, therapeutic and prophylactic rites, sorcery, mutilations, or the total inventory of ritual furnishings, symbols, dances, songs, musical instruments, melodies, paintings, carvings, recitations, and ceremonials, each reveals the same basic problems we have isolated in relation to totemism. How best may we make sense of these features? What are to be the basic units of study? To what kinds of rationally objective explanatory or analytic framework may we relate them?

Even if an anthropologist wanted to get "inside the skin" of an Aborigine, that skin — the socio-religious order which gives experience relevance — has to be experienced and comprehended. Though much has been done in this respect in the Australian field (particularly by R. M. Berndt, 1952; R. M. and C. H. Berndt, 1970; Stanner, 1966) there is little doubt that the greater advances in the analysis of religious life have been made elsewhere, by for example, Evans-Pritchard (1956), Lienhardt (1961), and Turner (1969) in Africa, and by Geertz (1960) in Java. What characterizes the work of these authors is the transformation of functionalism into varying kinds of structuralism. Abandoning the concrete institution, they have sought the units or elements of a total semantic field in which activities and institutions could be seen as particular selections and constellations of these units or elements, and in which the value or relevance of the latter differed according to position in a particular constellation. Making such advances has required not only intellectual imagination, but a firm commitment to the view that because religion explains, it is not to be explained away. Scientific technique, as thorough and painstaking as in other fields, has been kept wholly subservient to intellectual perceptions.

The study of myth, on the other hand, lends itself to positive, scientific evaluation; and the advances made have been due in large part to the breaking of relatively coarse units into relatively finer and finer units. But the one intellectual perception has sufficed: hosts of others may apply and refine the scientific techniques devolving from that perception. An investigator need not even collect the myth himself. Indeed, it was Lévi-Strauss' work on American myths — work that involved the application of methods and models borrowed from structural linguistics — which led him into his study of Australian totemism. The technique itself has become an indispensable tool. Yet neither in the field of myth nor in religious studies generally, it is fair to say, have anthropologists in the Australian field really begun to reap the harvest of old data transformed by new thinking. Still, the serious and scientific study of myth has been a relatively recent development in anthropology. Again, we have to look briefly into the past to see why.

While the Aryan Hindus, who shared a large stock of their mythology with their cousins the Greeks, were studying their myths in a spirit of exegesis, seeking truth from sacred texts, Anaximander, Heraclitus, Parmenides, Pythagoras, Socrates, Plato, and Aristotle were concerning themselves with the problem of relating their myths to their new-found philosophic truths grounded in rational objectivity. On the one hand, there were truths arrived at by logic, by inspection, by certain rules of investigation and procedure. On the other hand, there were the truths or statements of myth. While Indian sages regarded their myths, the Vedas, as true or truth as matter of axiom, the Greeks, always skeptical, were asking whether their myths were to be taken literally or allegorically; whether they contained traditional truths, intuitive truths, or religious truths; whether they were history in poetic style, or rather simple fictions designed to gull the people and maintain the priests in power. If myths explained or revealed anything, what was it they explained or revealed? Plato, in particular, was indignant and affronted that a virtuous and intelligent man should be expected to pay any heed to the silly and immoral sexual adventures of the gods, goddesses, and heroes of myth. Though in this instance Plato revealed himself as making the mistake of thinking of myths as always direct exemplars, in his allegory or myth of the man in the cave he invented a myth and demonstrated a universal property of myths: a mode of cognition and explanation.

This rejection of one myth or a set of myths only to invent another was to become prototypical. For the early Christians, most of whom were Neoplatonists, the Greek myths were anathema. Though they themselves were inventing their own myths — so many displaced persons and slaves, coming from disrupted communities, would need to invent new myths — at the intellectual level the idea of myth was directly opposed to the idea of history. The Bible was history, not myth. The continuities of principle from one generation to the next were to be preserved and recognized in history, not in myth. In an on-going situation characterized by rapid changes in social circumstances it was particularly important that history, not myth, should preserve the continuities and guide development. Rationality was based upon evidence, logic, and history. Myths were old wives' tales, so much fictional nonsense. History expressed the diachrony; the great chain of being expressed the synchrony, rationally and objectively. Yet, so far as it was a moot point whether God in his plenitude had created all things for all time, or was in the process of creating all becoming, thus far did the chain of being, though objectified, contain an essential quality of myth: it attempted to synthesize or reconcile the contradiction between the synchrony and diachrony. Still, what were thought of as myths had no place in the chain: they were childish figments.

Although from earliest times until the present day travelers have recounted the myths and stories of the peoples they have visited, these stories were regarded not as modes of cognition—having some affinity with alchemy, that magnificent attempt to marry man's psyche and perceptions to the physical world—but as an attractively decorated detritus from the past, possible evidence for history. Thus, for example, a story of a great flood could be used to show that a particular people's ancestors had attempted to hand down the experience of the historic flood of the Old Testament. Such myths reinforced the historicity of the biblical flood, supported the argument of a common humanity descended from Adamic stock, and posed the historical problem of what had happened in the interim.

With the Renaissance, and much more so in the eighteenth century, the Greek and Roman myths reentered the ambience of the European intellectual world. They were still, however, stories or tales which were figments or fictions, becoming the novel, and bearing much the same relationship to history and to the people who immersed themselves in them as the novel today or in the nineteenth century. Travelers and ethnographers could and did compare the myths of primitive peoples in the new worlds with the mythologies of the ancient world. But the same kinds of inference continued to be drawn: they were evidence of contact or common origin at some time in the past, and the history of what had happened in the meantime remained to be investigated.

When, toward the end of the eighteenth century, Sir William Jones' researches into Sanskrit, the laws of Manu and the Vedas became known, it was the historical implications of the relationship between Greek and Sanskrit that were deemed important. Even when, later on, the philological and linguistic implications were taken up, the inferences were used to elicit history. There was no attempt to study a myth as a construction in itself, as a coherent set of social representations. If, by virtue of their rational and objective creation, novels seemed, and were, a different genre, the family relationship with myth was recognized not in the cognitive mode that yielded an awareness of the synchrony in relation to the diachrony but in the quality of figment or fiction that both assumed in relation to history. Though, by the middle of the nineteenth century, folklore, myths, and tales were beginning to be collected and studied, few of those in Britain and America who thought of themselves as anthropologists took much notice. Myths and tales were hardly evidence for an evolutionist, a view confirmed by the overimaginative use of them by diffusionists as historical evidence. Not until Max Muller, orientalist and philologist, was driven by his studies of the Vedas into appreciating some of the significance of myth, did myth begin to enter the ambience of anthropological research as a field worthy of examination for its own sake and for the light it could throw on social life from a synchronic point of view.

In 1868 Max Muller delivered a series of lectures on the Science of Language to the Royal Institution of Great Britain. Two years later the same audience was listening to him on the Science of Religion. In 1878 he was lecturing on the Origin and Growth of Religion. The young James George Frazer, then twenty-six years old, may be supposed to have read them even though Max Muller was at Oxford and not at Cambridge. A decade later Andrew Lang, a classical scholar and prolific writer, published *Myth, Ritual and Religion* (1887), and Frazer had embarked on *The Golden Bough*, itself grounded in a puzzle arising out of classical mythology. Myth had arrived. In 1888 Max Muller was lecturing on Natural Religion, using myth to make his points. In 1897 Andrew Lang published *Modern Mythology*. In 1899 J. Mathew published his *Eagle-hawk and Crow, A study of the Australian Aborigines*, an analysis of social organization based on the myth of the eaglehawk and crow which, albeit varying in particulars, was widespread in Australia. Yet, although by the turn of the century the collection, study, and exegesis of classical and Hindu mythology as well as of European myths, legends, and folk-tales had become specialist scholarly topics in their own right, providing mines of information for the quarryings of historians, philologists, and linguists, nothing like this kind of attention (understandably) was given to the mythologies of the simpler or nonliterate peoples. In what respects, aside from the posing of historical problems, were these mythologies relevant to anthropology?

One obstacle to the perception of this relevance, the alliance of re-vealed religion and history, was to some extent overcome by Max Muller. He used Indian data and pointed to ritual. Within the Christian ambience ritual had always been relatively unimportant. Christianity had always emphasized faith, doctrine, dogma, and rationality, allowing rituals of different kinds to flower in profuse diversity. Andrew Lang, too, per-ceived the chief relevance of myth in the context of its relationship to ritual. Because myth was relevant to ritual, however, neither Muller nor Lang could avoid the inference that myth must bear importantly upon religion. Yet for both these authors as well as for others "myth," "ritual," and "religion" were quite separate chunks of culture which might be interrelated in a piecemeal way but remained clearly distinct universes. Further, the ascribed attribute of myths as "old wives' tales" or the like — Max Muller dubbed myth a "disease of language" — deterred many a scholar from bringing myth into the center of the stage. Even when, in 1919, Frazer published his *Folklore in the Old Testament*, a direct assault on the historicity of the Old Testament and both an application of anthropological comparative method as it was then conceived, and of textual analysis, few at the time seem to have considered that the methods appropriate for analyzing myths — analogous to the logical methods of textual analysis developed by medieval scholasts, and as illustrated in minor key by J. Mathew's handling of the myth of the eaglehawk and crow — might also be appropriate, as the logicians of old had held, to the analysis of other aspects of culture. To arrive at this position, however, it was first necessary to stop juggling with words which subsumed enormous chunks of culture, and to devise analytical tools which could be used to handle smaller units.

The main problem in the interrelations of myth and ritual concerned the logical and temporal priorities. Which came first, the myth or the ritual? Did people engage in a ritual and then, later, rationalize their activities in the form of a myth, or was the ritual a mode of acting out what had already taken shape as a myth? Given the temporal priority, logical priority would follow. Or, by finding out which was the more durable and rigid, and which the more flexible, the priorities might be deduced. In themselves vain issues clearly posed under the influence of historicist and evolutionist dogmatics, they nevertheless provided a stimulus for literary and classical studies. What was lacking was a good ethnographic field data. In the Australian field, Spencer, it is true, collected a number of myths and, almost a quarter of a century before it became fashionable, used them to adumbrate, explain or explicate more positive kinds of traditional Australian activity. That is, he used Australian myths to help him rationalize other aspects of Australian culture: functionalism of a kind. Himself a biologist by profession, Spencer trusted Gillen and his senses, knew what he knew, but was always diffident in the world of professional, intellectualized anthropology. Thus it was Marett, Spencer's friend and anthropological mentor, who gave expression to Spencer's functionalist mood in asserting that myths and rituals were built up together and generated each other.

Much later, Clyde Kluckhohn (1942, pp. 45–79) was to cap Marett by showing the futilities of talking about the priorities of myth and ritual. At the time, however, although a variety of ethnographers had begun to collect and translate Aboriginal myths, little else was done with them. To be sure, Durkheim, like Spencer, used myths in his classic on Australian religious life to explicate a situation. But again, neither scholar seems to have realized explicitly that in so doing they were treating myth as a mode of cognition. Despite Durkheim's insistence on the "social fact" and the "social representation," he was unable to realize the unparalleled opportunity presented by the Australian material: myth as an integral part of culture and the social situation. Even though linguists had begun to study Australian languages, the notion of studying myth and language in combination, or as in a vital dialectic relationship was not realized until much later. Following Max Muller, myth and language were wholly opposed. The one was a disease, a dark shadow on thought, the other a blessing, the basis of knowledge and philosophy.

Advancing into the new century, to the study of myth and ritual was added a growing interest in the relations between myth and history. Partly, as has been noted, this was a question of finding out how much good historical evidence was contained in myths and legends. It was also a question of looking at myths and historical studies and trying to discover the relations between them as modes of intellection, explication, explanation, and persuasion. Lying behind this was the growing realization in intellectual circles in Britain that the great British whig historians were in no small measure mythmakers as well as propagandists. There were no known whig historians among Australian Aborigines, but the intellectual problems posed by historians who were also mythmakers, and by mythmakers who might also be historians, were very much the kinds of problems that might attract anthropologists.

What was missing, however, were those reliable and documented events in the histories of these peoples which might provide the fixed points against which the historicity of myth might be evaluated. This did not deter Perry (1923, 1927), or indeed Rivers (1914) from using myths as though they were cryptic historical texts. Though this use of myths, within the constraints of a much stricter methodology, is bound to be taken up again (cf. Lévi-Strauss, 1964-1969, 1967) in relation to Australian Aborigines, in the past the Australian material did not easily lend itself to the task, and few professional anthropologists since Rivers have been willing to stake their reputations on such a slippery pursuit. Still, particular discoveries such as those made by Sir George Gray in 1837 of what are now known as *Wandjina* paintings (Gray, 1841; and see Crawford, 1968) or, more recently, near Haast's Bluff in central Australia, of anomalous artifacts and engravings (*People*, 1968) have fired the imagination and provided a lever for attempting to make particular myths historically relevant. Nor is there much doubt that as archaeologists continue in their attempts to build up a coherent picture of Australian prehistory, mythology will provide them with clues and may even achieve a fit. We know, for example, that Macassan trepang fishermen have been visiting the coasts of Australia at least since the early eighteenth century, and their activities have not gone unrecorded in Australian mythology. The fit has been established. But finding out from a myth what is historical in it presents difficulties. For though myth may enter history, it remains a myth albeit an historical myth; and when history enters myth it becomes a myth: the unique and unrepeatable event becomes a symbolic truth, a repeatable truth of principle.

After the First World War, with the professionalization of anthropology in Australia, studies of myth began to proliferate. Teams of linguists in Sydney and Adelaide began not only to map out the languages of Australian peoples, but to collect and publish texts of myths. Spurred by the Malinowskian doctrines of fieldwork and functionalism, myths were viewed as "charters" (Malinowski, 1926) of social activities and belief. But they were still used as auxiliary explications of the interdependencies of institutional life which they "reflected." There was little thought of myth as a logical model capable of overcoming a contradiction, particularly that posed by the diachrony and the synchrony. Nor was much attention given to the way in which myth could transform a primal event, temporal priority, into a first principle or efficient cause, logical priority, and then retransform the latter into event.

Though Max Muller had recognized the multivalences in mythical words and sentences, they were the very qualities he deplored and anathematized. He did not perceive that it was through these multivalences that myth effected, through language, those very transformations which people in a culture experienced directly. Myth, in short, was still myth—an unstructured and random figment that could be recruited as evidence in particular circumstances (when it suited) and neglected in others (when it did not suit). Its truths were fictional truths, as haphazardly useful to science or philosophy as the truths of a novel. The idea that an appropriate way of analyzing a novel or a myth might also be appropriate for the analysis of other aspects of culture was a long way off. Yet some approach toward the idea was made by psychology. Both Freud and Jung had stressed the significance of myths and dreams and, whether within the terms of professional discourse, or more naively, the content of

Australian myths began to be assimilated to general theories of psychology. Much was done. But, mainly through Malinowski, grave doubt was thrown on the transcultural validity of psychologies built wholly upon the European experience. It was, in a sense, Tylor and Frazer all over again. At what points was an otherness the same, or different? What criteria of relevance would bring differences in culture, social order, and scale into a proper perspective? Adumbrating the similarities was one thing, but what was needed was some kind of framework or model which, in revealing the similarities, would also demonstrate and perhaps account for the differences. Nevertheless, though it was in an eclectic and piecemeal way, myths were collected, set down as accurately as possible with respect to the vernacular and its translation, and used to adumbrate and explicate what were thought of as the more positive features of social life. This, indeed, was what anthropologists were doing with myth in other fields across the globe.

In Europe and the United States, however, the bases for a quite fresh appraisal of anthropological materials had been, and were being laid. Folklorists and linguists were borrowing from each other, cooperating, and combining their separate skills into a single endeavor (see Maranda and Maranda, 1971, pp. ix–xiii). The central features of this fresh stance — which was not wholly new in principle in the European experience, and which could include varying kinds of entry or approach to the material — may be characterized as resting on four main principles: (i) definition of elements or entities by logical criteria of inclusion/exclusion; (ii) elements or entities so defined have relevance and value only insofar as they are in specific relations with other elements or entities; (iii) when these specific relations alter, the elements or entities are transformed; (iv) the rules by which such elements or entities or their relevances and values are transformed are to be derived from the dialectical relationship between the particular categories of inclusion/exclusion which define them, and should be such as to generate the transformation under review. (See Maranda and Maranda, *op. cit.*) Now Durkheim, Hubert, and Mauss (Durkheim, 1895–1938; Durkheim, 1924–1953; Durkheim and Mauss, 1903–1963; Hubert and Mauss, 1898–1964) had been working within roughly these terms since the turn of the century. But, being stronger in the preaching than persuasive in the praxis, what they had to say did not make a wide impact at the time. Evans-Pritchard's brilliant implementation of these principles in *The Nuer* (1941) and in *The Sanusi of Cyrenaica* (1951) were only barely recognized as, in principle, a complete break with the functionalist studies of the time. It was not for a couple of decades that, with Lévi-Strauss' *The Savage Mind* (1962b) and *Totemism* (1963), analytic works specifically based on the methods developed by structural linguistics, it was generally recognized that something new had entered the scene.

The Battle of Britain was hardly an appropriate scenario for welcoming and acknowledging an intellectual advance made in relation to the Nuer, a then obscure people in the Southern Sudan. Nor was the aftermath of the war—more than a decade of preoccupation with the cold war, and the economic and political reshaping of the world—a wholly favorable ambience for appreciating the subtlety of an intellect which could, within the same analytic mode reveal the ontological relations lying behind the phenomenology. *The Nuer* did not go unnoticed in Australia, nor did *The Sanusi of Cyrenaica*. But there is little to show that the principles which guided the analyses had much impact on studies of Australian Aborigines. Nothing if not independent, scholars in the Australian field were not alone in being unable to separate ethnographic material from the mode of making it known. This was Lévi-Strauss' emphasis, made very explicit. Dealing with Australian data he showed that, whether the material was myth or a series of activities, both were statements and, therefore, susceptible and assimilable to the one mode of analysis based on logical criteria of inclusion and exclusion. Which Evans-Pritchard had already shown, albeit indirectly.

One feature in Lévi-Strauss' method, however, was not integral to it. As Tylor (1871–1958, p. 539) had pointed out, anthropology or, as he called it, ethnology, was a reformer's science. If through Lévi-Strauss the study of myth, and so of culture, had become a science in that there exists no necessary moral relationship between analyst and text, to many Australian anthropologists, for whom the Aborigines were partly a reformer's problem, the analytic model was at first but coldly received. It did not seem to contribute to the primary problem of understanding the people. People, the concrete reality—that glint of eye and animated gesture which revealed, so it seemed, the purposes of myth—seemed to have been voided from culture and replaced with a series of binary oppositions coupled to hypothetical history. Besides, participating in the Australian ambience of anti-intellectualism combined with an addiction to technological science, Australian academics were highly skeptical of Lévi-Strauss' intellectual agility and logical acrobatics. Nevertheless, in spite of continued opposition (see, for example, Hiatt, 1969), students have begun to take up Lévi-Strauss' ideas and submit them to the test of fieldwork. It has become clearer, as the Greeks might have assured us, that

with a more precise analysis of form has come a more accurate knowledge of content. Far from the reality being voided it has come to be
known more significantly. Moreover, since the analytic mode suggested is
appropriate to a computer, and not to make use of such a tool would be
like attempting to commit observations to memory when a pencil was to
hand, form and content may be tested against each other. The computer,
in short, provides that laboratory situation and precision which many
an anthropologist has been happy to do without, but now must use,
particularly in analyzing myth.

5   REALITY AND ILLUSION

Evans-Pritchard (1965, p. 121) has drawn attention to the fact that the
bulk of anthropological work on the religious lives of primitive peoples
has been done by nonbelievers, by those who have ascribed no reality to
the gods, spirits and souls of religion, by those who have sought to explain
by reference to what are optimistically called the more positive features
of social life why it is that an illusion like religion should exist. On the
whole, the statement holds true in relation to students of traditional
Aboriginal religion. In one way or another, paternalistically, charitably, or
in more forceful derogation, most authors leave the reader with an impression of systematic illusion. The bits and pieces of cultural life are made to
fit together right enough, but the vital departure point, the ancestral
beings, never "really" existed. The question who or what the ancestors
are has rarely been seriously asked. Perhaps, like ghosts, they are parts of
conscience and memory. We read of them as being ever-present, but they
emerge from analyses as figures and figments of the past. It might be that
the ancestral beings are not only necessary components of the spirit of
Aboriginal man but of the spirit of man in general. If so, under what other
name or names do we – Christians, atheists, whatever – evoke a statement
about ourselves and our being that corresponds with what the ancestral
beings are saying about the being of Aborigines?

Initiations, dances, ceremonies – rituals of all kinds – are evidently fun
to watch, photograph, and write about; and the serious business of analyzing the doing is absorbing. Clearly the Aborigines get a kick out of all
these activities. They make for social cohesion, yield identity, give the
Aborigines something to live for, make him feel secure in an essentially
insecure world. One could as well say in the same breath with equal
justification that they caused strife, stultified the personality, narrowed
the outlook and produced a sense of paranoid insecurity. Such ambi-

valences are surely the stuff of significance. For most Westerners the general categories of law, economics, or politics are scrupulously divided into numbers of aspects and segments of relevance. This division is carried over into the analysis of other cultures. But "religion" has tended to be regarded as an epiphenomenal chunk of ritual and — unhappy word — "belief." It emerges as good for some, particularly primitives who need that cohesion, but bad for others who think they can know themselves in a rhythm of bodily pollution and cleansing, work, drugs, parties and purgatives; or good in some respects, but not so good in others.

As with television and other media born of nineteenth-century thought, concentration on the elaborations of the medium that is ritual has tended to obscure the message, the statement being made by the ritual. The idiom of the message has only too often been mistranslated into that of the stock exchange or of Erewhon's musical banks: an adventitious psychological investment which happens to yield dividends for the unenlightened *them*; a monument to the formalities of man's absurdity. Marett's anecdote of the French senator realizes itself again and again. We need to remind ourselves that if social scientists can be the arbiters of the absurd and set it on one side, it is precisely in his absurdity that man reveals himself most truly. If it were not for his follies man would have remained a primate in paradise. Though the great bulk of anthropological literature has been concerned with religious life, Simmel's insight (1959, p. 10) into the central authenticity of religious life as something that emerges spontaneously from the human breast has rarely been taken up. It is as though we were afraid of what we might find.

It would be difficult to write of Aboriginal religious life without alluding to the intimate connections with the natural world of land, animals, plants, and meteorological phenomena, the interrelationships of those living in community, and the interventions of chance, fate, cataclysm or other features over which man has no control (cf. Simmel, *op. cit.*, pp. 6–10). What is lacking, however, is a sense of the integration of these experiences into an objective world of faith which the Aboriginal self — and the reader — may explore and so gain in total awareness. There is no map of the possibilities of experience. There has, too, been little systematic search for those occasions on which an Aborigine might or could seize the moment and find a harmony of personal feeling with outer conditions — though the data for doing just this are there in plenty (see, for examples, Berndt and Berndt, 1970; Mountford, 1968; Stanner, 1966). Rather than separate the cultural from the moral, and the animal and spiritual from both and each other, field observations are almost invariably fed into the hopper of normative moralities, modes of thought and forms of social organization. Yet what is distinctive about the human primate are the ways in which he transcends the "here-now" to give himself over to a past and future that moves into eternity; transcends his spatial limitations so that his essential self may move into regions where the animal apparently cannot; created morality and then attempts to transcend it.

Whether religion be regarded as illusion or reality, anthropological treatises on the topic, Aboriginal religion particularly, have also been affected by equivocations between gorilla and baboon theory. Just as, since the eighteenth century at any rate, the bias has been to illusion rather than reality, so has it been an implicit assumption in most anthropological work on primitive religions that man was a loner who had sacrificed a part of his being in order to live in community. The bonds of religion are emphasized, religion is a binding-in, the necessary cohesive cement required for survival under hazardous environmental conditions. From which it follows that when the hazardous conditions are removed there is no need of religion. Hence the assumption of illusion. Yet if we were to assume baboon theory, that aeons before a creature crossed the threshold to become man the animal was social, not a loner, a quite different scene unfolds. Religious life now becomes the ambience within which the self may realize its individuality, its uniqueness, its animality, its spirituality, its moral and cultural capacities. What had appeared as bonds and constraints now turns into invitations to adventures into awareness. This, the reality of religious life as the religious themselves have expressed it, has been almost totally lacking in studies of Aboriginal religion. Much of the necessary data is there to be culled. But as yet, apart from Stanner (1966), there is little sign of the quality of insight and methods of analysis of, say, Evans-Pritchard (1956) or R. G. Lienhardt (1961) or Turner (1967, 1968, 1969) being applied to the Australian material.

Finally, although we know the Aborigine as artist and artisan, as painter, carver, dancer, musician, singer, orator, and proficient worker in stone, quite able to fend for himself in his traditional environment, he emerges through history as on the one hand the free and independent noble savage, promiscuous, a child of nature, wandering where the spirit lists, and on the other hand so hedged about with rules, conventions, and ritual that these have of themselves often seemed more important than the man. On both hands distanced from ourselves, a central feature of Aboriginal religious life which, if perceived, might have closed the gap was, instead, used to widen the gulf. Whatever we may think *really* happens at conception, the Aboriginal child came into the world at the behest of the spirit. The essential self demanded to be born, came into the world to realize morality and then transcend it. Mediating between the articulate thought and an awareness and experience of power in the world, myths, rituals, and ceremonies provided the framework within which each Aborigine could find answers as to why the spirit within him had asked to to born. How *wrong* were those answers?

CHAPTER 6

Man Transformed

1 THE ENCOUNTER: ACTION DIMENSIONS

In 1510 John Major, a Scottish professor, apparently the first to apply to the American Indians the Aristotelian doctrine of natural slavery, published his conviction that force should be used as a preliminary to teaching Indians the faith. The next year, a Dominican friar, Antonio de Montesinos, asked "Are these Indians not men? Do they not have rational souls? Are you not obliged to love them as you love yourselves?" (Hanke, 1959, pp. 14–15). These preliminaries to the great debate at Valladolid show how deeply rooted, explicit and self-conscious within the European Christian tradition is the problem of how to conduct relations with primitive or simple peoples. We need to remind ourselves that the process of expanding into and absorbing other cultures into the European ambience has always taken place at two main levels: the intellectual, moral, or theological on the one hand, and the practical or political on the other. Given a necessary interaction between the two levels, what is characteristic of, and unique to, the European expansion is that the process of absorbing other cultures has taken place mainly at the former level, and has always involved this level even when practical and political considerations have seemed paramount.

Nor has this been simply because Europeans have occupied relatively sparsely populated lands inhabited by nonliterate and simple peoples. In the parallel situation of other expanding and imperialist cultures, the ways of life of the conquered peoples were of small or no consequence, or at least not of sufficient consequence to be recorded, studied, and seriously discussed. Because or in spite of the fact that Europeans, divided among themselves, have rarely been able to deploy the physical force and numbers of men required to subdue or overrun another civilization completely, their cultures have been recorded, studied and, in many ways, absorbed into the European tradition. What is worthy of note about the Spanish conquests of Mexico and Peru is not that they were carried out by mere handfuls of men in each case — though this in itself was remarkable enough and has yet to be convincingly explained — but that so much was preserved and recorded for future generations to ponder. There were no "conquests" of the Ottoman empire, India, China, Indo-China, and the Malaysian archipelago. They were penetrated by small numbers of men — adventurers, merchants, missionaries, and the politically adroit supported by small armed forces — who may have been ruthless, but who left a variety of gifts in exchange for the raw materials their machines required. Today, although only a few Europeans remain in these lands, the libraries of Europe and America contain most of what is known about their cultures and histories. The process of finding out more continues.

The Australian experience has not been atypical. Along with the expectable parleys and affrays that took place as settlers spread out over lands that had belonged to others — a course of events repeated times without number across the globe and through history as one people has expanded into the lands of another — there was that characteristic absorption of Aboriginal culture at the intellectual level. Aboriginal words and place-names entered the European Australian vocabulary. Following the example of Captain Cook, officials, sojourners, and settlers began to explore and describe Aboriginal ways of life. Settlers, prospectors, shearers, explorers, and escaped convicts were not too proud to learn from Aborigines how to survive in the Australian bush. But, as has been noticed, those Aborigines who entered the European ambience were ill-prepared to survive in it. It was this failure — the sight and experience of layabout Aborigines drinking, swearing, making themselves comical and ridiculous in their aping of the white man's ways — that seems to have been decisive in that general rejection of Aborigines as of equal worth as human beings. For, as much to the Aborigine steeped in his tradition as to the European — or indeed anyone else — the loss of integrity involved in the treason to one's heritage and progenitors must inevitably and significantly diminish the human. Those who, in principle, are true to themselves and their heritage, are most likely to command the respect and affection of others.

Though it was clear, from the earliest days of contact, that a nonliterate and technologically simple culture must be in some ways inferior to a literate and technologically advanced one, to sustain an argument of general inferiority some incontrovertible physical fact was needed. A dark skin was a favorite resort of those with political and economic interests to forward. Evolutionism seemed to clinch the case. The fact that most dark-skinned peoples were, existentially, palpably not so technologically capable as Europeans, was readily grasped, generalized, and transformed into an innate inferiority and backwardness. The idea that man's consciousness and mental ability derived from the social forms and so from the technological capability perhaps had much to do with this transformation. Just as rain and sunshine were immune to moral considerations, so the supposed "scientific fact" of innate inferiority provided a convenient escape from the moral problems involved in men and women encountering their kind. The loss of integrity could be offset by an appeal to the "facts" of science.

On the other hand, Cook's eulogies sounded a note that has echoed and reechoed down the years. From Hodgkinson (1845, p. 243) who was of the opinion that in everything requiring mechanical ingenuity and dexterity the Australian Aborigines were the most apt scholars, through Worsnop (1897a, p. 2) who found them highly intelligent and quick of apprehension, to Strehlow (1956) who, in adducing the values of any hunting and gathering people, or indeed any small community, could not do otherwise than hold the Aborigines up to admiration, there has been no lack of sympathy and admiration. Nevertheless, this admiration for Aboriginal culture and the Aborigine of integrity at the intellectual level has, since the earliest days of settlement, been accompanied by a generalized rejection of those Aborigines immediately involved in attempting to cope with so much that was strange and new. These poor trapped souls have only too often been made into objects of denigration, laughter, and pity. If the depersonalization could temporarily allay the loss of integrity on the one part, the actual loss of integrity on both hands could only result in mutual distaste and dislike. But the further reaction to this otherwise on-going and increasingly bitter relationship has been a long struggle on the parts of some European Australians to embrace the Aborigines as brothers and fellow citizens. The saga of the Trappist, Benedictine, and Pallotine missions in Western Australia, and the extraordinary efforts of Bishop Salvado and Daisy Bates (see Durack, 1969) were perhaps exceptional. But they are representative of the activities of many organizations and individuals who refused to close their minds to the troubles and difficulties of encountering fellow human beings with different cultural assumptions. Continuing into the present, and expressed in political, moral, and intellectual terms, the dialectic has a familiar ring.

In 1839, before evolutionism had become familiar to the laity, Lord John Russell was saying (Bonwick, 1863, p. 74) that it was "impossible that the Government should forget that the original aggression was our own, and that we have never yet performed the sacred duty of making any systematic or considerable attempt to impart to the former occupants of New South Wales the blessings of Christianity, or the knowledge of the arts and advantages of civilized life." But, then as now, it was one thing to wax indignant at the situation, quite another to detail how an "improvement" might be implemented. For even when and where some such implementation was embarked upon the difficulties increased rather than decreased. As Hodgkinson (1845, p. 241), pointed out, the areas to which salaried Protectors of Aborigines had been appointed were precisely those in which the Aborigines had committed the most serious outrages. For Bonwick (*op. cit.*, p. 83) this kind of compromise was no solution. Either the Aborigines should be left alone in suitable reserves, where they could maintain their own integrity, or they should be positively and explicitly inducted into the European ambience by systematic training and teaching programs. That is, the Aborigine in the contact situation should be initiated into a new law, a new integrity. Bonwick goes on to deplore the fact of the matter: that in exchange for "endearing relations, joyous freedom, and unanxious existence" the Aborigines were thrust into a keenly competitive society, exposed to the gibes and contempt of the worst scallywags in Australian society, invited to learn how to swear and drink, and expected to earn a living as best they might. Continuing, Bonwick quotes further eulogies of the Aboriginal—his intensity of life, his carefree freedom, his exemption from disease in the natural state, his integrity in refusing to cultivate—and yet is forced to conclude (Bonwick, *op. cit.*, p. 84): "But all this fine sentiment does not satisfy the Christian man; for he looks upon his dark brother as one possessed of a kindred soul, and an heir to immortality. He sighs, therefore, at the native gliding away without a sign."

Bonwick wrote in the early sixties of the last century. The main lineaments of the problem were as clear then as they were to Las Casas in the sixteenth century, or even to some anthropologists today. Is integrity simply the product of an educational training program? May different cultures and normative moralities coexist within the same polity without that minimum substratum of common values and allegiances capable of engendering mutual respect? Given the mutual respect, may individuals move from one ambience to another without loss of integrity? Although some white Australians have acted as though the only solution was the complete destruction of Aboriginal culture, and even of Aborigines, more generally and at the level of official policy this was never a practical proposition.

Nevertheless, particularly where and when a population seems clearly demarcated, such a course has always had a semblance of realism and, viewed as euthanasia, can even be made to seem ethical. In condemning the rounding up, capture, exile, and so the eventual disappearance of the Tasmanians, for example, it should be remembered that if this operation seems little different from the attempted destruction of the Jews in Europe by the Nazis, both are grounded in the same framework of assumptions as legalized abortion or the expulsion of Palestinian Arabs from their home-land. To leave peoples such as Australian Aborigines strictly and severely alone in reserved lands may be convenient for a while — especially when it is thought that the population is declining fast and will soon disappear. But eventually time runs out, as it now has, and the problem has to be faced. Besides, with an increasing Aboriginal population occupying lands with rich mineral deposits, the problems demand a solution. Yet forcibly to induct the Aborigines into a European ambience seems as distasteful and immoral as to leave them alone on restricted reserves with supple-mentary feeding arrangements as a kind of living museum, or zoo, for tourists to visit and for anthropologists to study. Inexorably, the problem is and always has been how the Aborigines can become one with our-selves. The alternatives involve losses of integrity on both hands.

For Christian missionaries the major question has always been how far Christian principles can or could be expressed in different cultural idioms. In general, missionaries from southern and mediterranean Europe, where diverse cultural forms and normative moralities exist in some profusion, have usually laid the emphasis on the principles, allowing varieties of cultural expression to take care of themselves. On the other hand, missionaries from northern Europe, where at least since the Reformation there has been a much tighter fit between principle, cultural expression, and normative morality, have usually insisted that their charges become Europeans as well as Christians. Again in general terms, the less formal the theology and the more evangelical the missionary, the greater the insistence that Aborigines should become temperate, nonsmoking, sexually inhibited, work-addicted Europeans for whom happiness is a starched white shirt on Sundays. Nevertheless, whatever the emphases none has met with much success in relation to Australian Aborigines. For

Christian Church organizations have been, and are, geared to the settled life, and are ill-suited to the nomadic habits of a hunting and gathering people. Since it was always foreseeable that the conditions which made possible a nomadic hunting and gathering way of life must at some time cease to exist, as they now have, the greater effort has gone not into adapting Christianity to the nomadic life, but into attempting to persuade the Aborigines to adopt a more settled way of life. Despite the formal antitheses, however, a solution to this particular problem is beginning to appear.

In the north of Western Australia some five mission stations belonging to the one missionary order (Roman Catholic Pallotine Mission) are grouped within reasonable nomadic walking or trucking distance of each other—from seventy to several hundred miles apart—among groups who, for nearly a century at least, have interacted with each other and traveled to each other's ceremonies. In much the same way as the indigenous pastoral nomads of Cyrenaica (see Evans-Pritchard, 1951) order their movements in relation to particular holy sites or shrines which house members of the religious order of the Sanusiya, so the Pallotine missions have become the fixed points between which the Aborigines may "go walkabout," visit kin and friends in the bush, or at a cattle ranch or sheep station or township or other mission station, reside for a while, engage in ceremonies and make transactions, and return again to the home mission. Though much remains to be done to realize the full advantages of the situation, there is little doubt that if this kind of pattern had been more general in Australia, many of the difficulties in the missionary endeavor might have been solved. But there has been no such general patterning. Even if sectarian rivalries had been overcome—and let there be no mistake, sectarian rivalry has had much to do with the missionary failure in Australia—not until relatively recently has it been possible to give such mission stations the necessary logistic support. Financial aid from the central and State governments, roads, and more efficient motor, air, and sea transport have made a world of difference.

It is necessary to stress the missionary effort. Despite mistakes, the crippling effect of sectarian rivalries, and a variety of peculiar attitudes and activities resulting from the frustrations and irritations of a lonely life in the outback without the active support of one's fellows, it has been the missionaries who have actually applied themselves to the practical problems of embracing the Aborigines as brothers. Poorly financed, having to live with the consequences of their mistakes, these missionaries should not be judged in their failure but in the enormous task they set themselves in devoting their lives to the service of their fellow men. Indeed, it is often convenient to forget that had it not been for the work of Christian missionaries, it is doubtful whether Australian Aborigines would have survived into the present.

Anthropologists, like Lord John Russell, only much more so than he, have done most of the talking and exhorting, have indulged their propensities for waxing morally indignant, have grappled with the problem at the intellectual or "theoretical" level only. Albeit for very different reasons, anthropologists along with administrative officials, ranchers, prospectors, mining companies, and the owners or managers of sheep stations have been the loudest critics of the missionary effort—this in spite of the hospitality afforded to them in the field by missionaries. To be fair, anthropologists have not hesitated to criticize their fellow critics. But these can hit back. Missionaries have to suffer in silence, are the easiest game. Always able to withdraw from the personal rancors of the field into the comparative quiet and security of their university posts, and given over to science, anthropologists have generally been strangely blind to the features of the situation as a whole. Shift the point of view into Xavier Herbert's perspective and the crusading self-image of the anthropologist fearlessly putting his finger on fault turns into the less noble building of academic reputations on the patience and kindness of others, a swallowing of financial grants and bursaries that might have been used by others to more purpose.

There is of course another side, a side which missionaries, government officials, and a variety of business and other interests have been coming to appreciate more keenly: the showing forth and analysis of the lineaments of the contact situation. Yet the standpoint generally taken has hardly been objective. The contact situation, especially on the reserve or mission station, has much in common with a prison. Most of us are familiar with the growing literature on prison life—how prisoners or detainees fight against and rise above the cruelties and asininities of prison or concentration or work camp rules and routines. But what of those cardboard figures, the commandant and his men? We know quite a lot about Aborigines in the contact situation, but we know very little about the missionaries and others involved in the same situation. Without the powers of a prison commandant, they too have to rise above difficulties—difficulties which are inherent in the situation and which the situation never fails to produce. Yet anthropologists have so far failed to provide a model of the total situation. In analyzing the situation from, for the most part, an Aboriginal point of view, anthropologists have failed to convince those most actively involved. Hence, intellectual appreciation of the contact situation has come only slowly. It is possible that it might have come the more swiftly had anthropological writing on the subject appeared less stuffed with moral indignation and political bias and rather more humble and painstaking in the face of the total situation. Bias of this kind was scarcely likely to breed confidence. Moreover, even if the contact situation be excepted, the general status of anthropology as a subject has not been such as to inspire the confidence of laymen. Old bones, monkeys, and varieties of savage esoterica were one thing. But a scientific knowledge of culture combined with political bias was asking too much.

Until the late twenties of this century anthropology as such was the hobby of amateurs, the leisure interest of those — including missionaries, soldiers, sailors, explorers, doctors, academics, and administrative officials — whose means of livelihood and professional appointments entailed a full day's work aside from their anthropological researches. Professional anthropologists could be counted on one's fingers and thumbs. Interests were purely intellectual, centered on the relevance of the data to history, evolutionary theory, diffusionist constructs, and what was to become known as functionalist theory. Work specifically and systematically directed toward the analysis of the contact situation — topics of "acculturation," "social change," and "applied anthropology" as they came to be known — only got started in the early thirties when, with the professionalization of the subject and the demise of the wealthy sojourner, financial support from foundations and government or university bodies became more readily available. Ten years of work by a handful of professionals, and the Second World War had begun to engage their attentions. Not until the late forties and early fifties, as more funds became available and governments applied themselves to postwar reconstruction and attempts to head off possible consequences of the cold war, did it become possible to send swelling numbers of trained, but only budding professionals into the field. Now, there are few universities which do not have their departments or schools of anthropology and/or sociology or social science. Nevertheless, given that in 1948 full-time professional anthropologists the world over numbered only a few hundreds, twenty-five years is not an overly long period in which to produce the numbers of interacting professionals required to generate significant advances.

During this period of professionalization, however, all those amateurs whose contributions had laid the basis for the profession were eased out onto the sidelines. Often excluded from professional discussion, they were in any case hardly able to keep up with professional requirements. If latter-day professionals have often been overcritical of their amateur forebears, it is hardly surprising to find criticism and opposition concentrated in the ranks of those whom they have shouldered aside. But it was not always thus. Before the First World War the interactions and interrelations of anthropologists, administrative officials, and missionaries were nothing if not harmonious in relation to anthropology. They had their differences, of course, both politically and intellectually. There was always that gulf between intellectual appreciation and practical experience and political considerations. But there was no doubt in their minds that, as educated men with a common substratum in educational background, each could be an equal partner in an intellectual enterprise. They corresponded with one another. Missionaries and administrative officials wrote treatises which are still authoritative ethnographies, tended to be anthropologists at heart. The missionary and social reformer were built into the being of an anthropologist (see Glynn Cochrane, 1970). After the war, however, in spite of the fact that colonial administrations had begun to finance professional field research, and were beginning to appoint "government anthropologists," a significant difference becomes noticeable.

Bronislaw Malinowski, that pioneer of professionalism, draws the divide. When he published his *Argonauts of the Western Pacific* (1922) and *The Sexual Life of Savages in North-Western Melanesia* (1929) few readers would have supposed that the Trobriand islands had been quietly and reasonably administered for many years, or that missionaries had been active in the islands for about the same time, or that there was a mission station on Kiriwina. Still, those who might have been offended at the break with tradition held their peace. The Trobrianders were allowed to become an image of the noble savage although, as became evident with the publication of Malinowski's diaries after his death (Malinowski, 1967), this image was quite at variance with Malinowski's private thoughts about the Trobriand islanders when in personal contact with them. If, at an intellectual level, Malinowski might have seemed to some the best kind of enlightened missionary and social reformer, at the practical and political levels he would have made an impossible missionary and a worse administrative officer.

Take the case of Mr. Rentoul. In 1931 a Mr. Rentoul, an administrative officer in the Trobriands, wrote to *Man* (Rentoul, 1931). Following tradition, wishing to participate in the enterprise of anthropology, but puzzled at some of Malinowski's assertions in *The Sexual Life of Savages*, he queried Malinowski's findings with some evidence of his own. Having spent much of his time as a magistrate deciding paternity cases in the Trobriands, and well aware that the Trobrianders knew precisely the how and why of the advantages of introducing prize boars into the Trobriands, he questioned whether the Trobrianders really were ignorant of the role of the male in human procreation. Malinowski's reply was over four pages long (Malinowski, 1932). Pronouncing shortly but, presumably, sincerely on the urgent need for cooperation between anthropologists and administrative officers, the professor then indulged at length his not inconsiderable gifts for putting people in their places. Poor Rentoul! His honest queries were hardly met, but the message was clear. The amateur trespassed on the complexities and subtleties of the professional preserve at his peril.

Today, after nearly half a century, the wheel has begun to come full circle. Not only do missionaries and administrative officials take courses in anthropology as part of their preparatory or "refresher" training, but they maintain the interest, write to the professional journals and even, in many cases, resign their posts to become professional anthropologists. The journal *Anthropos*, published by the missionary Society of the Divine Word, for long an invaluable source which, during the period of professionalization, had fallen into some decay, has become once again professionally respectable. Yet this developing rapprochement between those who write about and intellectualize a situation, and those who have to deal purposefully with people on the ground, is more the result of a common growing familiarity with ethnographic situations than the consequence of any particular scientific know-how. In fact the situation remains much as it was in the days of Las Casas. If a given moral and intellectual statement can be translated into political aspirations and action, difficulties arise when competing political courses are derived from numbers of different intellectual and moral statements based upon diverse assumptions. Moreover, since the most general assumption, only rarely questioned despite the persistent evidence to the contrary, is that the people concerned will consent to whatever is being prepared for them, further difficulties arise when they prove recalcitrant and refuse to do what is thought good for them. Force? Attempts at persuasion through parleys and reasoning? Indirect persuasion through economic measures or the provision of prizes? Or back to the drawing board?

The missionary effort in Australia has been generally characterized by the underlying assumption that the Aborigines are a collection of individuals each of whom, severally and individually, might be persuaded to enter the Christian ambience with or without European appurtenances.

Remaining on the mission in close relations with his pagan kinsfolk, however, the willing convert can hardly give expression to his Christianity without appearing to have lost rather than deepened the integrity of his cultural heritage. Becoming a black European as well as a Christian is no solution. The convert is alienated from his own, becomes the servant or follower of the resident missionary. If there happens to be a European, nominally Christian community close at hand, he has to steer a path between sectarian rivalries before, if at all, he can be welcomed into the homes of those with whom he is in communion. Even where it is possible, as with some mission organizations it is, to send a convert away to a training school in the city, he is hard put to it when his training has been completed to survive in a world where "Aboriginal" has become synonymous with "work-shy," "lazy," "no sense of time," "given to drink," "quarrelsome," "dirty," "rowdy," "thriftless," and so on. Sooner or later these prognostications become self-fulfilling, and the convert walks straight into his stereotype.

The facts that within their own environments Aborigines work hard, are not lazy, have an acute sense of timing in relation to nomadic life, do not drink, and simply cannot afford to be too quarrelsome, rowdy or thriftless, hardly signify. A European who has "gone bush" gets much the same treatment. Consequently, accepting that differences in social nurture always put the stranger at a disadvantage, missionaries have generally resigned themselves to the idea of the long haul. They have sought, through succeeding generations of individuals, to create Christian communities on the station. As has been noted, where several stations of the same missionary organization are sited reasonably close to each other there exist the seeds of a quite new kind of community based on a blend of the nomadic life with the settled. Given the necessary initial financial support, protection from the more powerful and rapacious business interests, and the sort of governmental encouragement that succeeds in helping without being meddlesome, this type of missionary endeavor might, in time, realize Las Casas' dream: the gradual assimilation of those of another culture into the Christian rather than European fold.

Missions might become, then, and in some instances are becoming, the incubators of quite new sets of social institutions. Despite the fact that it will not be easy to obtain what seem to be the necessary conditions under which communities of this kind might prosper, dogged perseverance might see it through. Yet little realization of these possibilities is as yet to be found in anthropological monographs. Paradoxically, perhaps, most of the criticisms of the missionary effort on the parts of anthropologists and administrative officials can be related to the assumption that these new communities are not European or white Australian enough. Behind the criticisms and assumption is the generalized Australian ideal of creating and maintaining in Australia a roughly homogeneous community with a common substratum of values and beliefs. Thus migrants from Europe are not only encouraged to become Australians, involved in the Australian way of life, as soon as possible, but there are also all sorts of pressures discouraging them from forming "quarters" in cities, or clubs and coteries based on common country of origin. Although implementation of this ideal has not been entirely successful, the ideal itself exists and is expressed in a multitude of ways. In neither case, however, have anthropologists been able to give much of a lead. Their descriptions and analyses have drawn attention to the existence of social problems, and remain as valuable historiographies. But their intellectualizations of the problem in relation to a variety of theoretical constructs have only served to widen the gulf between themselves and those who might wish to enter an informed program of action.

In the Aboriginal field anthropologists have, unlike missionaries, tended to neglect the individual and what can be done through him. Instead, Aborigines have verged on becoming a collection of so many interrelated categories and groups imbued with organic or even organismic lives of their own (for a notable exception to this see Stanner, 1960). On this level of the collective, culture tends to become not simply an abstraction referring to a melange of artifacts, traits, thoughts, and activities, but a solid lump of stuff with form and boundaries. Which is precisely what culture is not. Though "social structure" is merely an abstract analytical mode ideally in some sort of correspondence with the concrete reality, the latter tends to drop out of sight and concreteness becomes ascribed to the mode. Similarly, horde, local group, kinship system, section and subsection systems, totemism and so on very quickly become "things" which can be manipulated.

There is no doubt that within the profession, among those familiar with the idiom of discourse, such manipulations can be meaningful. But for those outside the profession who are unfamiliar with the idiom it can only be confusing. Hence the desirability either that the laity read more, or that anthropologists write not for each other but for the public. Missionaries open themselves to criticism because they work in a context of action-reaction and do not generally publish the principles which guide them in their particular endeavors: the opportunities for mistakes are legion. Few missionaries have succeeded in intellectualizing their situation in an idiom acceptable to anthropologists at large. Indeed, this exclusiveness of the anthropological idiom, born out of the workings of the professionally transcultural mind, is in itself an initiatory hurdle which a tyro has to master if he is to enjoy collegial relations. But the price is a certain isolation, an inability to convince outsiders. Although any profession is bound to produce its own specialized idiom of discourse, few have been so incomprehensible as the anthropological. It is not so much the meaning of the words as their differing contexts of relevance related to varying ethnographic situations.

Anthropologists, then, have not been able to provide viable alternatives acceptable to those actually involved in attempting to bridge the gap between ourselves and the "other." They have tended to talk to themselves. They have competed to deduce or adduce so-called "laws" of change or acculturation, much of it a plethora of eclectic and particularist special pleading. They have failed to appreciate that changes in a social order are not simply a question of circumstance but of defined political action. Nevertheless, allowing for point of view, their descriptions and analyses of the contact situation stand. They reveal more or less what the situation is or is like. Less on the specific merits of their professional work and more in virtue of current friendships, kin ties, or past childhood, school or university acquaintance, they have been able to persuade governments and administrations to dig into their treasuries, undertake programs of welfare, supplementary food supply, schooling, training and the like, finance research, and bring into existence bodies such as the Australian Institute for Aboriginal Studies. Though it could be argued that it is through anthropologists that the Australian public, concentrated in the large cities where only a few Aborigines live out of sight and mind, has been made aware that a problem exists, a better case could be made in favor of more popular authors who have not been professional anthropologists. Bates (1938–1949), Durack (1969), Hasluck (1942), Idreiss (1963), Marshall (1948), Moorehead (1966), Simpson (1951), and many others too numerous to mention here have probably had more impact on the general public than have anthropologists. On the whole anthropologists have failed to reach, let alone convince, the bulk of the laity.

2   A REFORMER'S SCIENCE

Like Plato, like Montesquieu, Comte, St. Simon and many others who have attempted, in intellectual vein, to build ideal societies founded upon the supposed "natural laws" of society or culture, many anthropological accounts of other worlds have a dream-like or mythical quality. The praxis of political action, of human ambitions, interests, envies, enmities, and loyalties are not so much absent as taken for granted: contingencies whose consequences are subsumed in the general construct. Habitually eliciting consistency, order, and logic from the messy empirical reality, it is tempting to conclude that the imposition of consistency, order, and logic will somehow result in a corresponding empirical reality. Although anthropologists claim to be social scientists, they can hardly be said to have convinced others that they have exposed the realities on which a program of social planning might be thought out and implemented.

Partly, the dilemma arises from the contradiction contingently expressed in Tylor's phrase, "a reformer's science" (Tylor, 1871–1958, p. 539). Reform and social planning cannot but spring from defined political aims. But, on one view of the meaning of science, anthropological findings must be set out without fear or favor, irrespective of political bias. The discoverable principles upon which a culture or social order rests are to be regarded as existing as independently of political bias as the principle that at a fixed temperature the pressure of a confined ideal gas varies inversely with its volume. The fact that no culture or social order could have a form other than that given by the traditional or dominant but foreign politico-religious ideology has tended to be brushed aside. Suppressing rather than unaware of the way in which political prejudices inevitably informed their analyses, anthropologists have been wont to sheer away from working out, detailing, and publishing the implications of a particular political involvement. As politically involved human beings they have done what they thought they ought to do. As scientists they have sought to assume a position above the noise of political battle. On the other hand, the overriding rationale of anthropology or sociology at least since the eighteenth century has been precisely in its applicability to political concerns.

Radcliffe-Brown (1931b), for example, held that while it was necessary for a scientist to pursue knowledge for its own sake, the value of science lay in its applicability, and that one ought to look forward to the time when the government and education of native peoples would make some approach to being an art based on the application of the laws of society or culture as discovered by anthropological science. Today, in a way that Radcliffe-Brown might have deplored and fought against, more and more anthropological works, no less systematic in their analyses of what are considered to be the significant realities of social life, are beginning to be more explicit in their adoption of political standpoint.

Nevertheless, the dilemma of "a reformer's science" is a real one. It is not wholly resolved by giving a meaning to "science" that is consistent with particular reformist attitudes, ideals, or action programs. For though no political ideology worthy of the name is not built upon the significance of perceived realities, and, in much the same way, no anthropological theory is not built on the perceived significances of certain kinds of data, what remains is scholarly doubt or scientific skepticism. Has all the data available been adequately accounted for? Is there not something there which, more or less usefully accounted for or interpreted in the terms of a political ideology, cannot be more fully accounted for in terms that are currently nonpolitical? Allowing that this doubt or skepticism can be used as an excuse, or even as a mask, for an outward posture of noninvolvement in political bias, without this doubt and skepticism the investigatory process would be rendered nugatory. There do exist those kinds of reality which a political ideology can afford to ignore or dismiss, but which an anthropological analysis must accommodate. It is an awareness of just this which on the one hand tends to emasculate any radical political bias in published anthropological works—though, ironically, alignment with a conservative or *status quo* position has been found generally acceptable—and on the other hand, tends to bring those who carry their politics into their analyses into some professional disrepute. The gap between observed behaviors, or direct experiences, and their intellectualization is a very real one. Though this gap may be bridged by the explicit resort to political ideology, it is precisely the aim of anthropology that data and intellectualization might so join hands as to make the political bridge unnecessary.

For administrative officials the bridge between the realities of the situation and that intellectualization which can contain them and their interrelations without distortion is largely contained in their roles and is, in a sense, prefabricated. Bound to implement policies which they may or may not have had a hand in formulating, and which, as often as not, go against the grain of their experience and personal views, administrative officials are nonetheless caught in a situation whose significant realities are determined by the administrative role. Aware of the discrepancies between the realities of experience and the realities brought into focus by an administrative policy, administrations have often turned to anthropologists for advice: What are the "scientific" or "objective" realities that current policies do not but should recognize? What changes in policy would bring about such recognition? Anthropologists, only too well aware of the different kinds of human misery which follow in the wake of piecemeal change, interested in spite of themselves in maintaining the culture as it is, and in any case wary and distrustful of interests lying behind adminis-trative policies, have tended to be conservative or, boxed in by the circumstances of the situation, have had to be satisfied with a variety of ameliorative measures. No more or less than others, anthropologists cannot be political arbiters.

A missionary who did not seek quite deliberately to bring about certain kinds of change – in the customary procedures of day-to-day living as well as in awareness or consciousness – would be failing in his office. But as missionaries themselves have been well aware, it is extremely difficult if not impossible in practice and on the ground to separate Christian values and principles from the ethnocentric and political expressions in terms of which particular missionaries must almost inevitably view those values and principles. In order to obtain that wider and more comprehensive view of the realities of the situation, missionaries, too, have had recourse both to anthropology and to anthropologists. On both hands, the personal contacts – which force the anthropologist to abandon his technical vocabulary and explain his perceptions of the reality in the terms of ordinary language – have been more valuable than recourse to published works.

Classically, missionaries have always identified themselves with the indigenous peoples against administrators and commercial interests. Anthropologists have identified themselves with an indigenous people against administrators, commercial interests, and missionaries. The struc-ture of the situation is such that in the interests of self-identification each of the European categories must stand in opposition to the others. Their common concern in or for the indigenous people is, nevertheless, com-petitive, and their diverse interests are opposed. Yet they are inter-dependent for a variety of services. Further, the indigenous people them-selves make their own varying contributions to a total field of competing interests within overlapping spheres of quite differently perceived reali-ties. Deceptively easy to understand on the surface, the realities projected by business and commercial interests seem in closest correspondence with those of the simple culture in question. But of course they are not as easy to understand as they seem. Antithetical instead of mutually advan-tageous, disruptive, skewing the entire environment, this is the field in which developments take place most rapidly, leaving anthropologists, administrative officials, and missionaries panting behind. Nevertheless, it is precisely in this field of realities determined by economic interests but abetted by missionary teaching that, paradoxically, a simple people is both most at a loss and also retains its most telling initiative: popular but either sporadic and disorganized or more concerted activities directed toward taking control of their own affairs.

Attempting to understand these activities, and attempting to analyze the multidimensional fields they project within a single conceptual framework, involves difficulties which anthropologists have not yet mastered. It requires the capacities of a dramatist, a subtle and sophisticated acquaintance of the relations between what is said and what is done, the ability to intellectualize and fix the movement of the drama within the terms of a few pertinent coordinates. Although work has certainly started on this problem, most of it is as yet between the covers of doctoral theses. Under the unimaginative rubric "social change" we can hope for little that is new or even particularly informative. An abstraction and application of some of Victor Turner's (1957, 1959) ideas on schism and continuity, on *communitas* and structure and anti-structure might yield much better results.

Thus far, however, anthropologists have tried to deal with the situation in a series of diadic relations: a linear and mythical technique which, without the subtlety of true myth, can only handle gross pairs (such as white versus black, imperialism versus subject peoples, money economy versus subsistence economy, and the like), rarely goes to the interplay of principle involved, and cannot grasp the complexities of the interrelationships as a whole. The activities or movements on which anthropologists have concentrated their attention have been called a variety of names: millenarian, adjustment, nativistic, messianic, revitalization and many others (see Burridge, 1969, for a general review, and R. M. Berndt, 1962, for an Aboriginal example). But whatever the name the basic underlying assumption of the analytic viewpoint has for the most part been entirely ethnocentric and even subjectively parental or paternal. The question has not been "What are the lineaments of the situation as a whole?" but "Where did we go wrong, how did we fail them?" The simple fact that human beings assert themselves from time to time, and that, as in a dramatic performance, the contact situation is one in which the actors are forced to assert themselves and play out their roles, express their selves, has received little notice. Moreover, the general conclusion has not been, as it might have been, "Let them go their own way"—for that would have been virtually impossible in the political circumstances obtaining—but redoubled efforts to make them come our way. The participatory values have won out and, in spite of a gallant if naive attempt to give the story a happy ending, the inevitabilities of tragedy keep insisting their truths.

In the Australian situation three main positions have emerged, though they have always been implicit. The first (let them go their own way) seems the most ethical or charitable but actually entails varieties of apartheid: leaving the Aborigines alone in strictly demarcated reserves to fend for themselves with or without a supervisory apparatus responsible for medical treatment and the supply of supplementary foodstuffs. Although, before 1940, this kind of situation actually obtained in a negative and existential way in the remoter areas — Europeans could do little to develop them at the time — the positive and rigid application of such a policy has never stood much chance of acceptance or success in Australia. Even if it were not for the fact that ranging animals require large regeneration or resuscitation areas, thus forcing the Aborigines into the European settled areas to find food, the mere presence of white folk in an Aboriginal ambience entails interaction. Interaction once started proliferates and deepens, implicates and draws in others. For very different reasons neither missionaries nor government, nor employers of labor nor mining companies could entertain the idea of leaving both land and people alone. It has always been possible, in Australia, to toy with the idea of confining Aborigines to reserves, even to imagine briefly the finality of the Tasmanian solution. Yet both these avenues have been in the nature of an escape from the very real problems posed by the two alternatives: assimilation and/or integration. The first, absorption into the greater Australian community, has never taken the form of a positive action program, though, as with European immigrant groups entering Australia, there have always been a number of overt and less explicit constraints. Given the Australian political situation, its ambience of individual choice, and the more subtle pressures to conform to a generalized Australian way of life, it is difficult to envisage the idea or implementation of any systematic program with assimilation as its end. Nevertheless, assimilation remained official policy until quite recently. Now, with a change of the central government, a new outlook is giving further stimulus to integration and the creation of what will be culturally distinct communities within the greater homogeneity.

It might be thought that, whether committed to integration or assimilation, anthropologists would be invaluable in implementing a program. Perhaps they could be. But scholarly doubt has a tendency to become an academic fetish rather than a technique of discovering the truth. Beyond this is the very human risk of putting one's money on the wrong horse. Behind the latter is the moral and intellectual background against which a decision that need not be made is expected to be made. On what grounds other than personal choice or political commitment may an anthropologist decide between integration and assimilation? Of themselves, his books and his learning can tell him nothing. Like any man faced with his myth, the myth can delineate but cannot decide. He has to decide for himself. That is the essence of moral problem. On the other hand, learning will surely enable him to rationalize the decision with greater or lesser dexterity if it does not, as it usually does, simply push him into expounding and refining his learning.

In a recent publication (Taft, Dawson, and Beasley, 1970) dealing generally with problems of assimilation, the thrust is not so much toward telling the reader about assimilation and how the problems might be resolved as about developments in sociology and how sociological as distinct from social problems might be resolved. Thus we learn that (pp. 116–117) "The study has also provided a certain amount of evidence to support Secord and Blackman's (1964) modification of exchange theory as a theory of inter-group relations . . . The lack of a device for measuring dissonance places certain limitations on the use of Festinger's (1957) theory of cognitive dissonance as a theory of attitude organization." A neat piece of academica, perhaps. But scarcely grist to the mill of a politician charged with initiating policies, and hardly the spur to action for a missionary, welfare worker, or government official.

By contrast, consider Schapper (1970) who boldly commits himself to a plan or program for integration. Sometime, maybe, some parts of the plan may find their way into the governmental machine, find favor, and be implemented. But one cannot be sanguine about it, well argued and persuasive as the statement is. Yet this is beside the point. What is of interest here is that to formulate the program, Schapper (an economist) is forced to commit himself to a point of view about human beings: ". . . human talent, ability, and potential is the most precious resource, from which follows the preference for a social order which reduces to a minimum, needless human suffering and degradation; which avoids human waste; and which stresses the development or utilisation of human resources" (p. xiv). As a view or assumption about the nature and purpose of human life, seriously proposed, one may well pause. In a familiar and contemporary entrepreneurial idiom it seems to echo the pleas of Montesinos and Las Casas. People, not structures, systems, and organizations, or orders are to be integrated, assimilated, converted, or whatever. And people make choices, have political ends to gain. On the other hand, the plan advanced also reflects John Major. For it is taken for granted that Aborigines will agree to the plan—they are merely a resource—or will have to accede to some sort of plan invented by others if they are to be "utilized," "not wasted" and so on. Plato would have smiled. Many a slaver would have cheered. Mining and business interests today could hardly do less. In like vein did Colonel George Arthur set about gathering up the Tasmanians.

Fortunately for the Australian Aborigines, however, and in the end more fortunately for ourselves, Aborigines dream. Always a source of inspiration for the formulation of new songs, dances, ritual, and other procedures, the dreams of Aborigines are now beginning to project a future as well as an ever-present past (see Tonkinson, 1972). Plans hatched in the universities or in government offices will have to run the gauntlet of Aboriginal dreaming. Perhaps the life that seems to one a wasted and unutilized human resource may be to another a life of fulfillment.

At bottom, the Christian missionary is concerned with man's spirit, man's soul; and that in whatever ambience of circumstances the person may find himself the soul, the spirit, shall be nourished, grow, and reach into God through the hearts of others. Prototypically, as with Christ and St. Paul, this concern for the spirit and soul of man has cut through the boundaries of political and moral orders, penetrated cultural exclusivisms, and held the soul worth more than the world. But the secular missionary, eclectic or doctrinaire, cannot but take departure from an extreme and narrow ethnocentricity: his own social circumstances further narrowed by his own egocentric view of them. If an intellect as broad as Plato's had to resort to the idea of physical force to keep reality in conformity with an intellectual ideal, what may we say of the missionary ideals which spring from the secular and highly specialized but usually spiritually impoverished intellectual background of today's academic?

It is true of course that only a relatively few missionaries have actually succeeded in communicating nourishment to the soul. Still, it remains an ideal, at the back of every religious missionary's mind. But the secular planner of other peoples' lives must needs become coercive, a serjeant-major with his triple stripes of expertise shouting, bullying, chivvying his charges into line. Yet this is not because a planner is by nature some sort of serjeant-major. It is because the contact situation makes particular kinds of demands on the participants. Just as Australian Aborigines must appear to be habitual drunkards, lazy, and shiftless to maintain their integrity over against those who insist they should be sober, hardworking, and frugal, so the drama demands that apparent aimlessness, uncertainty, and helplessness be met by carefully disciplined plans for progress. So far as a hand is held out to the soul the response is, as it always must be, positive: different kinds of human beings engage and cooperate. But so far as that hand, aware of the power behind it, curls to coerce, so far must the response be negative: an oppositional debate with integrity as prize.

If anthropologists have not on the whole been very impressive in their analyses of, and their inferences from, the contact situation, it is because Tylor was confused. Anthropologists may be missionaries and reformers, but neither ethnology nor social or cultural anthropology are a reformer's science. They were born out of a reach for otherness, an impulse to seize on the strange, a desire to fill in the detail of an ambience beyond or aside from the "here-now" and familiar. Though it is true that a reformer's vision of what might be, and the realization of an otherness that was, or is, or in imagination might be, spring from the same source, the lines of projection diverge. While the reformer develops the home ambience in his mind until it becomes an otherness, the anthropologist is presented with otherness, goes out to find it, is set the task of making that otherness intelligible. What an anthropologist says of his otherness may be grist to the mill of the reformer, whether in himself or another. "Reform" cannot exist in a vacuum but is a relation between what is and a positive idea of what might be. What emasculates the reformer in an anthropologist is the sure knowledge that reform will drain out the virtues and ideals of Aboriginal life as well as the disadvantages, and that these virtues may go for ever. Can the peculiar freedoms and warmths of Aboriginal life be separated from the constraints and hardships that go with them? We can learn, perhaps, what types of constraint are necessary to what types of freedom or warmth. The experience of otherness teaches us much about ourselves. But when that otherness has gone, from whom shall we learn?

The ways in which Aborigines accompany us into the future is partly in their hands, not in ours alone. Since a European cannot transform himself into an Aborigine, it is for the latter to work out and insist upon the kind of accommodation he is willing to make. Europeans will surely help best not by pressing their views but by extending a welcome. Yet a "mutual accommodation" would be entirely misleading and illusory if it did not imply, on both hands, the realization of that resolve, present in millennarian movements, to enter into a new life, new kinds of relationships pervaded by quite different qualities.

3 THE CONTACT SITUATION

Man's transformation is essentially a religious act and experience: a new perception of reality or the truth of things accompanied by a movement toward realizing the perception in action joined to a deeper under-standing of social relationships. It requires and entails a quite new integration of the levels of being. Hitherto constrained in a particular ambience of social relationships and categories of understanding, the new and burgeoning awareness of the relations between the animal, cultural, moral, and spiritual bursts its banks like a stream in spate and seeks new boundaries. Destructive unless supplied with these boundaries, the new awareness demands political shape. Within the normally functioning community this shape is already there: transformation involves move-ment from one well-defined field of awareness into another as well defined. The crisis of the self becoming other is met and surmounted by providing the individual with a framework of action and understanding that is pitched at the level of the collective. If the crisis seems necessary, if each individual has to meet that crisis by the exercise of qualities that inhere uniquely in himself, the instruction and support of friends and kinsfolk as well as the myths and procedures of his community carry him through. Once launched, the neophyte is gathered into a series of ritual activities and rites of passage which are the vehicle of his transformation. The drama of the vehicle takes command. Participants become actors constrained in their parts. The myth, necessarily an unfolding in linear time, is given expression in space. The spatial expressions in pictures or carvings flow into successive events.

The same basic configuration describes the contact situation. An initial chaos of new understandings and new social relationships quickly be-comes ordered in relation to crisis, and is successively reordered in relation to further crises. But the final climax to the drama is not known; many of the actors assume the additional roles of producers and directors. Continually giving directions and not wholly aware of their parts in an improvised drama, they give support and direction, try to steer a situation that has already enfolded them. In spite of their ministrations the play moves on. Others take up position, speak their parts. The would-be direc-tors are forced to become actors or make an exit. If we were to use our eyes we would see that the transformation we speak of is for people, not cultures. It takes place at the level of individuals who can seize the relations between one idea and another, who can perceive the conse-quences of certain kinds of social relationships, whose awarenesses can reach toward, grasp and rationalize experiences which could not be so comprehended within the terms the home ambience had supplied. It does not take place at that level where, for example, for intellectual or scientific purposes, cultures are regarded as "functioning wholes." If cultures can indeed change or be transformed into different kinds of cultures or social orders it is because people have been, or are being transformed, and seek to shape an appropriate ambience for their new awareness.

Were the ghosts of Tylor and M'Lennan to visit the United Nations they would see there the descendants of those whom they called "savages" — men and women as able as any the world has to show, as or more sophisticated than were Tylor and M'Lennan themselves. Ethnologists and anthropologists did not provide the frameworks of their transformations. Their task was and is to inform the home ambience of particular kinds of otherness, to expound the meanings and relevance of otherness. Missionaries, government officials, traders, and merchants supplied the transformational frameworks. These are and were the people who, acting out their own several parts, have also tried to lend support as well as direct the course of events: a crucial ambivalence and ambiguity of role which is as necessary to the transformational framework as it is to the development and resolution of a play. Corresponding with that resolution of basic paradox or contradiction essential to myth, movement from one kind of being to another, becoming what one is not, requires the ambiguous element.

The drama, in truth, is the best working model we have of the relations between the diachrony and the synchrony. Characters, situations, roles, normative modes, and underlying principles mesh together; people who represent principle demonstrate the mutual interaction of principle and character. Whether it is a Javanese *wayang*, a Greek tragedy, *Hamlet*, or a mother's brother severing the foreskin of his sister's son to induct him into manhood, ambiguity and paradox are the essence of what makes for change or transformation whether these take place on the surface or at that deeper level of awareness connoted by metanoia. Yet it is precisely ambiguity that is anathema to science. The data has to be laid straight, either one thing or the other, but not both at the same time. The fruitful literary device of anomalous justaposition is either eschewed or, when used, laid aside by the reader as a misprint at best, an unnecessary and unscientific flourish at worst. But if investigation must entail laying out the properties of that which is ambiguous in order to explain why it is ambiguous, not to return those properties to their essential ambiguity in the situation only obscures the realities of that situation. It is apt to lead into models, theories, and plans whose only concession to the situation as it is resides in the cautious designation, "tentative" or "provisional." The fact that the crisis to be found in any transformation is the resolution of paradox, contradiction, or ambiguity, and that a transformation cannot take place unless the crisis is encountered, challenged and overcome is not so much forgotten as neutered.

Indeed, such are the conditions of life in Western society today that that personal sense of crisis – even threat – so necessary to transformation and the development of awareness tends to be shifted into areas outside the individual's capacity to come to grips with it in a personal way. If some can so arrange or structure their environments that a crisis can be defined, recognized, and overcome, most environments are so loose and flexible that trivial and transient crises have to be fabricated. Otherwise, transformations have to depend on the procedures of mental hospitals or commitment to one or other of a number of readily available cults or political or quasi-political ideologies. Accepting that a pubertal circumcision under traditional conditions provided the transformation of boy into young manhood with a context of anticipatory anxiety, fear, pain, shock, and crisis – all of which had to be appropriately overcome – one may well consider whether the rite did not achieve more than the surgical operation under anaesthetic.

Turning the pages of any anthropological work on Australian Aborigines should make us at once aware of the element of crisis in their lives. The presence of ritual should alert us to crisis. Birth, puberty, marriage, initiations, and death are called "life crises." But the content and meaning of "crisis" is so much taken for granted that in spite of the detailed richness of the ethnography it is not always easy to grasp what, precisely, goes into the nature of these crises. The academic desideratum of fit and logical consistency in explication tends to obscure the realities of contradiction and ambiguity. Perhaps, again, the Aborigines are too far away from us, so far that if we can recognize we cannot appreciate the crises in their lives. Or perhaps, like so many adults in relation to children, we have forgotten how real those crises can be, that defining and overcoming crises is what makes us ourselves. On the other hand, so soon as the situation is brought nearer to ourselves the element of dilemma can be clearly recognized and analyzed (see C. H. Berndt, 1962). If an Aborigine wants to transform himself he has to make a transition. Either he remains an Aboriginal within an ambience of mutual support, sharing and affection, or he has to forego these securities, become a "White Aboriginal" and enter into the conventions, forms of thought and organization of the competitive and open community. Lacking a specific transformational framework, however, this leap in awareness has, on the whole, been too difficult to achieve. The risks are great, the ties of the nestling environment too strong, too suffused with the warmth of given interpersonal relationships to sacrifice for a life among strangers so many of whom would be actively hostile. Still, real as they are such considerations are secondary. Just as there are those amongst ourselves who gladly sacrifice the warmths of particular companionships for the sweet smell of success, so are there Aborigines who would do the same if opportunity offered — and do when it does. Movement into a new organizational ambience demands a reordering and reintegration of the emotions This is precisely what is involved in the crisis of transformation. But such a reintegration can hardly take place unless new ways of thinking and discriminating are there to contain it.

When Père Lafitau drew attention to the relations between modes of thought and forms of social organization, he did so in the assumption that modes of thought formed systems from which flowed the systems implicit in the forms of social organization. About a century and a quarter later Marx asserted the reverse. Almost simultaneously, M'Lennan, approaching the same problem through totemism, took much the same view. For Tylor the relationship was generally one of independence: the evolution of forms of thought ran parallel with, but separate from, the evolution of forms of society. It was this standpoint combined with the psychic unity of mankind and a geneticist-evolutionary position that enabled Tylor to put himself into the head of primitive man, adduce his mode of thought, and allowed him to compare the intelligences of primitive men with those of children of various ages in his own culture. Frazer, in his later work, avoided any determined position on the question. For although he derived his trifold evolutionary forms of thought — Magic (mistaken views on natural laws of cause and effect), Religion (super-natural interference with natural laws of causality on request), and Science (correct views on natural laws of cause and effect) — from varied chunks of custom, he did so eclectically. Yet since he was clear that magical, religious, and scientific ways of thinking were to be found in most societies and in most human beings, so that societies and persons could be characterized by that mode which seemed to dominate, he leaned toward Tylor: differing views of the flight of the causal arrow could he held independently of the social or cultural matrix.

For this Durkheim (Durkheim and Mauss, 1903–1963) took Frazer to task: man's modes of thought, his logic, the ways in which he analogized, perceived difference and similarity, classified and discriminated, were derived from his social relationships, from the ways in which his society was organized. Lévy-Bruhl (1912–1926, 1922–1923), was not always as clear to some as he might have been, but his main thrust — that there are two main modes of thought, prelogical (or associational and participatory) and logical (subject to specific and articulated rules), associated generally and predominantly but not exclusively with nonliterate and literate societies respectively—indicates an interdependence leaning toward priority in cognition. From the twenties until the sixties of this century the major assumption informing the many empirical monographs touching on or focusing on the problem was one of interdependence: priorities, whether in time or in logic, were generally eschewed in the attempt to probe ever more deeply into the detail of the situation. Culture-pattern and other psychologically based studies, it is true, gave explicit priority to modes of child nurture. Yet since these could be derived either from the forms of society or from the modes of thought obtaining, interdependence must be taken to be implicit. With his *The Savage Mind* (1962b) and *Totemism* (1963), Lévi-Strauss forced the problem back into the structure of the human brain which, everywhere operating in the same way, has selected but a few of the almost infinite variety of permutations and combinations at its disposal. First the brain, then the perception of phenomena, then the thought which articulates the perception.

These few and but briefly mentioned landmarks in a topic occupying the attention of ethnographers and anthropologists over a period of two and a half centuries indicate the importance of the problem: the attempt to resolve in a context of otherness a perennial preoccupation of European scholars. Yet despite the constant animadversions to change and development, particularly by nineteenth-century scholars, it is only with Marx, in his ideas of alienation and class conflict, that we are really brought face to face with the fact that changes and developments in modes of thought and the forms of society put human beings in crisis, entail a radical reorientation of heart in relation to mind. If Lévi-Strauss can be distinguished from many of his colleagues because transformations are his main concern, this concern is almost wholly in intellectual terms: transformation at the level of language and articulate thought. Perhaps the pervasive notion of inevitable process present in evolutionary thought, in much of historical philosophy, and in marxist exegesis, has something to do with this neglect of crisis in anthropological literature. Perhaps the concentration on the regularities of social life as distinct from the anomie or irregularity is partly responsible. Or again, since the rationalization of crisis can seem to emasculate it, personal crises can be made to seem an illusion, or irrelevant to the particular mode of discourse. Yet, as Weber made clear, if crises are social and at the level of the collective, it is for people to resolve them. Viable social orders depend upon crises, people make them inevitable.

For Australian Aborigines all transformations were crises not only for the individuals concerned but for the whole community. They could not afford, as we sometimes think we can, to lose a life let alone its potential in thought and awareness. Each transformational occasion meant a rearrangement of social relationships, a reallocation of tasks. If the main structure of the community did not change, the relative positioning of the people who gave that structure expression certainly did change. The action was suited to the word rather than vice versa whatever the misgivings of the heart. The structure allowed for those progressive alienations which, produced by the process of getting older, demanded a reintegration within a different framework of at-oneness. A structure that did not do this could not survive. If man does not seek crisis, he is by nature prone to it and makes his arrangements accordingly.

Few studies of millenarian, adjustment or nativistic and similar movements do not give us an idea of the fact of crisis. The activities are often bizarre and frenetic. Strange things are said and done. Administrations become worried, police forces are mobilized. A sense of crisis of some sort could scarcely be missed. Still, many of these studies have been so clouded with bland psychologisms and intimations of irrationality, foolishness, fantasy and lack of education or proper perceptions of reality that one is forced to ask whether something else is not in the heart of the matter. It is so easy to fall victim to the propaganda of fashionable intellectual assumptions. Because the activities are explicitly political and invite a political response, the significance and attention they have gained is only appropriate. But because the participants in these movements are relatively few in numbers, and the movements must succumb on the surface to overwhelming force, the import of the political event tends to be minimized. Further, if the activities contained in these movements are not representations in the mass of the experiences of countless individuals who have made the transformation from one mode of being to another, at least the two kinds of transformation are analogous. For however these movements are interpreted, into whatever molds they are poured by particular kinds of analysis, very much the same sorts of things could be said of individuals attempting the transformation on their own or being conducted through an established rite of passage. Just as a social structure has to allow for the successive transformations of the individuals who sustain it, so, perhaps, millenarian type activities may be that very dynamic of the evolutionary process for which scholars have so far sought in vain. Could it be that it was this kind of activity that provided the framework of the transformational drama that enabled bands of hunters to become the first cultivators, and enabled cultivators to found the first city? On the whole, because it is generally considered more useful to move into the unknown on a basis of what is known, our new knowledge of the ways in which forms of thought and society actually do change should not lead us to suppose that the processes were all that different in prehistoric times.

In Australia as elsewhere in history as well as the present time, the transition from country to city life has never been easy. But rather than risk the full impact of city life, its initial rush, lonelinesses, and anonymity, those Australian Aborigines who have migrated to the connurbations have become fringe-dwellers in the slums and outskirts. In a sense they have to live this way if they are not to follow the example of so many rural Elizabethans who, flocking into London, ended in Bedlam. Their ambience is a liminal 'tween-world between the downs and deserts of tradition, and the buses, cars, office towers, and bright lights of the modern city. Yet however wretched the conditions of existence, the warmth of mutual support and companionship is secured. Planners rarely remember that a human life which gives warmth to others is fulfilled rather than wasted. But of course this kind of thing cannot continue for long. Just as the mass of individual Black Americans in North America were too few and too weak to assure their own several and private transformational frameworks, and had to organize themselves politically if, as individuals, they were to enter the life of the greater society on equal terms with others, so too Australian Aborigines must presently organize themselves, define their crisis, and make their challenge explicit.

Yet conditions in North America and Australia are by no means the same. The division in Australia does not seem to be based on color, on sexual anxieties, on fear, on social acceptabilities, on the loss of a source of cheap labor. Nor is there any heavy sense of guilt. Australian Aborigines have always been too few, too far away, out of sight, too marginal to the mainstreams of Australian life for that. Rather is it based on the same features which divide one Australian from another and born Australians from new migrants: that within competitive egalitarianism each should be relied on to recognize the contexts appropriate to individual and collective action, self-interest and the collective interest, and accept the consequences. As C. H. Berndt (1962) has pointed out, this means bowing to a continuing interplay between the warmths of true comradeship and the cold isolation of success. But once the crisis has been defined, made explicit, and overcome, the choice will not seem so traumatic.

It has already been suggested that if assimilation was the official policy, integration is occurring. Nor is this inappropriate. It appears as a necessary step in the transformational drama that requires a series of successive mediations of the contraries contained in the central ambiguities. Otherness approaches, halts, becomes less ambiguous; and the process is repeated. Each mediation requires giving full rein to controlled expressions of the participatory values. Particularly where different cultures or antithetically related principles are concerned, no true dramatist can ignore the fact that once the participatory values are engaged it is impossible for the parts to remain what they were. They qualify and develop each other until it is convenient to terminate. So, after a century and a half of experience, Aborigines are beginning to make demands of their own, are beginning to shape the framework of their transformation into something other than they were traditionally or more recently. Like it or not anthropologists are themselves involved in the developing situation. Indeed, one of the first signals of developing incorporation is the positively stated objection to being anthropologized. The fact that anthropologists study otherness is recognized by the peoples whom they study, and objections to being so studied stem from the realization that that otherness is dissolving or has dissolved.

When in the past, as now, a traveler, settler, sojourner, trader, merchant, missionary, businessman, or administrative official went into otherness to stay or tour, the roles and purposes were explicit and recognizable. The merchant came to buy, to haggle, bargain, and make his profit; the missionary came to educate and enlighten; the administrative official came to implement the variety of activities implicit in his notions of good order and due process; the traveler came, was hospitably received, entertained, and duly went his way. No human group could fail to recognize the familiar essentials of their roles. The nature of ambiguity was clear and overt; opposition and hostility derived either from misunderstandings which could be cleared up, or from well-founded appreciations of interests, motives, and purposes. But when anthropologists started going to the field a new dimension was added. Deception as to purpose and interest was entailed; the nature of the ambiguities involved could never be clear. An anthropologist went to the field to ask questions, to find out, to probe into the being of others: an invasion which the members of no human group would tolerate among themselves. He put his foot in the door and, if most often graciously, sometimes more peremptorily, beckoned forth or demanded his information. He sat and observed, taking notes. He counted and measured. He was, as is a spy or secret agent, a wholly ambiguous element insinuating himself into an otherwise reasonably ordered set of expectations.

The picture of a lone anthropologist penetrating a jungle fastness or desert wilderness is largely figment. That kind of achievement belongs only to a few. Most often, fieldwork has depended on the support of administrative prestige and power. To traders a source of temporary and adventitious amusement and small profit, anthropologists could not but attract the doubts and suspicions of missionaries. Such ambiguity is not to be trusted, spies are apt to become double-agents: a feature as well appreciated by the administrative officials who overtly supported the project. For whom did these anthropologists act? What were their interests, their stakes in building up close but temporary social relationships? To what use would they put the information they obtained? Although such questions might be fully and honestly answered, it is difficult to believe that the answers were wholly communicated.

In earlier days and on into the forties and fifties of this century, say, anthropologists could afford to ignore the essential ambiguity of their position in the human situation. The forseeable consequences in relation to themselves and the outer world were either immediate or could be discounted as being in the nature of things: the necessary quotient of risk implicit in the initiation of any kind of social intercourse. Besides, the warm social relationships actually established by anthropologists in the field did not point to a problem of substance. Anthropologists were adopted into families, gained temporary kinsfolk, made friendships — features regarded as proof of incorporation into the strange culture, indicative of the rapport established and the trust and confidence gained. Few have been able to sustain the thought that these features might equally have been protective devices to ensure mutual trust. The euphoria and warmth of having crossed the divide and found a common humanity has tended to screen the fact that the people being studied must have some way of turning uncertain ambiguity into a semblance of reliability, some basis on which to ensure that information given would not be turned against them. So long as a people was remote and non-literate, anthropologists could afford to persuade themselves that they were the best judges of what should or should not be divulged to whom, what should or should not be published. They were, virtually, immune from legal suit. Whether the people were literate or not, irrespective of the sensibilities and sensitivities of the Europeans on the spot, it could always be claimed despite the confidence accepted, the word given, the promise made, that the needs of science were paramount. The "truth" must be revealed. Academic immunities provided the necessary protection.

In practice, of course, the hard edges of the characterization must necessarily soften. There is no doubt of sincere friendships, continuing interests, skill and tact in the mode of making information available to scientists and others. But there is no cynicism in pointing out that if most can rise above the realities of a situation, some cannot. The confidence has been betrayed, the word and promise broken. In knowing that he can (and will) betray a trust or break a promise if the needs of science beckon, the field anthropologist reveals his essential ambiguity and amorality: he seeks a trust and confidence in order to betray it if he finds it "necessary." Having crossed a cultural barrier, he can never wholly participate in a normative morality. He has to serve two masters. But unlike the spy, who pretends to serve one while actually serving another, or the double-agent with his double pretence, an anthropologist's masters are conscience and science: both notoriously manipulable. It is an enormous responsibility. That only a few have failed to carry it speaks volumes not so much for those who have borne it honorably as for those currents of tradition on which they have been carried. Nevertheless, it is not a responsibility that can ever find favor in relation to others. The good tyrant is an accident. The means must exist for enforcing the correct exercise of responsibility. Once published, bits of knowledge are no longer any one person's exclusive property. There is a special and childish naivete in supposing that information or technique made over to those whom one considers "good" is not at once going to fall into the hands of those with quite other intentions. Thus, not only have anthropologists been forced into developing codes of conduct in relation to field research, but the peoples they study and the administrations which govern them have joined in the process.

It is too early yet to project the consequences of this. What is quite clear is that anthropologists will not be able to draw up their codes by themselves. The role of the double-agent answerable only to himself, always implicit, has been exposed and made explicit. Administrations and agencies responsible to a central government and assembly of representatives have begun to insist upon safeguards to protect themselves as well as the individuals involved. Information and data may be made subject to subpoena or confiscation. Communities being studied have begun to insist on their right to make conditions or refuse to be studied. The regular and standardized payment of informants, which was once thought to vitiate the evidence, is already in some parts obligatory. The scrutiny and censorship of field notes by the subjects or a third party, the particular interests and political sympathies of the investigator, the right of subjects to terminate an interview or the whole study — all these are within view and now under discussion.

If these features point to realities always implicit in the fieldwork situation, they make nonsense of the anthropological ideal of establishing a truly moral relationship with the people being studied. Perhaps realizing that ideal was never really possible, and was always quite simply an anthropological fantasy built on the necessity for establishing some kind of moral relationship between investigator and investigated. Perhaps those who are wont to use the phrase "establishing rapport" – evoking the kind of smoothly machined friendliness of the door-to-door salesman – have been more closely in touch with reality. Developing techniques to extract information in order to employ people who can work on that information and develop further techniques to extract more information so that processing the information can give rise to a competitive economic situation which will provide more jobs – the cycle is familiar – may seem an unkind prognosis. But it is not wholly unreal. The "good old days" of anthropology have gone. Attempting to maintain the form of those days without their substance can only lead into the kind of mechanical cycle described above. It is useful to remember that the substance of anthropology has only been contained in that word for little more than a century and a quarter. It is possible that others, who do not call themselves anthropologists, but whose exploratory reach into otherness is informed by an engagement between the participatory values and rational objectivity, are more closely in touch with the substance.

4   CONCLUSION

Throughout this essay we have stressed the nature of anthropology's European signature. The main theme has been that in relation to Australian Aborigines as well as in relation to other peoples the problems and endeavors of the set of disciplines contained within anthropology are, and always have been, integral and authentic to European civilization. The opposition between rational objectivity and participation in oneness has always informed the substance of anthropological thought and investigation. Given the Christian synthesis, the lineaments of God were to be sought in those whom He had made in His image. Attempting to "save the data" by seeing it as God – the epitome of the rational – might have seen it, through the device of a rationally objective intellectual construct, has always been qualified by the exhortation to engage the participatory values. Since there can be no investigation of other peoples without an acknowledgment of moral relationship, political values have always colored the variety of theoretical constructs which have, through the years, expressed the meaning of rational objectivity. Though the primary problem contained within the notion of rational objectivity has been the construction of an intellectual framework capable of resolving the relations between the synchrony and the diachrony, and the broad issues could be thought of as resolved in, first, the great chain of being, and second in evolutionary theory, working constructs have generally allied themselves with one or the other. Nevertheless, if for many the basic and fundamental issue has been to separate questions of how things are from questions directed to finding out how things came to be as they are, for others the opposite has been true: how things are can in no way be separated from how they have come to be as they are. Since, in practice, neither kind of analysis or explication can afford wholly to ignore the other, a proper synthesis rather than mix seems appropriate.

On the one hand, synchronic analyses entail assumptions of equilibrium, interrelatedness, interdependence, integration, and a hierarchy of logical priorities — (in terms of which the smaller is derived from the larger, the parts from the whole) — which come to a head in the overarching ideas of pattern, function, structure, and structure-function. On the other hand, the diachrony has found expression in two general but opposed modes: First, history and diffusionism have attempted and continue to attempt to elicit order from the apparently random scatter of events in time. Second, protohistorical or evolutionary, extensionist and genetic points of view, which are combined with the search for origins, assume order, move from the smaller physical entity to the larger, from the less differentiated to the more differentiated. Intersecting in evolutionary or culture-pattern studies, they inevitably lead into or lean on biology and psychology. Yet whatever the mix or attempted synthesis between the synchronic and diachronic — and it is here that politics — social assumptions and aspirations attempt to bridge the gap — description, analysis and explication must take departure from assumptions which seek to contain that multifaceted node of the mysterious in man's affairs: the source or sources of the on-going processes of growing awareness, transformation and change at the level both of the individual and the collective.

Whether fixed in the nature of man himself, as essentially social or a loner, or in the implications of his culture or social order, man's fate has been variously referred to divine providence, the movements of the heavenly bodies, the Spirit of History, Nature, natural selection at the level of the animal or species or gene, the circumstances relating to conception and birth and child nurture, the struggle for economic resources, territoriality, the lust for power, charismatic gifts, the consequences of patricide and the incest taboo, exchange relationships combined with natural egalitarianism, the principles which appear to underly overtly expressed purposes and motives .... One might go on. For it is this node of mystery in man's affairs, which the Greeks assigned to the Fates, and which we tend to see as an entwining of character traits, values, and social and physical constraints, that at bottom draws anthropologists to their tasks, takes men and women into Aboriginal reserves.

Separating people from culture has always been difficult. It has never been easy to maintain the distinction between an untidy variety and continua of empirical reality, and the sharp but elegant logical discriminations in terms of which that reality may be comprehended. Rational objectivity and the participatory values have gone hand in hand. Feeling out or absorbing a people or situation through the skin has ever been qualified by fields of relevance projected from received intellectualizations. The perceptive flash must be transformed into the steady illumining of the articulate thought. The data has always been on two levels: an otherwise adventitious happening or doing on the one hand; a saying or more or less ordered rationalization or articulate comprehension of that happening or doing on the other. This leads naturally into the attempt to discover the relations between modes of thought and a complex of patterned activities. Yet this, the study of values or social representations, the attempt to understand how others understand themselves, frequently and inevitably lends itself to judgments on the parts of those who feel they know how things really are. How far another culture is but the artifact of the intellectualization which is thought to comprehend it, and how far the actual business of living corresponds with that intellectualization, has always been a matter of acute concern in the writing of a field monograph. The distinction between an analysis that purports to be existential and one that assumes purpose or a variety of contextually defined means-to-ends relationships has been hard to sustain. For so soon as contexts of time and space are opened or contracted, things become different, their relevance quite other.

Analyzing the interrelations and transformations of values or social representations is, formally, quite different from attempting to piece together the developmental process indicated by different organizational forms or patterns, whether in evolutionary or historical terms. But because the findings of one must affect the assumptions of the other, each tends to slip into the other, and each requires a dialectical interplay between scientific techniques of investigation and an intellectualization which can direct the investigation. For the Greeks "anthropology" meant "talking about man and his affairs." This "talking about man," engaging the freedoms of the spirit and the animal with the constraints of morality and the physical world within a cultural framework, has always been a central and continuing theme of European intellectual life. Differentiated through the centuries into different, particular, and more and more systematic kinds of "talking about," subject to continual regrouping in relation to changes in technique and dominating points of view, from Plato and the Christian synthesis the same questions occur and recur. They are not summed up in the question "What am I?" but in "What is man, Whence his becoming, Where his going?" These questions have always entailed looking outward into otherness, have always required that the discourse move into other social and cultural ambiences both in time and in space. "What am I?" is in the first instance, and tends to remain, culturally bounded: an exploration of being within the terms of a dialogue between received tradition and personal insights and circumstances. But in the European tradition this discourse has always been qualified by what has been learned from a study of other traditions, other circumstances, other kinds of insight. Which returns us to the authentic in anthropology's European signature.

The difference between the two kinds of questions needs to be emphasized. "What am I?" relies upon ethnocentric dogma, implies the dimensions of a closed society which alone can provide the question with a reliable departure and allow the answers a context of certainty. "What is man, Whence his becoming, Where his going?" are questions which inherently require the critique of dogma, the critique of self, identity, and context from varying points of otherness. The continuing reach into otherness, into other kinds of identity, self, and context, always qualifies, changes, opposes the questions and answers that have cohered into a temporary orthodoxy. The questions imply an open society, are such that the answers can never be complete. Rather are the answers contained in a continuing endeavor to find out what the bases of temporary answers might be. Again, the dialectic between the two sorts of questions and their answers lies at the heart of the European experience. Elements of the triune Godhead became man, were man, were in man, and were beyond and outside and above man. Paradoxically but characteristically, the exclusive community of Jews became the medium through whom all men might be reached and the nature of the relation between the self and God more nearly comprehended. The union of *The Republic* with the scriptures brought in its train the creation of innumerable alternative social orders which, wrought from the imagination, investigation, or compounds of both, have explicated the same major themes. Man was a special sort of animal. His nature was bound up in culture, the social order, and the ways in which he transcended their limitations and constraints. Probing the mystery of his being has always required the mobilization of all available intellectual resources and techniques.

Rooted not, as is often supposed, in the eighteenth century, but in the first beginnings of European civilization, the on-going interests and pre-occupations that were to become "anthropology" did not differentiate themselves and cohere into anthropology until the middle of the nineteenth century. As such, anthropology remains a typical nineteenth-century creation. Never a synthesis, nor even an amalgam, it mirrored the structure of its ancestry and birth. The professional men with different expertises who gathered together to talk and give papers, and who finally decided to group their interests into a set of more or less related disciplines to be called anthropology, had a common concern in otherness. Held together and flowering within the disciplined constructs of evolutionary theory and structure-functionalism, these interests were all but torn asunder in the chaotic eclecticism of diffusionism. Now, again, anthropology is beginning to disintegrate into a variety of specialisms. The same questions are asked, but the answers are being sought in ever narrowing contexts. The jobs of asking and answering are being further differentiated and reallocated. The central desiderata for social or cultural anthropology—fieldwork, participant observation (which summarizes the dialectic between rational objectivity and the participatory values), and learning a strange language—are on their way out. Departments, foundations, and institutes no longer enfold a gathering of scholars with a common literary background, the lived experience of otherness, and a wide ethnographic knowledge. Instead, there are biologists, dieticians, physicians, geographers, demographers, linguists, mythologists, economists, political scientists, methodologists, psychologists, pediatricians, mathematicians, ecologists, systems experts—a legion of specialists. Human biologists have always been in and out of the subject, tenuously connected through evolutionary theory and their interest in prehistory to the mainstream of sociological endeavor: and much the same is true of the prehistorians who are themselves going off on their own or joining the museologists. Those interests in law, history, and comparative religion which formed the core of the subject in the past are rapidly fading in significance.

While it is true that all the specialists mentioned have some sort of interest in, and experience of, otherness, they owe their primary interest and allegiance to developing the methodologies of their specialist crafts.

What joins them together is less a common intellectual endeavor and much more their employment in foreign aid programs and international agencies. What used to be attempted in holistic vein by a few with inadequate financial support is now being done by tens of thousands of specialists on vastly greater budgets. Though there are some anthropologists who still cling to the notion that there will always be a place for the scholar who can see the whole picture, who can address himself to a total structure of activities, ideas and values through, mainly, the study of kinship and customary usages, it is wholly against the trend of things. As well might the last dinosaurs assure themselves that they had always managed in the past. With the transformation of otherness into something more like ourselves, social and cultural anthropology must themselves become transformed. Their content must, and indeed has already started to, seep into other disciplines whose specialist rigor and methodology must always be more impressive than those available or appropriate to the wider ranging traditional anthropologist.

The tremendous growth in wealth, technology, population, and means of communication in the Western world over the last thirty years all entail such proliferations and differentiations in the division of labor that the social or cultural anthropologist as we have known him since the beginning of the century must become obsolete. Even if the kinds of peoples traditionally studied by anthropologists were not moving toward making their traditional tasks virtually impossible, the traditional anthropologist will have disappeared by the time the measures become truly effective. Still, however widely the substance of the subject is differentiated, there can be little doubt that the same sorts of questions will continue to be asked. The historian of ideas, the satirist, novelist, and dramatist will continue to pick up both questions and answers and weave a coherence from them. Bowen's *Return to Laughter* (1954–1964), Lévi-Strauss' *Tristes Tropiques* (1955) or *World on the Wane* (1961), Read's *The High Valley* (1965), Castaneda's *A Separate Reality* (1971) counterpointed by works such as Arthur Miller's *The Crucible* (1952), those of the Australian authors already mentioned and of a growing number of science fiction writers, are portents of what will become much more common. These are genres which, long before the "subject" of anthropology was invented, traditionally contained its substance. If anthropology is to survive as a subject it will surely have to provide the scientific basis of such genres, take the relations between word and deed as its center, and address itself to the ways in which man continually creates the environments in which he imprisons himself.

The temporary coherence of a set of problems into "anthropology" was a Victorian achievement, maintained thus far not without struggle, pain, and continuing threats of dismemberment. It is wholly in the nature of things, implicit in the history of European civilization, that in the perspective of twenty centuries the coherence of a century or so should revert into its constituent parts. Still, within the space of that coherence studies of Australian Aboriginal life have always had a special place. Dampier's best seller foreshadowed this place even if Cook's eulogies went virtually unnoticed at the time. Given the intellectual stimulus of evolutionary theory and structure-functionalism, however, through Howitt, Fison, Mathew, Mathews, Durkheim, Van Gennep, Spencer, Gillen, Malinowski, Radcliffe-Brown, Elkin, Strehlow, Warner, Mountford, R. M. and C. H. Berndt, Lévi-Strauss and Stanner among many others, Aboriginal life has always had a central importance. There is no traditional anthropologist who has not cut his teeth on Durkheim and Australian totemism. There can be few theories about the nature of man, society, and culture which have not found a testing ground in Australian Aboriginal life, and few anthropologists staking a claim to theoretical significance have not tried their hands at unraveling the complexities it contains. Captain Cook had indicated the happy simplicities of that life. But with the first real investigations it became apparent that these simplicities were bound up with rules and conventions of tortuous complexity. Had Bushmen, Hottentots, Veddas, Patagonians or the hunters of India and Southeast Asia revealed this juxtaposition of simplicity and complexity, difficulties of access would have been overcome and they too would have received the attention that Australians have had. It was taken for granted and generally accepted—by Frazer and Durkheim among others, for example—that Australian Aborigines were the "most primitive" representatives of man. Howitt, Spencer, and Durkheim himself revealed the Aboriginal as perhaps the most complicated representatives of man. It is this paradox that has kept Australian Aborigines at the center of anthropological intellectual life. It was, and could only be, ignored by those who were dogmatists rather than true scientists.

Though there were many features of Aboriginal life which were supportive of evolutionist schemes, in its totality Aboriginal life would not fit into evolutionary theory. The whole was at variance with its kinds of differentiations. Beautifully illustrative of the structure-function framework, and so stimulating fieldwork within those assumptions, Aboriginal life has shown the deficiencies of that framework. The time comes when, as the medium for containing and revealing the significance of data, a theoretical framework begins to preen and display only itself.

The "Murngin controversy" and the continuing problems relating to marriage, kinship, section and subsection systems demonstrate that new data found by old assumptions can only lead into impasse. It is not the data that lead into the impasse but the theoretical framework or set of assumptions by which they are ordered and made intelligible. Hence the need for new theory, new sets of assumptions. Though, paradoxically, diffusionism in its anthropological expression could do little with the circumstances of Aboriginal life at the turn of the century, it is now becoming apparent that, with so many new techniques available, diffusionism will provide the kind of intellectual stimulus and problem which Rivers outlined in *The History of Melanesian Society* (1914), but which the excesses of Perry and Elliot-Smith obscured. Apart from the American Indians and, perhaps, the Eskimos, no simple people has received such detailed ethnographic investigation over so long a period through so many different theorctical assumptions as have the Australian Aborigines. They provide the ideal situation for a revitalized diffusionism.

Aboriginal carvings and bark and cave paintings have been voluminously described and reproduced. But they have been related to Aboriginal life in an entirely superficial way. There has been little analysis of them and their relevances by people who know the Aborigines in the terms that would be familiar to a European connoisseur or art historian. What is the relevance of the painting of Albert Namatjira and his descendants? What are the assertions of Aboriginal art in relation to, for example, the identity of Aborigines *vis-à-vis* Europeans, the changing circumstances of life, status relationships, or intellectual development? Almost wholly shadowed by the professional urgencies and automaticisms of standard structure-functionalism, primitive art has only recently begun to gain the close attention it deserves. Collected and preserved in Australian museums, the paintings, carvings, and sculptures of Australian Aborigines still await the iconologists who will bring them into life and relevance. Dances and rituals have been described, some have been filmed. But the inherent dramatic values of dance and ritual, the ways in which dances and rituals change and develop, and the kinds of innate or improvised activities — so well described by Stanner (1966) — have not yet received the sophisticated attention that similar kinds of activities are beginning to receive elsewhere. Nevertheless, the intellectual basis for such studies is being laid (see Peacock, 1968; Mellema, 1954; Gargi, 1966), and they will surely be presently taken up in Australia. When man first knew what he scratched on a bone or stone he or she was human. Something was being *said*.

Though Kaberry (1939) was a pioneer in the investigation of the concomitants of sex differences in a given social milieu, and her work could not have been informed by the kinds of considerations later raised by Mead (1949) and Beauvoir (1952) and now being developed, challenged, and investigated in relation to North American life today, systematic investigation of these problems within an Aboriginal context has started (see Gale, 1970; Goodale, 1971). Much of what had been done tended to be riddled with the cliches of a male orientated anthropology — even though female anthropologists are almost as numerous as, and better known than their male colleagues. Yet Aboriginal life, where women are so often barred from ritual activities, where women were the main providers and are as strong, athletic, enduring and prone to physical combat as the men, should be an ideal base from which to derive something new. Traditionally, women have been denied the width and depth of social experience available to men, and they have been unable to transcend their roles as childbearers, helpmeets, and cooks. Men, on the other hand, mainly through ritual activities, are given successive opportunities to transcend their past and move into new areas of consciousness. No more or less subject to metamorphoses than women, men nevertheless experience a range of transformations which women are not normally permitted.

Does the key to this difference lie in biology — extended into psychology; in the economic consequences of a particular division of labor which allows men opportunities for initiatives which women may not claim; or are men's ritual activities the necessary and appropriate framework for transcendence? If there are serious underlying correlates in not allowing women the kind of community ritual life in which men participate so fully — What are the relations between the differing projections of sex and gender, man and woman, male and female, masculine and feminine, round which so much of ritual turns? These are not the sorts of questions which structure-functionalism could either pose or answer effectively. Balance, equilibrium, complementary opposition, polarity, and integration are notions which tend to seek expressions of themselves. They are strangely blind to the imbalanced and ambiguous which spell out part of the difference between human societies and insect societies. Inevitably, too, they are concerned with activities which, however obscurely, we tend to envisage as interlinked in the same kinds of relations of physical cause and effect which we perceive in our machines. Yet man lives in a complex environment of images and statements which, coded and communicated in a variety of ways, do not seem to be interrelated like the parts of a known machine. Perhaps this is the framework in which to discuss the war of the sexes.

Because of Australia's geographical position, intellectual as distinct from scientific and technological concerns and developments generally lag behind those in Europe and the Americas—between whom interaction is constant and concentrated. It was so with evolution, functionalism, and structure-function, and is so with that particular brand of logical and mathematical analysis called "structuralism"—and this despite the fact that neither Europeans nor Americans have always appreciated the details of Australian ethnography (see R. M. Berndt, 1967), and although it was precisely this ethnography which has been a primary stimulus and illustration of those intellectual developments. On the other hand, linguists in Australia have mapped, analyzed, and ordered just about all the languages and dialects spoken by Aborigines. Although all these languages can be interrelated within a structural framework, ultimately the exercise calls for an essentially diffusionist position. In addition, the much looser intellectual assumptions guiding the researches of demographers, geographers, ecologists, and prehistorians, and the active cooperation between them (see Mulvaney and Golson, 1971) has resulted in a situation which, when the linguists are added, promises just that kind of happy coherence of technique and question which leads on to significant scientific rather than intellectual discovery. It is in these areas rather than those which were the traditional concern of social or cultural anthropologists that one can expect the most exciting advances in the near future. From this, perhaps, there may emerge questions of more purely intellectual concern.

It would be impossible, and inappropriate to try to summarize all the problems that Aboriginal life poses for interested scholars. Whether it be social organization or kinship, history or myth, drama, painting, song— T. G. H. Strehlow has at last found a publisher for his massive *Songs of Central Australia* (1971)—carving, ecology, demography, prehistory, political life, economics or the variety of questions hinging on the contact situation, the main thrusts must be toward salvage and developing techniques of historical and prehistorical research, and toward eliciting the semantic fields which make up the more significant environment in which man lives. Both require not only imagination and intellect, but making full use of the varied resources of scientific technology. Over a period of some forty years social and cultural anthropologists have concentrated their attention on techniques of participant observation in fieldwork within a framework determined by the functionalist or structure-function models. The result has been more and more detailed configurations of, essentially, the values of Aboriginal life. Preceded by some seventeen papers on a variety of aspects of Aboriginal life, *Social Organization of Australian Tribes* in 1930 by Radcliffe-Brown laid the basis for future research. In 1938 Elkin's *The Australian Aborigines* summarized what was known of Aboriginal life, gave that knowledge a certain coherence of interrelatedness, and indicated the gaps. Since then, little of what has been done has not been in the nature of correcting, qualifying, and filling in the detail of Elkin's framework, and taking these advances into the study of groups that had not yet been studied. With the publication in 1964 of *The World of the First Australians* by Ronald M. Berndt and Catherine H. Berndt, former students of Elkin, the wheel comes full circle. Elkin's framework is filled out to capacity, the results of the prodigious labors of a mere handful of researchers are faithfully recorded and interrelated. So far as structure-functionalism is concerned, the picture is more or less complete.

It is only in the nature of things that, having shown how the parts fit into the whole, each of these parts should become a specialist concern; that having exhausted an impetus to find out how things are, attention should now be devoted to finding out how things came to be as they are. Discovering the lineaments of the semantic environment is perhaps the greater intellectual challenge. For this, structure-functionalism has laid the basis. But the interrelations of people, things, and specific categories have become subject to the law of diminishing returns. It is now time to move purposefully forward into that field of images, statements, and themes which, whether made by or derived from people, things, categories, activities, and their interrelations, provide the determinitive cultural environment in which man has being.

Australian Aborigines are people. Their cultures are sets of ordered behaviors, systems of interrelated categories, images, and statements in terms of which people interact, understand one another, themselves, and the physical environment. Tearing people from culture makes the one an animal, the other a more or less abstract set of relations. Yet man is an animal who can articulate his dreams, who quickens both his existential relations with others, and the environment which provides the relations with significance, with the ambiguity of his dreams. It is possible to ignore the dreamer and examine the relations and their environment — to attempt to perceive the lineaments of the whole, divide this whole into significant parts, analyze increasingly smaller parts. It is also possible to examine the animal, to pursue the features of biological patterns and processes that accompany and perhaps interlink more cogently the act or event and their perception and rationalization. In both cases at least since the eighteenth century the general movement has been from macrotheory to microtheory, from global and all-embracing theories about the nature, origin, and development of man and culture to micro-models of specific kinds of relations within carefully defined environments. Each kind of study necessarily proliferates into a number of specialisms; mathematical and logical models, quantitative techniques and scientific outlook and technology become the necessary companions of imagination and intellectual perception.

At the center of this web of techniques and approaches lies the dreamer who spun it. Organism and word, natural or accidental or proposed, certainly purposeful, yet converging in mystery. It is from this focus that the radii of specialisms proliferate, and toward which they should look if they are not to become simply mechanical tasks. Yet specialisms tend to look inward on themselves. Even though it has been the common quality of dreamer that has drawn anthropologists into the study of Australian Aborigines, this impetus tends to evaporate in the heat of professional specialism. Which is why others whose imaginations are freer, whose vision is broader, are beginning to make the dreamer their own. In the meanwhile, as Aboriginal cultures melt into history, Aborigines have to explain themselves not only to themselves but to those others in the differentiated community they are joining.

Works Cited

Abbie, A. A. *The Original Australians*. Frederick Muller, London, 1969

Abu Talib Ibn Mohammed, Isfahtani. *Travels of Mizra Abu Talib Kahn in Asia, Africa and Europe* (Translated by Charles Stewart). Longman, London, 1810.

Adam, L. *Primitive Art*. Pelican Books, London, 1940–1954.

Angas, G. F. *South Australia Illustrated*. Thomas McLean, London, 1846.

Ashley-Montague, M. F. *Coming into Being Among the Australian Aborigines*. Routledge, London, 1937.

Ashley-Montague, M. F. *The Concept of the Primitive*. The Free Press, New York, 1968.

Australian Institute of Aboriginal Studies. Annual Report, 1 July 1969–30 June 1970. Canberra.

Australian Institute of Aboriginal Studies. Newsletter, Vol. 3, No. 2, April 1971. Canberra.

The Australian Medical Journal. Melbourne.

The Australian Museum Magazine (founded in 1921). Australian Museum, Sydney.

Bachofen, J. J. *The Matriarchate*. (*Das Mutterrecht*). Krais and Hoffman, Stuttgart, 1861.

Barnes, J. A. Inquest on the Murngin. Royal Anthropological Institute Occasional Paper No. 26. London, 1967.

Basedow, H. *The Australian Aboriginal*. Preece, Adelaide, 1925.

Bates, Daisy. *The Passing of the Aborigines* (Foreword by Alan Moorehead). John Murray, London, 1938–1949.

Beauvoir, Simonde de. *The Second Sex*. Knopf, New York, 1952.

Berndt, Catherine H. The Quest for Identity: The Case of the Australian Aborigines. *Oceania*, Vol. XXXXII, No. 1. Sydney, 1961.

Berndt, Catherine H. Mateship or Success: An Assimilation Dilemma. *Oceania*, Vol. XXXIII, No. 2, pp. 71–88. Sydney, 1962.

Berndt, Catherine H. Uses and Misuses of Anthropology. *Anthropological Forum*, Vol. 1. University of Western Australia Press, Perth, WA, 1964.

Berndt, R. M. *Djanggawul*. Routledge and Kegan Paul, London, 1952.

Berndt, R. M. "Murngin" (Wulamba) social organization. *American Anthropologist*, Vol. 57, p. 104. Washington, D.C., 1955.

Berndt, R. M. *An Adjustment Movement in Arnhem Land, Northern Territory of Australia.* Cahiers de L'Homme, Mouton, Paris, 1962.

Berndt, R. M. Social Anthropology and Australian Aborigines. *Oceania,* Vol. XXXVII, No. 4, pp. 241–258. Sydney, 1967.

Berndt, R. M. (Ed.) *Australian Aboriginal Anthropology.* University of Western Australia Press, Perth, WA, 1970.

Berndt, R. M. and C. H. *The World of the First Australians.* Angus and Robertson, Sydney, 1964.

Berndt, R. M. and C. H. *Man, Land and Myth in North Australia.* Ure Smith, Sydney, 1970.

Birket-Smith, Kaj. *Primitive Man and His Ways.* Mentor Books, New York, 1957–1960.

Bonwick, J. *The Wild White Man and the Blacks of Victoria.* Fergussen and Moore, Melbourne, 1863.

Bowen, Elenore Smith. *Return to Laughter.* Anchor Books, Doubleday & Co., New York, 1954–1964.

Bowler, J. M; Jones, Rys; Allen, Harry; and Thorne, A. G. Pleistocene human remains from Australia: a living site and human cremation from Lake Mungo, Western New South Wales. *World Archaeology,* Vol. 2, No. 1, June, pp. 39–60. London, 1970.

Buchler, Ira R. and Selby, H. A. *Kinship and Social Organization.* The Macmillan Company, New York, 1968.

Burridge, K. *New Heaven, New Earth.* Basil Blackwell, Oxford, 1969.

Capell, A. E. *New Approach to Australian Linguistics.* Oceania Linguistic Monograph No. 1, Sydney, 1959. *Studies in Socio-Linguistics.* Mouton, The Hague, 1966.

Casagrande, J. B. (Ed.) *In the Company of Man.* Harper & Row, New York, 1960.

Casteneda, C. *A Separate Reality.* Simon and Schuster, New York, 1971.

Cochrane, G. *Big Men and Cargo Cults.* Clarendon Press, Oxford, 1970.

Cook, Captain J. *The Journals of Captain Cook on his Voyages of Discovery.* (J. C. Beaglehole, Ed.). Volume 1. The Voyage of the Endeavour. The Hakluyt Society, Cambridge University Press, London, 1955.

Coon, C. S. *The Origin of Races.* Knopf, New York, 1962.

Coulanges, Fustel de. *The Ancient City.* Doubleday, New York, 1959.

Crawford, I. M. *The Art of the Wandjina.* Oxford University Press, Melbourne, 1968.

Crequinière, de la. *Customs of the East Indians.* W. Davis, London, 1705.

Curr, E. M. *The Australian Race.* J. Ferres, Melbourne, 1886.

Dampier, William, *Dampier's Voyages,* John Masefield (Ed.). London, 1906.

Darwin, C. *Origin of Species.* John Murray, London, 1859.

Darwin, C. *The Descent of Man.* John Murray, London, 1871.

Dawson, J. *Australian Aborigines.* George Robertson, Melbourne, Sydney and Adelaide, 1881.

Dixon, R. M. W. (correspondence). *Man,* Vol. 3, No. 4, pp. 653–654, 1969.

Dumont, L. Descent or Intermarriage? A Relational View of Australian Kinship Systems. *Southwestern Journal of Anthropology,* Vol. 22(3), pp. 231–250. Albuquerque, 1966.

Durack, Mary. *The Rock and the Sand.* Constable, London, 1969.

Durkheim, E. *The Rules of Sociological Method.* (Translated by Sarah A. Soloway and J. Mueller). George E. Catlin (Ed.). The Free Press, Glencoe, Illinois, 1895/1938.

Durkheim, E. *Les Formes Élémentaires de la Vie Religieuse.* Bibliothèque de Philosophie Contemporaire, Paris, 1912.

Durkheim, E. *Sociology and Philosophy* (Translated by D. F. Pocock, Introduction by J. G. Peristiany). Cohen and West, London, 1924–1953.

Durkheim, E. and Mauss, M. *Primitive Classification* (Translated and Introduction by Rodney Needham). Cohen and West, London, 1903–1963.

Elkin, A. P. Anthropology in Australia, past and present. Proceedings of the Australian and New Zealand Association for the Advancement of Sciences, Vol. 2, pp. 196–207. Sydney, 1935.

Elkin, A. P. *The Australian Aborigines*. Angus and Robertson, Sydney, 1938.

Elkin, A. P. Anthropology in Australia. *Oceania*, Vol. 10, pp. 1–29. Sydney, 1939.

Elkin, A. P. Anthropology in Australia: one chapter. *Mankind*, Vol. 5, pp. 225–242. Sydney, 1958.

Elkin, A. P. A Darwin centenary and highlights of field-work in Australia. *Mankind*, Vol. 5, pp. 321–333. Sydney, 1959.

Elkin, A. P. The Development of Scientific Knowledge of the Aborigines, in *Australian Aboriginal Studies* (Helen Shiels, Ed.), pp. 3–25, Oxford University Press, London, 1963.

Elkin, A. P. *The Australian Aborigines*. Doubleday and Co., New York, 1964.

Elkin, A. P. Before it is too late, in *Australian Aboriginal Anthropology* (R. M. Berndt, Ed.), pp. 19–26, University of Western Australia Press, Perth, WA, 1970.

Evans-Pritchard, E. E. *The Nuer*. Clarendon Press, Oxford, 1941.

Evans-Pritchard, E. E. *The Sanusi of Cyrenaica*. Clarendon Press, Oxford, 1951.

Evans-Pritchard, E. E. *Nuer Religion*. Clarendon Press, Oxford, 1956.

Evans-Pritchard, E. E. *Theories of Primitive Religion*. Clarendon Press, Oxford, 1965.

Falkenberg, J. *Kin and Totem*. Oslo University Press, Allen and Unwin, Oslo, 1962.

Fison, L. and Howitt, A. W. *Kamilaroi and Kurnai*, G. Robertson, Melbourne, 1880.

Flower, W. H. *Journal of the Royal Anthropological Institute*, Vol. 18. London, 1889.

Fraser, J. *An Australian Language*. Government Printer, Sydney, 1892.

Frazer, J. G. *Folklore in the Old Testament*. Macmillan and Co., London, 1919.

Frazer, J. G. *The Golden Bough*. Abridged Edition, Vol. 1. Macmillan and Co., London, 1960.

Freud, S. *Totem and Taboo*. Routledge, London, 1913–1960.

Gale, Fay (Ed.) *Woman's role in Aboriginal Society*. Memoir of the Australian Institute of Aboriginal Studies, Canberra, 1970.

Gargi, B. *Folk Theatre in India*. University of Washington Press, Seattle, 1966.

Geertz, C. *The Religion of Java*. The Free Press, London, 1960.

Goldenweiser, A. Totemism. *Encyclopedia of the Social Sciences*, pp. 657–660. The Macmillan Company, New York, 1934.

Goodale, Jane. *Tiwi Women*. University of Washington Press, Seattle, 1971.

Gough, Kathleen. New Proposals for Anthropologists. *Current Anthropology*, Vol. 9, No. 5, pp. 403–407. Chicago, 1968.

Gould, R. *Yiwara*. Charles Scribner's Sons, New York, 1969.

Gray, G. *Journals of Two Expeditions of Discovery in North-west and Western Australia*. Vol. 1, London, 1841.

Greenway, J. *Bibliography of the Australian Aborigines and the Native Peoples of the Torres Strait to 1959*. Angus and Robertson, Sydney, 1963.

Hanke, L. *Aristotle and the American Indians*. Hollis and Carter, London, 1959.

Hart, C. W. M. and Pilling, A. R. *The Tiwi of North Australia*. Holt, New York, 1960.

Hasluck, P. *Black Australians*, Melbourne U. P., 1942.

Henry, A. *Travels and Adventures in the years 1760–76*, pp. 294–295. Milo Milton Quaife (Ed.). Lakeside Press, Chicago, 1921.

Herbert, X. *Seven Emus*. Angus and Robertson, Sydney, 1959.

Hiatt, L. R. Totemism Tomorrow: The Future of an Illusion. *Mankind*, 7, pp. 83–93. Sydney, 1969.

Hocart, A. M. *Kings and Councillors* (Introduction by Rodney Needham). University of Chicago Press, Chicago, 1970.

Hodgkinson, C. *Australia*. T. W. Boone, London, 1845.

Howitt, A. W. *The Native Tribes of South-east Australia*. Macmillan, London, 1904.

Hsuan-Tsang. *The Travels of Fa-Hsien* (Translated by H. A. Giles). Cambridge University Press, Cambridge, 1923.

Hubert, H. and Mauss, M. *Sacrifice: Its Nature and Function* (Foreword by E. E. Evans-Pritchard). Cohen and West, London, 1898–1964.

Huxley, T. H. *Man's Place in Nature*. Williams and Norgate, London, 1863.

Ibn Batuta. *The Travels, A.D. 1325–1354* (Translated by H. A. R. Gibb). Cambridge University Press, Cambridge, 1958.

Ibn Khaldun. *The Muquaddimah* (Translated by F. Rosenthal). Routledge and Kegan Paul, London, 1958.

Idriess, I. *Our Living Stone Age*. Angus and Robertson, Sydney, 1963.

Kaberry, Phyllis. *Aboriginal Woman, Sacred and Profane*. Routledge, London, 1939.

Kluckhohn, C. Myths and Rituals: A General Theory. *Harvard Theological Review*, Vol. 35. Cambridge, 1942.

Korn, Frances and Needham, R. Permutation Models and Prescription Systems: The Tarau Case. *Man*, Vol. 5, No. 3, Sept. London, 1970.

Lafitau, J.-F. *Moeurs des Sauvages Ameriquains*. Paris, 1724.

Lang, A. *Myth, Ritual and Religion*. Longman Green, London, 1887.

Lang, A. *Modern Mythology*. Longman Green, London, 1897.

Lang, A. *The Secret of the Totem*. Longman Green, London, 1905.

Leach, E. *Virgin Birth*. Proceedings of the Royal Anthropological Institute. London, 1966.

Lescarbot, M. *Histoire de la Nouvelle France*. Paris, Bk. vi, 1609.

Lescarbot, M. *The History of New France*, Vol. III, (Translated by W. L. Grant). The Champlain Society, Toronto, 1914.

Lévi-Strauss, C. *Tristes Tropiques*. Plon, Paris, 1955.

Lévi-Strauss, C. *World on the Wane*. Hutchinson, London, 1961.

Lévi-Strauss, C. *Le totemisme aujourd'hui*. Plon, Paris, 1962a.

Lévi-Strauss, C. *The Savage Mind*. Weidenfeld and Nicholson, London, 1962b.

Lévi-Strauss, C. *Totemism* (Translated by Rodney Needham). Beacon Press, Boston, 1963.

Lévi-Strauss, C. *The Raw and the Cooked* (Translated by John and Doreen Weightman). Harper & Row, New York, 1964–1969.

Lévi-Strauss, C. *Du Miel aux Cendres*. Plon, Paris, 1967.

Lévy-Bruhl, L. *How Natives Think* (Translated by Filian A. Clare). Allen and Unwin, London, 1912–1926.

Lévy-Bruhl, L. *Primitive Mentality* (Translated by Filian A. Clare). Allen and Unwin, London, 1922–1923.

Lewis, C. S. *A Preface to Paradise Lost*. Galaxy Books, Oxford University Press, New York, 1961.

Lienhardt, R. G. Religion, in *Man, Culture and Society*, H. L. Shapiro (Ed.). Galaxy Books, O.U.P., New York, 1956.

Lienhardt, R. G. *Divinity and Experience*. Clarendon Press, Oxford, 1961.

Locke, J. *An Essay on Human Understanding*. Thomas Bassett, London, 1690a.

Locke, J. *Two Treatises on Government*. London, 1690b.

Lommel, A. Changes in Australian Art, in *Diprotodon to Detribalization*, A. R. Pilling and R. A. Waterman (Eds.). Michigan State U.P., East Lansing, 1970.

Long, J. K. *Voyages and Travels of an Indian Interpreter and Trader*. London, 1922. Edited by N. N. Quaife. R. R. Donnelly & Sons, Chicago, 1922.

Lubbock, J. (Avebury). *Origin of Civilization*. Longman Green, London, 1870–1912.

McCarthy, F. D. *Australia's Aborigines: Their Life and Culture*. Colorgravure, Melbourne, 1957.

McConnel, Ursula. *Myths of the Mungkan*. Melbourne University Press, Melbourne, 1957.

McLaren, J. *My Crowded Solitude*. Ernest Benn, London, 1926.

M'Lennan, J. F. *Primitive Marriage*. A. & C. Black, Edinburgh, 1864.

M'Lennan, J. F. The Worship of Animals and Plants. *Fortnightly Review*, Vols. 6 and 7, p. 427. London, 1869–1870.

Maddock, K. Rethinking the Murngin problem: A Review Article. *Oceania*, Vol. XLI, No. 2, December, pp. 77–89. Sydney, 1970.

Maine, H. *Ancient Law*. John Murray, London, 1861.

Malinowski, B. *The Family Among the Australian Aborigines*. University of London Press, London, 1913.

Malinowski, B. *Myth in Primitive Psychology*. London, 1926.

Malinowski, B. *The Sexual Life of Savages in North-Western Melanesia*. Routledge, London, 1929.

Malinowski, B. Pigs, Papuans, and Police Court Perspective. *Man*, 44, Vol. XXII, February, pp. 33–38. London, 1932.

Malinowski, B. *Argonauts of the Western Pacific*. Routledge and Kegan Paul, London, 1962.

Malinowski, B. *A Diary in the Strict Sense of the Term* (Preface by Valetta Malinowski, Introduction by Raymond Firth). Harcourt, Brace and World Inc., New York, 1967.

Mankind. Journal of the Anthropological Society of New South Wales, founded in 1931. Sydney.

Maranda, Pierre and Elli Köngäs (Eds.) *Structural Analysis of Oral Tradition*. University of Pennsylvania Press, 1971.

Marett, R. R. *Anthropology*. Home University Library, London, 1925.

Marett, R. R. and Penniman, T. K. (Eds.) *Spencer's Scientific Correspondence*. Clarendon Press, Oxford, 1932.

Marshall, A. *Ourselves Writ Strange*. F. W. Cheshire, Melbourne, 1948.

Mathew, J. *Eaglehawk and Crow: A Study of Australian Aborigines*. D. Hutt, London and Melbourne, 1899.

Mathew, J. *Two Representative Tribes of Queensland*. T. Fisher Urwin, London, 1910.

Mead, Margaret. *Male and Female*. W. Morrow, New York, 1949.

Meggitt, M. *Desert People*. Angus and Robertson, Sydney, 1962.

Meggitt, M. Social Organization: Morphology and Typology, in *Australian Aboriginal Studies*, pp. 211–217. Helen Shiels (Ed.). Oxford University Press, London, 1963.

Mellema, R. L. *Wayang Puppets*. Royal Tropical Institute, The Hague, 1954.

Miller, A. *The Crucible*. The Viking Press, New York, 1952.

Moorehead, A. *The Fatal Impact*. H. Hamilton, London, 1966.

Morgan, H. *Systems of Consanguinity*. Smithsonian Institution, Washington, 1871.

Morgan, H. *Ancient Society*, H. Holt & Co., New York, 1877.

Mountford, C. P. *Winbaraku*. Rigby Limited, Adelaide, 1968.

Muller, M. Essay on the Philosophy of Mythology. Lecture delivered at the Royal Institution. London and Oxford, 1871.

Mulvaney D. J. The Australian Aborigines 1606–1929. Historical Studies, Vol. 8 University of Melbourne, 1958.

Mulvaney, D. J. *The Prehistory of Australia*. Thames and Hudson, London, 1969.

Mulvaney, D. J. The Ascent of Aboriginal Man: Howitt as Anthropologist, in *Come Wind, Come Weather*, H. M. Walker (Ed.). Melbourne University Press, 1971a.

Mulvaney, D. J. *Discovering Man's Place in Nature*. The Australian Academy of the Humanities, Sydney University Press, 1971b.

Mulvaney, D. J. Fact, Fancy and Aboriginal Australian Ethnic Origins, *Mankind*, Vol. 6, No. 7, June, pp. 299–303, 1966.

Mulvaney, D. J. and Golson, J. (Eds.) *Aboriginal Man and Environment in Australia*. Australian National University Press, Canberra, 1971.

Oceania. Sponsored by the Australian National Research Council, founded in 1930. Sydney.

Peacock, J. L. *The Rites of Modernization*. University of Chicago Press, Chicago, 1968.

People. Vol. 19, No. 8, June 5. Sydney, 1968.

Perry, W. J. *The Origin of Magic and Religion*. Dutton, New York, 1923.

Perry, W. J. *The Children of the Sun*. Methuen, London, 1927.

Piddington, R. *An Introduction to Social Anthropology*, Vol. 2. Oliver & Boyd, Edinburgh, 1950–1958.

Radcliff-Brown, A. R. Three Tribes in Western Australia. *Journal of the Royal Anthropological Institute*, Vol. 43, pp. 143–194. London, 1913.

Radcliff-Brown, A. R. Notes on the Social Organization of Australian Tribes. *Journal of the Royal Anthropological Institute*, Vol. 49, pp. 222–253. London, 1918.

Radcliff-Brown, A. R. *The Andaman Islanders*. Cambridge University Press, 1922.

Radcliff-Brown, A. R. Notes on the Social Organization of Australian Tribes. *Journal of the Royal Anthropological Institute*, Vol. 53, pp. 424–447. London, 1923.

Radcliff-Brown, A. R. The Sociological Theory of Totemism, in *Structure and Function in Primitive Society*, pp. 117–132. Cohen and West, London, 1952.

Radcliff-Brown, A. R. *The Social Organization of Australian Tribes*. Oceania Monographs No. 1, Melbourne, 1931a.

Radcliff-Brown, A. R. *Applied Anthropology*. Report of the Twentieth meeting of the Australian and New Zealand Association for the Advancement of Science, D. A. Herbert (Ed.), Brisbane, pp. 267–269, 1931b.

Rapaport, A. (Ed.) *Clausewitz on War*. Pelican Classics, London, 1968.

Read, C. No Paternity. *Journal of the Royal Anthropological Institute*, Vol. 48, pp. 164–150. London, 1918.

Read, K. E. *The High Valley*. Charles Scribners, New York, 1965.

Reay, Marie. *Aborigines Now*. Angus & Robertson, Sydney, 1964.

Reclus, Elie. *Le Primitif d'Australie*. Denton, Paris, 1895.

Rentoul, A. C. Physiological Paternity and the Trobrianders. *Man*, 162, Vol. XXI, August, pp. 152–154. London, 1931.

Ridley, W. *Kamilaroi and other Australian Languages*. Government Printer, Sydney, 1866 and 1875.

Righter, Anne. *Shakespeare and the Idea of the Play*. Chatto and Windus, London, 1962.

Rivers, W. H. R. *The History of Melanesian Society*. Cambridge University Press. Cambridge, 1914.

Roheim, G. *Australian Totemism, A Psycho-Analytic Study in Anthropology*. Allen and Unwin, London, 1925.

Roheim, G. *The Eternal Ones of the Dream*. International Universities Press, New York, 1945.

Rose, F. *Classification of Kin, Age Structure and Marriage Amongst the Groote Eylandte Aborigines*. Deutsches Akademie der Wissenschaften zu Berlin, Berlin, 1960.

Roth, W. E. *Ethnological Studies among the North-West-Central Queensland Aborigines*. Government Printer, Brisbane, 1897.

Roth, W. E. Scientific Report to the Under Secretary on the Natives of (Lower) Tully River, 20 September 1900, Cooktown. Uncatalogued MS 216. (Mitchell Library, Sydney), 1900.

Roth, W. E. *North Queensland Ethnography*. Bulletin No. 5, January. Government Printer, Brisbane, 1903.

Rousseau, J.-J. *Social Contract*. (J. M. Dent and Sons, London, 1935) Orig. M. M. Rey, Amsterdam, 1762.

Rowley, C. D. *Aboriginal Policy and Practice* (3 vols.). A.N.U. Press, Canberra, 1970–71.

Sadlier, R. *The Aborigines of Australia*. Sydney, 1883.

Sagard, G. *Le Grand Voyage du Pays des Hurons*. Paris, 1632.

Sagard, G. *The Long Journey to the Country of the Hurons*, George M. Wrong (Ed.), translated into English by H. H. Langton. The Champlain Society, Toronto, 1939.

Salter, E. *Daisy Bates*. Angus and Robertson, Sydney, 1971.

Schapper, H. P. *Aboriginal Advancement to Integration*. Australian National University Press, Canberra, 1970.

Sharman, G. B. and Pilton, Phyllis E. The Life History and Reproduction of the Red Kangaroo. Proceedings of the Zoological Society of London, Vol. 142, pp. 29–48. London, 1964.

Shiels, Helen (Ed.) *Australian Aboriginal Studies*. Oxford University Press, London, 1963.

Simmel, G. *Sociology of Religion* (Translated by Curt Rosenthal). Philosophical Library, New York, 1959.

Simpson, C. *Adam in Ochre*. Angus and Robertson, Sydney, 1951.

Smith, B. *European Vision and the South Pacific, 1768–1850*. Clarendon Press, Oxford, 1960.

Smith, R. B. *The Aborigines of Victoria*. Government Printer, Melbourne, 1878.

Spencer, H. *Proper Sphere of Government*. W. Brittain, London, 1843.

Spencer, H. *Principles of Ethics*. Williams and Hargate, London, 1893.

Spencer, W. B. and Gillen, F. J. *The Native Tribes of Central Australia*. Macmillan, London, 1899.

Spencer, W. B. and Gillen, F. J. *The Northern Tribes of Central Australia*. Macmillan, London, 1904.

Stanner, W. E. H. "Durmugam," in *In the Company of Man*, J. B. Casagrande (Ed.). Harper & Row, New York, 1960.

Stanner, W. E. H. Religion, Totemism and Symbolism, in *Aboriginal Man in Australia*, R. M. and C. H. Berndt (Eds.). Angus and Robertson, Sydney, 1965.

Stanner, W. E. H. *On Aboriginal Religion*. The Oceania Monograph No. 11, The University of Sydney, 1966.

Stanner, W. E. H. Reflections on Durkheim and Aboriginal Religion, in *Social Organization*, pp. 217–240. M. Freedman (Ed.). Franti Cuss & Co. Ltd., London, 1967.

Stocking, G. W., Jr. What's in a Name: The Origins of the Royal Anthropological Institute. *Man*, Vol. 6, No. 3. pp. 369–90. London, 1971.

Strehlow, T. G. H. *Aranda Traditions*. Melbourne University Press, Melbourne, 1947.

Strehlow, T. G. H. *The Sustaining Ideals of Australian Aboriginal Societies*. Adelaide, 1956.

Strehlow, T. G. H. *Songs of Central Australia*, Angus and Robertson, Sydney, 1971.

Taft, R.; Dawson, J. L. M.; and Beasley, Pamela. *Attitudes and Social Conditions*. Australian National University Press, Canberra, 1970.

Taplin, G. *The Folklore, Manners, Customs, and Languages of the South Australian Aborigines*. Government Printer, Adelaide, 1879.

Thomson, D. F. *Economic Structure and the Ceremonial Exchange System in Arnhem Land*. Macmillan, Melbourne, 1949.

Tillyard, E. M. W. *The Elizabethan World Picture*. Vintage Books, New York, 1942.

Tonkinson, R. *Da: wajil: A Western Desert Rainmaking Ritual*. Ph.D. thesis, University of British Columbia, Vancouver, 1972.

Turner, V. *Schism and Continuity in an African Society*. Manchester University Press, 1957.

Turner, V. *The Forest of Symbols*. Cornell University Press, New York, 1967.

Turner, V. *The Drums of Affliction*. Clarendon Press, Oxford, 1968.

Turner, V. *The Ritual Process*. Aldine Press, Chicago, 1969.

Tyler, S. A. Review of Kinship and Social Organization, by Ira A. Buchler and Henry A. Selby, Macmillan, London, 1968, in *American Anthropologist*, Vol. 71, No. 4. Washington, D.C., 1969.

Tylor, E. B. *Researches into the Early History of Mankind*. John Murray, London, 1865.

Tylor, E. B. The Religion of Savages. *The Fortnightly Review*, No. XXX, pp. 71–2. London, 1866.

Tylor, E. B. *Primitive Culture*, Vol. II. Harper Torchbooks, New York, 1871–1958.

Tylor, E. B. Remarks on Totemism, with Especial Reference to some Modern Theories respecting it. *Journal of the Royal Anthropological Institute*, Vol. XXVIII. London, 1899.

Walkabout. The journal of the Australian Geographical Society, founded in 1934. Sydney.

Warner, W. L. *A Black Civilization: A Social Study of an Australian Tribe*. Revised Edition. New York: Harper, 1958.

Weiner, J. S. *The Piltdown Forgery*. Oxford University Press, London, 1955.

Wilson, K. Co-operatives, Leadership and Assimilation, in *Aborigines Now*, Marie Reay (Ed.). Angus and Robertson, Sydney, 1964.

Wilson, K. Pindan: A Preliminary Comment, in *Diprotodon to Detribalization*, A. R. Pilling and R. A. Waterman (Eds.). Michigan State U.P., East Lansing, 1970.

Worsley, P. Totemism in a Changing Society. *American Anthropologist*, Vol. 57, No. 4, pp. 851–861, 1955.

Worsley, P. The Utilization of Food Resources by an Australian Aboriginal Tribe. *Acta Ethnographica*, Budapest, Vol. X, Parts 1–2, Budapest, 1961.

Worsnop, T. *Aborigines of Australia*. Government Printer, Adelaide, 1897a.

Worsnop, T. *The Prehistoric Arts etc. of the Aborigines of Australia*. C. E. Bustow, South Australia, 1897b.

Young, G. *Two Worlds Not One*. Ad Hoc Publications, London, 1969.

Index